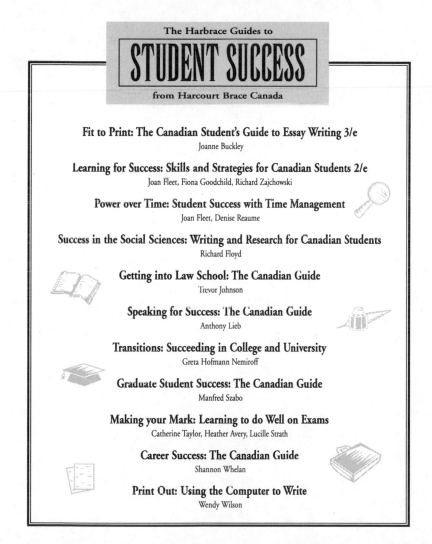

Ideas and Details

A Guide to Writing for Canadians

M. Garret Bauman
Monroe Community College

Clifford Werier
Mount Royal College

HARCOURT
BRACE
CANADA

Harcourt Brace & Company, Canada

Toronto Montreal Fort Worth New York Orlando
Philadelphia San Diego London Sydney Tokyo

Requests for permission to make copies of any part of the work should be mailed to: Permissions, College Division, Harcourt Brace & Company, Canada, 55 Horner Avenue, Toronto, Ontario M8Z 4X6.

Every reasonable effort has been made to acquire permission for copyright material used in this text, and to acknowledge all such indebtedness accurately. Any errors and omissions called to the publisher's attention will be corrected in future printings.

Canadian Cataloguing in Publication Data

Bauman, M. Garrett
      Ideas and details : a guide to writing for Canadians

Includes index.
ISBN 0–7747–3472–8

1. English language — Rhetoric. I. Werier, Clifford M., 1954–   .
II. Title.

PE1408.B38 1995 808'.042 C95–930824–5

Publisher: Heather McWhinney
Editor and Marketing Manager: Kelly Cochrane
Projects Manager: Liz Radojkovic
Project Co-ordinator: May Su Mei Ku
Director of Publishing Services: Jean Davies
Editorial Manager: Marcel Chiera
Supervising Editor: Semareh Al-Hillal
Production Editor: Louisa Schulz
Production Manager: Sue-Ann Becker
Production Co-ordinator: Sheila Barry
Copy Editor: Dallas Harrison
Cover Design: Opus House
Interior Design: Priscilla Mingus, Vicki Whistler
Typesetting and Assembly: Sharon Moroney
Technical Art: Sharon Moroney
Printing and Binding: Best Book Manufacturers, Inc.

Cover Art: Phototone from Letraset, by permission of Curry's; and Dick Hemingway

This book was printed in Canada.

1 2 3 4 5 00 99 98 97 96

PREFACE

Like most writing teachers, I am constantly frustrated by textbooks. The standard handbook/rhetoric is a dense tome that overwhelms both teachers and students—more like a grammatical reference work than a useful guide to writing. My other criticism of standard texts is that they tend to be formulaic; they suggest that to be an effective writer one must simply follow the prescribed steps and emulate the characteristics of each mode. This approach often results in essays that have all the formal elements, but lack creativity, style, and content.

When I first read the American edition of *Ideas and Details*, I was struck by the simplicity and importance of its key concept: the notion that powerful writing must always have a dynamic balance of ideas and details. Writers must have something to say, and they must make sure that their central idea is clear and well developed. And writers must learn how to give life to their subject by animating it with details. This notion is not limited to thesis and support in argumentative writing, but applies to every act of communication—there must always be an idea at the heart of an essay, and it must be exemplified by vivid particulars.

The approach of *Ideas and Details* is fresh, not radical. It covers all the important material—process, modes, documentation, and grammar—but in a style that is accessible for students because of its practicality and lucidity. For example, in chapter 2, the text does not simply theorize about the need to generate ideas in everything we write, but offers a comprehensive selection of "Brainteasers," innovative strategies to unlock creativity. Likewise, the tone is always clear and very readable, without needless jargon. The text has been very popular in the United States because it avoids the clichés of most writing instruction.

Ideas and Details is also highly interactive: it challenges students to try all of the methods it advocates. Student examples are frequently used as models to demonstrate both effective and weak writing. These examples help students to see that rhetorical and stylistic considerations are not the sole property of professional essayists. The innovative list of "Writing Suggestions" at the end of each chapter helps students to develop ideas and details in their own essays. Likewise, the practices throughout the text engage the reader's interest and make the lesson more than just a passive absorption of theories. Instructors and students will find that the questions in the "Peer-Review Checklist" at the end of many chapters are helpful in the editing of drafts.

The chapters on research and grammar (chapters 13 and 14) offer concise yet thorough coverage. Rather than attempting encyclopedic overkill, the "Handbook of English" provides a grammar review along with a detailed examination of the most common errors in student writing. The chapter on research takes the student through each step of the process and provides instruction in current methodologies, including the use and citation of CD-ROM databases and electronic sources. The sections on APA and MLA documentation are based on the latest revisions. Both MLA and APA systems are demonstrated by fully documented sample student essays.

In preparing this edition, I have tried to incorporate numerous examples that reflect current Canadian experience. Everywhere in *Ideas and Details*, Canadian readers will enjoy seeing reflections of their own culture, whether it is in a detailed examination of Canadian literary works in "The Literary Essay and Review" (chapter 12) or in the many examples of student writing.

Ideas and Details is not just a slimmed-down version of a traditional handbook. Instead, writers will find innovative approaches on every page— new ways of looking at the process and practical methods for generating lively, engaging, and rhetorically sophisticated prose.

The making of a Canadian edition involved much more than plugging in place names. The text was reworked to satisfy the needs of Canadian instructors in both community colleges and universities. To this end, I have received help from many places. I would like to thank my colleagues at Mount Royal College, a dedicated and innovative group of writing teachers, who work wonders under less than ideal conditions. I would also like to thank Michael Young for inspiring this project and getting it started and Reid Gilbert (Capilano College) for his helpful review. The people at Harcourt Brace & Company, Canada, have been immensely helpful, and they deserve my thanks: Marguerite Martindale for her work in the middle stages; Heather McWhinney and Kelly Cochrane for wise advice throughout the process; and Su Mei Ku for her perseverence and understanding. A special note of thanks goes to Dallas Harrison for his thorough and perceptive editing. Finally, I would like to thank my wife, Sabrina Reed, whose patience, suggestions, and feedback were and are invaluable.

Several quotations in this book have been taken from *Colombo's New Canadian Quotations*, by John Robert Colombo. Used by permission of the Canadian Publishers, McClelland & Stewart, Toronto.

A NOTE FROM THE PUBLISHER

Thank you for selecting *Ideas and Details: A Guide to Writing for Canadians*, first Canadian edition, by M. Garrett Bauman and Clifford Werier. The authors and publisher have devoted considerable time and care to the development of this book. We appreciate your recognition of this effort and accomplishment.

We want to hear what you think about *Ideas and Details: A Guide to Writing for Canadians*. Please take a few minutes to fill in the stamped reply card at the back of the book. Your comments and suggestions will be valuable to us as we prepare new editions and other books.

Contents

10 Informative Writing: Telling Your Audience What It Doesn't Know · 139

11 Persuasive Writing: Seeking Agreement from an Audience · 153

12 The Literary Essay and Review · 172

13 Research   194

14 Handbook of English   242

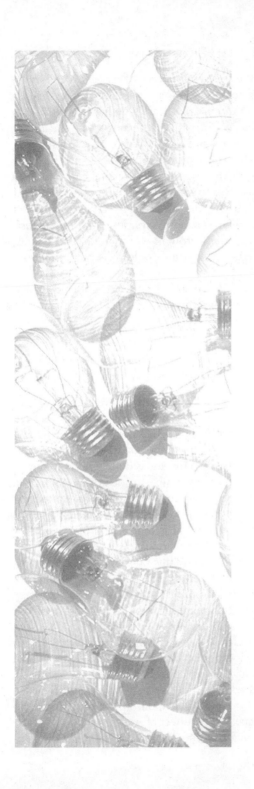

Chapter 1

The Two-Part Secret of Good Writing:

Ideas and

Details

Eternity is in love with the productions of time.

William Blake

*Y*ou probably didn't expect the best-kept secret of writing to be given away so soon, but here it is. All successful writers—whether businesspeople or professionals—have this ability, and many writers who have serious flaws in other aspects of their writing can get by with just this one skill: *the ability to combine ideas and details.* Another way of saying this is that the successful writer must continually move between the general and the specific.

Ideas and details are the heart of your writing. They alone cause readers to say, "This is great!" or "Let's take this to the board of directors." No one I know ever received an award, a job offer, a kiss, or a promotion for perfect spelling or punctuation. Readers of magazine essays, love letters, or business reports care about interesting ideas brought to life with vivid details, and that is what your reader will pay attention to unless distracted by poor spelling and organization.

Let's look at what *ideas* and *details* mean, why they're both necessary, and how you can work with them comfortably.

IDEAS

An idea summarizes, concludes, highlights, or generalizes. It's usually abstract. Here's an example to study. Marshall McLuhan, Canadian philosopher and media theorist, was internationally recognized for this intriguing idea: "The medium is the message." If your first reaction to this sentence was like mine, you found it vague or confusing. Most ideas do take time to unravel. I would loosely interpret McLuhan's sentence to mean that there is a direct connection between any form of communication and its content. It brings to mind a number of questions. How do the visual "media" of television and movies shape their "messages"? What is more important, words or images? If "the medium is the message," is it ever possible to separate what is said from how we say it? In the act of reading this book, you see no moving pictures and hear no music. That must mean the medium of print is shaping and limiting, in a very specific way, the kind of message you receive.

I'm not sure if you understand all the implications of McLuhan's ideas, but notice what's happening. *My comments are already moving away from the general to the specific.* McLuhan's idea stands above specifics. It can apply to many possible situations, and it leaves room for readers to supply their own examples. Because it does not move to specifics, its meaning is vague. In McLuhan's book *Understanding Media*, this idea was tied to specific details— he used it to summarize a principle about the relationship between new technologies and their consequences, such as the effect of automation on the number and kinds of jobs that people perform. The details gave the idea vitality.

■ *Practice 1-1:* Below are three more ideas. Any of them could be the seed from which an entire essay grows. Examine them carefully to see what *expectations* a reader might have after reading them. What details might you want the writer to move to next in order to explain them?

1. Preston Manning is a clever politician.
2. Technology today is humanity's greatest hope and greatest threat.
3. Growing up on a farm prepared me for life.

 DETAILS

Let's look at *details* in the following little story.

A young man strolls a sandy beach at dawn, picking his way along the line of discarded shells, seaweed, and crab legs brought by high tide. He picks up several souvenirs. He plans to display them on his bookshelf when he returns home from vacation. A fisherman casts in the surf a few metres off, and nearby is a pool of water left by the retreating tide. The young man notices a fish in the tidal pool.

"It's a bottlenose skate," the fisherman says. "A lot of them get trapped by the tide."

The fish is flat like a flounder, white on the bottom, brown on top, with a long, whiplike tail. It thrashes the water.

"Skates are garbage fish," the fisherman says. "They compete with the game fish."

The young man looks more closely. The pool is sinking into the sand, and the skate gasps. It thrashes, searching for deeper water, then settles into a five-centimetre-deep puddle.

"A half-dozen get stranded every day," the fisherman says. "People don't eat them. Look—" he gestures down the beach where gulls are pecking at another skate, which is still alive.

The young man bends, touches the skate. It's slimy. He tries to grasp it, but his hand slips off.

"All right," the fisherman says, setting his pole in its holder. "Grab the other side." Between them, the men drag the skate down to the surf. The skate jerks free as it hits water. It surges, tail splashing. The young man's souvenirs jangle into the frothy water and are lost.

The skate disappears.

Notice that this story is a collection of sights, sounds, and touches. It is easier to visualize the first time through than McLuhan's sentence because it is concrete and specific. We're not talking about dozens of possibilities here, but of one day at one beach with one fish. Details can be *facts, descriptions, stories, examples.* They give us life close up, one piece at a time. Ideas, on the other hand, give us life from the mountaintop, in grand scale. Details make a reader feel in touch with a writer. They make what you write about seem present and real. An idea does something else for a reader—it gives a sense of purpose and importance to the writing, more significance to details than first meets the eye. You might consider details and ideas to be sight and insight—the physical presence and the mental meaning. Readers need both to feel satisfied with a piece of writing.

The story about the skate might end as it is, leaving the reader to figure out what insight is behind these details. Fiction does not usually tell, while narrative essays often make the meaning clearer by climaxing the story with a generalization. One thing seems clear—the young man understands better the life that has inhabited his souvenirs. In a sense, both men have been fishing. Has the older man been resensitized to the lives he takes for sport, or is he just being polite? The loss of the shells in the frothy sea and the fact that gulls eat many skates each day suggest it is futile to save one life. Is it?

Notice that we had to move to details with McLuhan's idea to clarify and develop it. The story about the skate is a collection of details; to clarify and develop it, we must move toward ideas that give meaning and purpose to the details. Alone, neither is enough.

Read the following and try to figure out what each paragraph needs to satisfy a reader.

1. Is it fair for a woman who gets raped and pregnant to have to deliver her rapist's baby? Then there's the possibility she may be in danger of dying. But there are lots of women who use abortion as birth control, and they don't give a damn that a little life is involved. And I know of at least one anti-abortion protester who had an abortion herself! On the other hand, if we say a woman has total rights over her own body, doesn't that also give her the right to use drugs, be a prostitute, or commit suicide?

2. Education today needs to be more personal. Too much that goes on in schools is theoretical and professional; students and teachers both forget they're dealing with people, because they focus too much on the job.

The overall effect of the first paragraph is confusion; it has interesting examples, but it's difficult to figure out what the writer's main point is. The writer needs to help us along with *a unifying idea.* The second paragraph is just the opposite. It has a clear, forceful idea, but it hasn't come to life with details to illustrate that idea. See if you can complete the second paragraph with vivid details from your experience and provide an idea that would tie the first together. As you write, don't hesitate to *add details or change the idea a bit.* That is how writing gets better! Ideas and details enhance each other, build each other up.

The skilled writer and thinker tests ideas against details and draws ideas from details. If your employer says, "Do you think we ought to start a day care centre for company employees?" you've been given an idea to work with. Your first step is to test it against some details—how many employees would bring their children to the centre, how much will it cost, is there room, and a dozen other specific questions. This test should help to develop the original idea. If your boss says, "We get forty percent more damaged merchandise returned from our shipments of widgets to New Brunswick than anywhere else in the country," you've been given a fact (a detail) in search of an idea to explain it. Could it be transport (bad New Brunswick roads), personnel (a truckdriver on that route who throws boxes), manufacturing (widget psychopaths on the assembly line), or something else?

WHAT MAKES A GOOD IDEA

What makes a good idea? The best ideas are original, but because true originality is rare, your teachers will probably be happy if you present an *unusual* or *fresh* idea and avoid clichés and commonplace ideas. Fine, but how do you get unusual ideas? It's easy to grab the first ideas that come to mind. The problem is, those ideas come to everybody else's mind first too. Chances are, if you take the first idea off the top of your head, you'll be saying something trite and dull. Look at your facts or story more closely—what truth might be lurking there that isn't obvious? Here's an example. A student writes a fairly predictable essay about being in a car crash. After the wounded are put in the ambulance and the tow truck hauls the once-sparkling car to the dump, the writer concludes that he or she has learned how serious driving is and will drive more carefully in the future.

The essays you remember, however, say things like this: "Being in an accident made me realize how close I am to death *all* the time and not really aware of it. A loose bolt, a piece of glass, a flying rock, one drink too many, and I'm gone forever." If the writer then goes on to speculate how people block this realization out of their minds and still drive, he or she is brewing a good idea.

■ *Practice 1-2:* Can you think of additional meanings to be drawn from car accidents?

Being *brutally honest* helps to make good ideas. Social pressure to say the acceptable thing and fear of embarrassment or of being different hold back fresher ideas more than a lack of brain power does. No one deliberately tries to come up with boring ideas, but too often we censor ourselves.

There will be more on this in the next chapter, which is devoted to getting ideas. But for now, ask if your idea has an unusual twist or slant to it. If not, dig deeper.

A second aspect of a good idea is *complexity,* because the truth is usually complicated. One trick to make your ideas deeper is to *develop several competing ideas.* Writing seems shallow if the writer implies there's only one way of seeing the topic. To develop deeper honesty, force yourself to look for ideas that compete with your first ones. Put them on trial.

This method is tricky, because students sometimes generate so many ideas in preparing to write an essay that they can no longer figure out *which* side to take in an argument. A student in a first-year writing class decided to write about television advertising.

"Everybody hates TV ads," Carrie said. "They try to get you to buy things you don't need or even things harmful to you. They lie and deceive. But everybody knows that. I can't write a paper telling people what they already know."

"So what do you think ought to be done about commercials?" the instructor asked.

"Well, first I thought we could just not allow them anymore. But who'd pay for the shows on TV? Maybe we could charge people to watch, like with cable TV. Then I thought, well, what about poor people? And legally, don't the advertisers have a right to say what they want? But what about my right not to hear the same dumb ads over and over? I'm so sick of dogs selling beer! Well, then I thought, why not just turn off the TV set? Maybe enough people not watching would make them create better commercials. Suppose a lot of us wrote letters...."

"How about that?" the instructor replied.

"Oh, no! People are too lazy. I don't know if I'd even bother. The other night I caught myself laughing at a new ad. And I hum the jingles sometimes. I don't know what to write. It's just a mess. I need another topic."

Carrie should be glad, not upset. Her conflicting emotions and ideas made her better informed, even though the only research she'd done—the most important kind—was in her internal library. The temptation for a writer in Carrie's position is to glance at her watch and say, "I've got to get this paper done by Friday. I'm just going to pick a side, call it 'Just Say No to Commercials,' and state that the answer to bad advertising is to twist that little dial to the off position." Then the real idea she's come so close to shrivels and dies. But don't kid yourself. The paper will still be hard to write, because it's tough work to tell only half the truth.

The honest response to confusion is to accept it. Don't worry. Most people are confused when they think. All research into creativity and idea-getting shows that you must tolerate chaos for a time until the confusion rearranges itself into a good idea. You have time to sort out the contradictions later in the last three stages of writing: the order stage (chapters 3–4), the draft stage (chapter 5), and the revision stage (chapters 6–7). In the thinking stage of writing, don't pick *one* side—gladly choose two or three sides before deciding what the truth is. If one idea comes to you at the start of your paper and never changes, red lights and buzzers should rattle your head to warn you that you're not really thinking.

Work patiently through competing ideas, testing each with details to see if it is supportable. If one answer doesn't emerge during thinking or outlining, perhaps it will in drafting or revising. If *the* answer doesn't come by then, the worst you have is a paper that says, "There's no simple answer to television advertising—the sellers, the station owners, and the viewers are all to blame. No one solution can satisfy the rights of everyone involved." This is essentially what Carrie wrote.

But here's a warning: deliberately trying to be complex *just to be complex* usually leads to confusing writing. Complexity should be the *result* of honestly exploring an idea—of opening yourself to see as many possibilities in it as you can. It's not something you add to a paper like a pinch of salt.

■ *Practice 1-3:* Which of the following ideas promise the most originality? Which could you expand into essays? Does any go too far?

1. Suicide is a reasonable response to misery.
2. Many teenagers make great parents.
3. Racial discrimination continues to make our society unfair.
4. Discrimination hurts those who hate as much or more than those who are hated.
5. We love innocence in others, but not in ourselves.
6. Television commercials should be limited to no more than ten minutes of any hour's programming.

 # WHAT MAKES A GOOD DETAIL

What makes a good detail? Most readers and writers would agree that details should be *vivid*—a word derived from *life* (*vivre*, meaning "to live"). Details should put abstract ideas in motion. They must be specific, dramatic if possible, and direct, not second-hand. Suppose you wanted details to bring the following idea to life: "College and university athletics do more harm to the student than the supposed benefits of character-building we hear about so often." Which of the following gives the most vivid details to support the idea?

1. College and university athletes spend so much time practising they have very little time left for studies, and they're too tired to do a good job anyway. What does playing hockey, football, or basketball teach them about their field of study? Yes, they're taught competition, winning at any cost, but will that get them a good job when they graduate? Most athletes take easy courses and do poor work. They miss the real meaning of education. A lot of them never even graduate, and when the coaches get years of effort out of them, they couldn't care less what happens to them.

2. Bill Peterson limps back to his dorm from hockey practice, where he skated hard for two hours. The coach yelled at him: "Hit harder, Peterson!" He's limping because somebody hooked him and sent him flying into the boards. "Put your whole body into the check, Peterson," the coach said. Peterson is a starter this year, but has no hope of playing in the NHL or of making the big money. At his room, he picks up his history notebook, then heads for his night class—scheduled around practice. He sighs. The professor has been talking about the importance of the Canadian Charter of Rights and Freedoms, which legally protects freedom of the press or peaceful assembly and association. "What a crock!" Peterson says. "Maybe I'll sit in the back and catch a few Z's."

Is there any doubt that the second example involves us more, makes us think more? The first example is general, relying on abstract terms such as "the real meaning of education"; the second is specific, making its ideas concrete by talking about the protection of "freedom of the press or peaceful assembly and association." The first is bland (athletes are "too tired" or have "very little time"); the second is vivid, *showing* us how tired Bill is, not just *telling* us.

Finding the powerful detail can be just as creative as developing an interesting idea. The eye, as well as the intellect, must be trained to see better. One student, who wrote of hugging an old woman, said: "Her chest was as hard and flat as a weatherbeaten plank." The story of years of living was in that comparison. Another student, writing about working in a nursing home, gave intimate, honest details: "I have put diapers on a one-hundred-year-old woman, helped to quiet an old man after a bad dream in which he called on his long-dead wife, and put countless people on bed pans only to have them miss and urinate on me instead."

Good detail may look a bit different in informative writing, but it follows the same principles. If you heard that you will probably earn more money after finishing a degree, you might not even bother to yawn. But if you read details that told you university graduates' starting salaries for 1993 averaged $27,000 per year to high school graduates' $15,000, then you have something specific to visualize (you can visualize $12,000, can't you?).

The chapters on descriptive, narrative, informative, and persuasive writing will suggest ways of creating vivid details for specific writing assignments. But for now, remember that details plant the reader's feet on the ground. Support each idea with at least a couple of examples, descriptions, or facts. Only then will the reader be able to see your idea clearly.

■ ***Practice 1-4:*** Make the following general ideas more specific by enriching them with vivid details.

1. Nurse O'Hare is a real witch.
2. Many homeless people are mentally disturbed.
3. The Young Offenders Act is too soft.
4. Casinos are a great way for governments to generate income without raising taxes.
5. The price of food has shot up in the past five years.

 # SHOULD YOU START WITH IDEAS OR DETAILS?

Should you start with an abstract idea and then add details to liven it up? Or should you start with details and then develop the overall idea from them? Both sides have their advocates, and either method will work as long as you *move back and forth between ideas and details* during the thinking process. Remember: the thinking process is not neat; neatness is for the final draft. But let's consider the pros and cons of each method as a starting point.

In life outside school, we usually learn things by starting with details and then drawing conclusions after experiencing enough examples. As children, we first touch hot stoves or slobber out half-words, and later theories about heat and language emerge. The idea of death may not be real until we see someone we loved looking like wax in a casket. Divorce may be an empty abstraction until we live through one. As we experience things one by one, our brains work to develop ideas that summarize or explain our experiences. Most of our self-learned ideas grow this way over years.

On the other hand, most teaching starts with ideas and asks you to apply them to specifics. Moral guidance from religion or family begins with abstract ideas such as "Thou shalt not kill," rather than letting you kill to see how it feels and discovering what punishment follows. Biology professors give you the abstract plan behind a frog's internal muscle and digestive systems and then ask you to dissect a specimen, rather than handing you a frog and scalpel and letting you figure out the principles by trial and error.

For a writer, details sometimes offer the best place to start—when you're doing personal writing, for instance, in which recalling specific places, people, and incidents will lead you to ideas. In *Heart of a Stranger*, novelist Margaret Laurence describes how her vivid memories of the prairie landscape influenced her writing:

> In everything I have written which is set in Canada, whether or not actually set in Manitoba, somewhere some of my memories of the physical appearance of the prairies come in.... I doubt if I will ever live there again, but those poplar bluffs and the blackness of the soil and the way in which the sky is open from one side of the horizon to the other—these are things I will carry inside my skull for as long as I live, and the vividness of recall that only our first home can have for us.

However, your professional writing tasks may start with ideas given to you. Your employer may ask you to come up with a plan to reduce employee absenteeism or to persuade a client to stay with your firm. Your job is to supply details. This might also be true with informative essays or reports in which the topics are assigned to you.

Details are easier to get than ideas. They tend to come to us whole. Ideas, on the other hand, rarely, if ever, emerge complete—like a light bulb flashing on. We need to play around with an idea, rub it up against details before we can say clearly what it is.

Think about how you might create ideas and details when you consider topics for papers. Examine the following as potential essay topics. What will be hard or easy in each?

Democracy

Your favourite vacation spot

Airport terminals

Artificial intelligence

Democracy is the most abstract topic. Therefore, an idea will be easy to get, and details harder, because the topic does not help you to visualize it. But much has been said about democracy, so even though *an* idea will be easy to get, saying something fresh will be harder. However, competing ideas will be readily available. Your favourite vacation spot and airport terminal are both visual, so you'll have an easy time with details, but a harder time creating an abstraction about them. The vacation is one of the most common topics assigned, so coming up with a fresh idea will be even harder. Beware the topic that looks familiar or easy at first glance! The airport topic is more unusual, so as long as you stay away from the obvious approaches (hijacking problems and delays), almost anything you say will be fresh. Artificial intelligence (or computer intelligence) is less abstract than democracy, but not nearly as specific as the other two. Visualization will be a problem. Because it's a technical topic, details will be hard to get unless you're well read on computers or do some research.

One last point: there's a classic formula for details and ideas. It says about 75% of your writing should be details, 25% ideas. There's nothing sacred about this formula, but it's a handy guideline. Many students think abstractions sound more intellectual, more important, than homely details. Your professors are likely to tell you, however, that most papers suffer from too few details rather than from too few abstractions. They may complain that the ideas lack honesty, originality, or depth, but almost all want more and livelier detail.

Highlights of Chapter 1

1. Good writing combines ideas and details, and the writer who hopes to be in touch with a reader must continually move back and forth from abstract ideas to concrete details.

2. Ideas give meaning and purpose to writing; they tie things together. Details help readers to visualize ideas; they are memorable and touchable.

3. Honest ideas should be both fresh and complex. Strive to develop competing ideas in the thinking stage of writing.

4. Good details should be specific and vivid—the more nitty-gritty they are, the better.

5. You can start with either details or ideas in developing topics to write about, but both are necessary, and writers usually have several supporting details for each idea they present.

Writing Suggestions and Class Discussions

1. "If this were my last day alive, I would,…." Make a list of ten specific things you might do. Then pick two or three and list details about them. Be vivid, concrete, and honest. Don't write to impress people. Now, review the ones you developed for a unifying idea—the values that best capture the philosophy of your last day. Write a short paper based on these notes. Turn in your rough notes, clearly labelled, as well as the finished essay.

2. What follows are some generalizations—ideas that need details. Pick one and use it for your core idea. Illustrate it with three or four concrete details and build it into a coherent paragraph.

   a. "All evil will shun a place where people are happy."—Igjugarjuk, Inuit shaman

   b. "The only critic is time."—A.J. Casson

   c. "Canada is a hard country to govern."—John A. Macdonald

   d. "And God said unto [Adam and Eve]…replenish the earth and subdue it."—The Book of Genesis

e. "Fear not that your life shall end, but rather fear that it shall never begin."—Cardinal Henry Newman

f. "A short story is what you see when you look out the window."—Mavis Gallant

g. "Any woman who tells the truth about herself is a feminist."—Alice Munro

h. "Work is love made visible."—Kahlil Gibran

3. What follows are collections of details in search of an idea. Choose one of the groups and list two or three ideas that these details suggest. Also, add several new details to the list.

a. AIDS:

AIDS may be transmitted from mother to fetus.

AIDS may lie dormant in a person for as long as ten years, while the person infects other people.

AIDS is not confined to homosexuals or intravenous drug users.

Promiscuous sex occurs more often than ever before.

Many people in Third World countries resist using condoms.

b. The teaching profession:

"Those who can do; and those who can't teach."— (proverb)

The pay of the average starting teacher is just behind that of a sanitation worker or police officer.

Studies have shown that teachers and religious leaders have the longest life expectancy of any group.

Teachers report that they are among the most contented with their occupation.

Teachers are used as scapegoats for the large and complex problems of an increasingly underfunded system of public education.

4. For one of the following topics, generate a list of details that can be used in a paper: quotes, stories, facts, descriptions. But also move to ideas as they occur to you. Try for three ideas and nine or ten details on the topic you choose. Mark each item on your list as "I" or "D."

Teaching morals to today's children

Physical education classes

Your favourite vacation spot

War movies

Abuse of the elderly

5. Follow the instructions for 4, but start with ideas first, freely moving to details.

   An ethnic group to which you do not belong

   Canada-U.S. relations

   Personality of the last person you dated

   Dentists

6. Write down three competing ideas to explain one of the following:

   a. Men under 25 cause far more automobile accidents than women under 25.

   b. Why do bad things happen to good people?

   c. If teenagers today know more about sex than other generations did, why are there more teenage pregnancies than ever before?

7. Write a list of ideas and details for a topic that interests you.

8. Write a list of ideas and details for a professional writing task you might have someday. Imagine, for instance, that you have been asked to deliver a speech to your local business group or library or church group, or to write a press release or a memo on hiring procedures.

9. Write a list of ideas and details for a paper due in another course.

10. Write down three ideas you believe in deeply. These may be technical (passive solar heat is the most efficient energy source), argumentative (people over 70 ought to be required to repass the driver's test to keep their licences), or philosophical (happiness is easier the less you want). These ideas may be kernels from which papers may grow.

11. Make a list of half a dozen details to support each of your three ideas in 10.

12. What is one idea you have mixed feelings about and would like to explore more deeply? Explain why you have mixed feelings and give a few details. (One of mine is how much freedom a teacher ought to allow students in writing assignments. One side of me says students should develop their own topics completely from scratch so they control them. It's democratic. The other side of me says students need to be shown that they can write on anything and that in their careers they will most often be assigned topics. It's less democratic, but more practical.)

13. Write a two- or three-page essay based on one of the previous writing suggestions. Aim for a fresh idea with some complexity and plenty of vivid details.

14. Evaluate the following list of potential paper topics. How hard would it be to come up with a fresh, complex idea and vivid, specific details for each? Also consider how these topics match your experiences, knowledge, and biases: what are your personal strengths and weaknesses in each?

The national debt

Concepts of beauty and ugliness

Stereotypes of grandparents

City parks

Lesbian parents

Your first encounter with violence

15. Write a letter to your boss asking for a promotion or raise. Present several reasons (ideas) why you deserve this reward and support your ideas with specific details.

16. Write a brief summary of a key concept you're learning about in another course. Write out the main idea so it's accurately complex and clear, then illustrate the idea with several examples. Imagine your reader is a student in the class who doesn't "get" the concept.

17. Write a brief criticism of an afternoon talk show. Point out what you don't like, then support it with at least three specific examples.

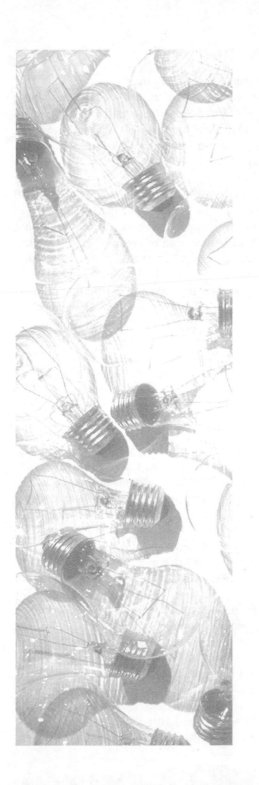

Chapter 2

Getting Ideas:

Brainteasers

to Help You Write

on Almost Anything

---

*The wise possess ideas;
the greater part of
mankind are possessed
by them.*

Samuel Taylor Coleridge

A former editor-in-chief of a major women's magazine once said that she learned to be an idea person when she first started working as a young assistant editor. Each Monday, she and every other staff member had to bring to a meeting a list of 25 great ideas for articles. This brainstorming gave her boss, the editor-in-chief at that time, hundreds of ideas from which to choose for the dozen or so she needed each month. It also gave the young assistant editor a headache.

Then the ideas began to come more easily. Some weeks she had 30 or 40 ideas—better ones her boss could use. The important trick she learned was to let her subconscious mind work on the problem during the week and not to sit down at three o'clock on Friday afternoon to create 25 ideas spontaneously. All week long she'd jot down ideas as they came to her, stimulated by all sorts of things—a taxi ride, a meal in a Hungarian restaurant, an unusual garden she saw, a newspaper article. Soon she realized that almost anything could become an idea for a magazine article. "Just knowing I had such an assignment made me remember things I'd otherwise have forgotten," she said. One of the side benefits of becoming an idea-creating person was that she lived at a more intense pace, appreciated life more.

This is *incubation.* You plant a seed of an idea, and your subconscious mind—which is far more powerful than your conscious mind—will work on the problem. The solution that finally comes to you has been growing in your subconscious, which thinks about it while you go about your normal life, unaware of its activity except in flashes here and there. When the idea has ripened, it rises to the conscious level. The point is, you don't have to wait helplessly for a magic moment to strike in order to write. You can arrange your own inspiration. In fact, working with ideas creates inspirations.

There are two things to remember about using your subconscious brain power. The first is that better ideas come if you give your subconscious mind subtle reminders from time to time. The subconscious needs to be tickled once or twice a day if it's to keep going. The second thing to remember about incubation is that ideas often don't come out fully formed like newborn babies. They usually emerge in bits and pieces—the arm or leg of an idea. I'm using this grotesque image to describe ideas because most people don't want to accept such fragments as the offspring of their minds. Have faith. Be prepared to write down the fragments as they're delivered. You don't need index cards or a computer—although they work for many people. Novelist H.G. Wells had an unusual system to keep new ideas organized as they emerged in bits and pieces. He kept a dozen big barrels around his home, one for each book he planned to write. When fragments of an idea or details came to him, he'd jot them on a slip of paper and toss it into the appropriate barrel. When a barrel filled, Wells knew he had enough material to write a book.

There's no need to buy barrels. Two pages of notes are plenty to create a two- or three-page paper. "Two pages of *notes*?" I imagine some students protesting. "Why not just write it out? I thought you were going to save us work in this book."

This chapter will address this question, but a few comments are in order now. First, notetaking is rarely wasted. Researchers into creativity in many fields have shown that this is how the best idea people operate. They've proved it's dependable, saves time, produces more interesting ideas, and helps blocked writers to get going again. Why shouldn't it help you? And remember: notetaking is *easy writing*, because you pay no attention to spelling, word choice, or complete sentences.

Suppose your anthropology professor tells you to write on the notion of personal space. Start by observing the way people stand and sit in public places. For example, the way people arrange themselves in elevators—where do they direct their attention, and how much space do they give each other? Perhaps you notice two women of Indian background touching while talking, and you consider that personal space might be culturally determined. Later, you watch how your friends arrange themselves around a table in the cafeteria, or the way lovers stand together talking, face to face.

At this point, it is important to find a piece of paper or boot up the computer and start writing; it doesn't matter how you write, but it is crucial that you start keeping lists of all the details you observe and all the ideas you generate. This is the way to "prime the pump," to get your mind engaged in the consideration of the topic and the generation of innovative approaches. These activities will fuel your subconscious, and when you write your paper, deeper, more original ideas are likely to arise. Inspiration results from *many* good ideas banging into each other.

■ *Practice 2-1:* Take five minutes (maximum) to recall some specific cultural differences that distinguish groups of people where you live. Write in list form and do not worry about spelling or sentence structure. Tomorrow, up till class time, add to the list new things that occur to you from school, your job, travel, or television.

 # IMPROVING YOUR IDEAS

It's easy to come up with dull ideas—they're the ones off the tops of our heads. The tops of our heads are notoriously dull—clichés, television jingles, routine responses, and pass-the-salt ideas live there. The Greek writer Euripides once said, "Among mortals, second thoughts are best." Believe him! Second, third, and fourth thoughts create the unusual angles that make ideas creative. To be interesting, to make people think, you cannot simply repeat what they already know—that is, what fills the tops of our heads. Put ideas on trial; call them into question.

So *how* do you go deeper and draw out more original ideas? Most professional writers *make a habit of creativity* through regular notetaking and incubation; you can get yourself into the groove of having ideas just as ball players groove a batting swing. Novelist Morley Callaghan once described the writer's challenge as finding "the extraordinary in the ordinary," being fascinated by the strangeness of the life that surrounds us. Keeping a journal, reading stimulating books, and jotting down observations are ways of maintaining this perception. But there are other techniques that help writers to discover fresh ways of looking at old subjects.

The following *brainteasers* are *systematic ways* of stimulating and exploring regions of your mind to find out what ideas lurk there subconsciously. These are *the ways people think.* At first, these brainteasers may seem artificial and awkward to use, but after a semester or two of practise, they will become part of the way you think and will help you to create ideas more quickly and with less agony. They will make it possible for you to think or write on almost anything. Brainteasers also help you to be more honest, for they draw out the complex, conflicting ideas you may be holding back.

Brainteasers go beyond what you tried in the last chapter. There you *randomly* bounced between ideas and details—a kind of free brainstorming. It's a great technique to get started and may be enough to bring some papers to the order and draft stages. But there will be times when you're stuck, times when simple brainstorming doesn't evoke fresh enough ideas, times when you want more focus. Brainteasers get you going again, and some even organize papers. If you feel blocked or empty, try one or two brainteasers to reenergize yourself. You can use several or all to get started on any topic.

All the brainteasers follow the same overall process. First, *make long lists.* Since your mind contains thousands of ideas, you must never settle for the first few that appear. Write down the obvious ones, but keep going, for the longer the list you create, the more likely better ideas will turn up. Sure, you'll throw away many of your ideas, but we're only talking about a scratch list anyway. I recommend a half-page minimum for a brainteaser list. One page is better. It takes time to wake our deepest mind. Why a list and not freewriting in sentences and paragraphs? Items on a list are easier to organize than in a paragraph. Also, freewriting tends to focus you on one idea; a list forces you to find many alternatives.

Part of the problem any writer has is translating a non-verbal concept into words. How many times have you thought, "I know what I want to say, but I can't put it into words." Second, to eliminate this problem, *make a list of ideas in rough form, not worrying about wording or grammar.* Turning the ideas into words is a separate step. A little sloppiness is good compost—don't rewrite brainteasers for neatness. In the early stages of writing, concentrate on *what* you want to say (the ideas and details), not on the structure (which comes next), the words (which come during the draft and revision), or the mechanics (which come last). Brainteasers are not word-association but a list of ideas. One-word items are too vague to help a lot; phrases of three to ten words or occasional sentences will tweak your brain more.

Third, *you must not prejudge ideas or details as you compose your list.* Write everything down, no matter how dumb some items sound. Judge later, when you choose which ones will appear in the paper. If you judge at the list-making stage, you may shut off the flow of ideas. Good ideas have a way of hiding underneath weak ideas. Research into the creativity of scientists, businesspeople, artists, writers, and many others proves that self-criticism kills creativity if done too early—so save criticism until later.

To summarize:

1. Make a long list (at least half a page).

2. Concentrate on ideas/details, not on words.

3. Move quickly and do not prejudge items.

TEN BRAINTEASERS

1. USE YOUR SENSES

List sensory details about your topic. Doing so will help you to get into the topic and supply you with vivid details for the draft. Our senses connect our minds to the world around us, so by recalling sensory impressions, you re-create the subject for yourself, engaging brain and feelings, stirring subconscious memories. Drenching yourself in sensory impressions is enjoyable once you catch on—one of the secret pleasures of most professional writers.

Try an exercise. List all the sensory details you can about your mother. Start visually—describe her face, the way she walks, favourite gestures, the way she looks when angry, sad, or laughing. Then become more specific—try her teeth, hair style and colour, her favourite clothes. Bring up other things.

Now move to touch—the way she felt your forehead for a fever, a time she struck you in anger, the temperature and texture of her skin, what it feels like to kiss her cheek.

Now sounds—the tone of her voice, the noise of her steps, peculiar expressions she uses when she speaks, unusual sighs or other nonverbal noises such as snores, wheezes, or gurgles. (Yes, mothers do these things. Be honest.)

Now smells—smell her perfume or kitchen or work odours, the unique odour of her room.

You can't just read these words to understand; try the exercise. Write down as much as you can about your mother, letting your mind go. Probe deeply, especially for the forgotten or unusual detail. Think sensuously. Recall key scenes.

Not only does this brainteaser prepare details and get you into a topic, but it also leads inevitably to ideas. Write down any *ideas* that occur to you as well as details. For example, perhaps memories of your mother lead you to recall how your father so dominated her life that she really had little life of her own at times. This is an abstraction, not a sensory detail, but it could become the main idea of an essay. This is exactly how brainteasers move writers from rough notes to core ideas.

Using senses doesn't just apply to personal topics such as mothers. Suppose you're writing about public-smoking laws. Use your senses to visualize scenes of smoke-filled cafeterias or restaurants. If you're a nonsmoker, get down all the sensations you've experienced in a smoke-filled room— your burning eyes, your raw throat, the film on the windows, the stale odour of your sweater afterwards. If you *are* a smoker, use your senses to describe the agony you suffer wanting a light—your dry throat, your nervous hands, your eyes involuntarily glancing at the door. The sensory brainteaser is an excellent way to start almost any topic. It draws you into your topic and provides sharp details.

■ *Practice 2-2:* Make a half-page list of sensory details about bus or airplane travel. Move quickly; pay no attention to spelling or writing complete sentences. Be as specific as possible. In class, your teacher may ask you to read your list and discuss how to develop it into a paper.

2. See the Topic from Alternative Viewpoints

This brainteaser gives you *perspective* by making you see the topic from outside your own narrow viewpoint. This is another secret of honest writing. When trying alternative viewpoints, you must try to see the topic as someone else would, to inhabit another's mind and eyes for a little while and not impose your views on others. Doing so helps to open our own eyes.

For example, if you want to write on a personal relationship that has soured, first list all the people whose viewpoints might be different from yours:

Igor (your ex-boyfriend)

Igor's mother

Igor's friends

Your parents

Your friends

Igor's new girlfriend, Bertha

Your new companion, Lars

Your children (if any)

Now spend time with each viewpoint, trying to see the break-up as each of them would. What would they think in their secret hearts about it? How would they explain its causes or place blame? Remember that each of them will have a different focus. Lars may care less about the past than the future; friends may think Igor was tied down to you; your mother might take your side, but underneath her sympathy, perhaps she hopes the experience has taught you a lesson about jumping too quickly into relationships. Ask yourself as you proceed how much truth is in these ideas.

If you still don't feel as though you have enough ideas, you can create a list of *character types*, who always have viewpoints on any topic. This is a kind of cross-section of human opinions. How would the following view your topic?

An accountant

A lawyer

Your religious leader

Your favourite singer

Someone in the year 2050

An ecologist

A psychologist

A child

A politician

You are doing a little bit of stereotyping here, but just imagine what a lawyer might say about the break-up. He or she would consider it a legal/contractual problem. What new facets would that view bring up? Your religious leader might relate the break-up to your moral and spiritual beliefs. Obviously, some of these character types may not be very helpful on this topic: the ecologist and socialist perhaps. The person from the future may simply say, "It doesn't matter now," and suggest not worrying about it. Give each one a few minutes. If nothing comes, move to another. We all have little bits of these perspectives inside us. To cultivate your deep, honest ideas, give each perspective a chance to speak. See who speaks loudest and clearest to you, and listen for new ideas. Alternative viewpoints help to free you from your surface or normal self so you can probe your deeper, more unusual self.

The competition among the different viewpoints will lead to more honest and sophisticated ideas. Good ideas toughen up under pressure from other ideas; poor ones fade away. Alternative viewpoints will also help you to relate better to your audience because you will think of things your readers may want discussed. As the English novelist W. Somerset Maugham once said, "the measure of a writer is the number of selves he encompasses."

Suppose you're writing on a less personal topic for a communications course, such as how television affects our views of marriage. You can start by listing some alternative viewpoints:

Young children

Advertisers

Teenage couples

Program writers

Actors/actresses

Lesbian and gay people

Marriage counsellors

Religious leaders

Senior citizens

People in troubled marriages

People in wonderful marriages

Write down each viewpoint. Remember, no matter how you feel about this conflict, each group will feel it is doing what's right and will justify its viewpoint. When you finish, you can begin sorting through the viewpoints to decide which to use. If you decide on your message before honestly exploring all sides, you'll be a little bit like the Queen in *Alice in Wonderland*, who wants to have the punishment first and then the trial.

Examining alternative viewpoints is best for honesty, for widening your perspectives, and for audience awareness. Doing so may help you to organize, but may tend to pull a draft in many directions.

■ *Practice 2-3:* Your college or university is suffering budget problems and is considering reducing costs by eliminating the required writing course. List five people or groups who would have different perspectives on this plan. Explain each viewpoint in half a page.

3. BREAK STEREOTYPES, BREAK UNQUESTIONED IDEAS, AND BREAK SLOGANS

Stereotypes, unquestioned ideas, and slogans are enemies of creativity—blocks that prevent honest, imaginative thinking. All three encourage us to think in accepted, common patterns.

Stereotypes place people or ideas in close-minded categories:

1. He is from Alberta, so he must be a redneck.
2. A woman can't build a house.

3. Most white people are probably racists.

4. Fat people are so jolly.

Sentences such as these portray a writer who does not look carefully at life, who sees groups and generalities, not individuals. Stereotypes are comfortable lies that make the world seem more simple and predictable than it really is. They're hard to break because they make thinking easy.

A creative thinker must also peek behind *unquestioned ideas* once in a while to keep from being close-minded. Doing this has led to some of humanity's most creative concepts. A good example is the discovery of insulin to treat diabetes by Sir Frederick Banting and his associates at the University of Toronto. Although diabetes had been linked to the pancreas, Banting came at the problem with a new idea. He jumped out of bed and wrote in his notebook in 1920: "Tie off pancreas ducts of dogs. Wait six or eight weeks. Remove and extract." Sceptics did not believe it was possible, but Banting persevered, eventually isolated insulin, and received a Nobel Prize.

For centuries, dissection of the human body was forbidden. Until this unquestioned injunction was lifted and the body dissected, people believed our emotions came from our hearts (not our minds) and even such strange things as that a man's erection came from air in his lungs! Unquestioned ideas are invisible to us because almost all of us take them for granted, as we do eyesight or the ability to walk. If challenging these ideas is upsetting, it's because our belief in them is deeply ingrained.

Slogans are the stereotyped use of words. If you find yourself concluding, "Man does not live by bread alone," or "Guns don't kill people; people kill people," watch out! You're not thinking; you're repeating something off the top of your head. While stereotypes are comfortable and unquestioned ideas are invisible, slogans come to us with a sense of discovery: "Ah, I've got it!" But just as we have the chance to move into new territory, we have found our way back to the worn, common road of thought. Students sometimes protest, "But this slogan is true! I've seen it!" Perhaps. But if it's true, put it into your own words at least to make it your truth.

Stereotypes, unquestioned ideas, and slogans are lumped together because the same brainteaser applies to each. To get fresher, more honest ideas, imagine yourself as a puncturer of balloons. *Become a cynic who suspects all commonly held ideas and sayings have little lies in them that need exposing.* Think like the philosopher Nietzsche, who said, "Joyous distrust is a sign of health."

To break these three idea-killers, first list all the stereotypes, unquestioned ideas, and slogans you can about your topic, all the "common" truths. These are what you'd write in your essay if you wanted to create a below-average paper. Next, find *exceptions* to items in this list. Think of people and cases that may contradict the common belief. Write as long a list as you can. After you've attacked the stereotypes, unquestioned ideas, and slogans, you can honestly decide what you really think, and you will have plenty of material for an outline or draft.

For example, let's assume your sociology professor assigns an essay on the topic "Women in the workplace." Here are some idea-killers on this topic:

Women can't do the heavy work a man can. (stereotype)

A woman's place is in the home. (slogan)

Working mothers hurt kids by not being home. (unquestioned idea)

Men will not go to a woman doctor. (unquestioned idea)

Keep women barefoot and pregnant. (slogan)

Equal pay for equal work. (slogan)

Would you want women shot if they were allowed in combat? (unquestioned idea)

Women are too emotional to be in public office. (stereotype)

All male bosses are chauvinists. (stereotype)

Women bosses aren't feminine. (stereotype)

Notice that these stereotypes, unquestioned ideas, and slogans come from both sides of this controversial topic. Now, the creative task is to puncture these balloons. Some, such as "A woman's place is in the home," are easy to pop. Suppose Queen Elizabeth I, Monica Seles, Sheila Copps, Marie Curie, Jane Goodall, and Kim Campbell had stayed home? The list could go on for pages. See if you can poke other holes in this slogan.

Other statements are harder to attack. Some people think it's awful to shoot women in battle because they have been brought up to believe women should be treated with respect and a gentler touch than men. Maybe, however, they need to get behind the "manners" they've been taught. Are those manners sexist? Maybe the real issue is that it's also awful to shoot men in battle.

We may agree on the concept of "Equal pay for equal work," but our job in this brainteaser is to question what we believe on the surface. Here's how we might puncture that slogan: how do we ever know work done is equal? Doctors may earn as much in two hours as truck drivers do in a week. People with seniority often earn far more for the same job than newer employees. What about quality of work? Many mediocre workers get the same pay as outstanding workers.

My conclusion: equal pay for equal work sounds good in theory, but variables not related to the worker's gender make such an idea hard to define, to put into effect, or to enforce. We may not be happy with this conclusion because we want to believe in gender fairness and justice, but until we think some more about this slogan, we will be forced to qualify its generalization. Can you find some exceptions to this conclusion?

This brainteaser shows us some of the walls we or our upbringings have built around our inner worlds. Tearing down these walls, or at least peeking over them, is one way people think. Loren Eiseley, the great nature and science writer, once warned any thinking person "not to love anything *official* too fondly, otherwise one is easily destroyed."

Breaking stereotypes is good for creativity and challenging established ideas, and it's a great approach to most essays you will write.

■ *Practice 2-4:*

1. List five stereotypes about men and break two of them with examples, facts, or logic.
2. Treat "All men are created equal" as an unquestioned idea and poke two holes in it with specific cases in which this is not (or should not be) so.
3. List five common slogans used to debate public policy (for example, "Guns don't kill people, people kill people") and pop holes in two of them.

4. CLASSIFY YOUR TOPIC

To classify is another way to think—one used by scientists, businesspeople, and others. Classifying breaks a subject into categories and places individuals or things in each of the categories. For example, biology divides all living creatures into two main classifications: plants and animals. It further classifies types of animals according to whether they have backbones, lungs, give live births, and so on. Then biology decides to which classification individual species such as the monkey or dolphin belong. The thinking you do here is to figure out sensible, inventive categories that show underlying qualities among members of the same group that may not be obvious at first glance. People classified whales as fish, for instance, until realizing that some not-so-obvious qualities such as lungs and feeding offspring with milk make whales closer to land-inhabiting mammals than to fish.

In this brainteaser, break your subject down into categories *several times* until you come up with a creative pattern. For example, suppose your topic is "Dreams." You could break dreams down into daydreams and night dreams. You could further classify night dreams as follows:

Dreams in which you're chased

Sexual dreams

Falling dreams

Replay-of-the-day dreams

Dreams in which you can't run or speak

To finish this brainteaser, list examples and descriptions of each category.

Suppose your topic is "Education." Off the top of your head, you might generate the following:

Elementary school

High school

College or university

This classification is pretty boring, but it *is* a starting point. Now try working just on high school. How about:

Good high schools

Bad high schools

Average high schools

Again, it's not fresh enough because the categories are too vague. How about this:

Preppie high school

Learn-nothing high school

Vocational-technical high school

Private high school

This is getting better. It's easy to think of people and facts to put under each. You might get even more specific by classifying types of private schools.

Now go back to the original topic, "Education." We could have taken a different route. Instead of schools, we could have classified students, courses, or teachers. Take a minute or two to imagine several classifications for each.

The more specific your subject, the more you can do with it. This seems like a contradiction, since you might think the broader the topic, the easier it is to think of things to write down. Not true. It's easy to call up common thoughts on big topics, but harder to say something fresh. Suppose you start with "Technology" as your topic. The possibilities are too overwhelming. Narrow it to "Medical technology" and you can classify it more vividly. Narrow that to "Types of gynecologists" or "Types of sports doctors," for instance, and the paper almost begs to be written.

You might have one objection to classifying—it seems to create stereotypes! It puts individuals in categories. Isn't that what we were fighting in the last brainteaser? Yes, it was. However, our main objective in this chapter is to increase the ways we have of thinking. Breaking classifications that have become stereotypes is one way people think; creating classifications is another. Classifying need not be stereotyping—if you keep in mind (and remind your readers) that not all individuals fit their categories perfectly. Classification helps us to see patterns; it is only close-minded if it's applied too strictly. If you're worried that your classification is dishonest, try breaking it down as in the previous brainteaser. Classifying works well for scientific and technical writing and for many assignments. It is a strong organizer.

■ *Practice 2-5:* Classify types of television programs, poems, art works, or music. Have at least five categories. Now pick one of these types and classify it into at least three subcategories. Give a specific example of each.

5. COMPARE AND CONTRAST YOUR TOPIC

You can get more ideas by comparing your topic with another. This is another basic way people think. We contrast socialism and capitalism, urban life and country life, retailing and wholesaling, the Blue Jays and the Expos. To understand our world, we stretch one thing to meet another, thereby creating meaning. If you must write a paper on British Columbia's emerging status as a trader in the Pacific Rim, you might discover ideas by comparing it to Newfoundland and the Atlantic economy. Start listing differences:

BRITISH COLUMBIA

The BC economy is booming.

The forest industry is partly responsible for the strength of BC's trade surplus.

BC is taking advantage of proximity to Southeast Asian markets.

NEWFOUNDLAND

The Newfoundland economy is depressed.

The collapse of the Atlantic fishery has contributed to the current crisis.

Newfoundland does not have the same strategic relationship with European markets that BC has with Asian ones.

This list should continue for half a page, but it's probably not meaningful to you unless you know a little bit about the economies of the two regions. What do I do next with this list? Well, I might create my main idea by combining a number of these contrasts, or I might go into one difference in depth: say, to figure out why the forest industry is so much stronger in BC than in Newfoundland.

Sometimes comparison or contrast is implied in the topic given to you—"Contrast the democratic and totalitarian views of the press," or

"What similar techniques do the French painters Monet and Renoir use?"
Simply start listing. At other times, you may be given a topic and can discover a useful comparison to bring it to life. If you must write a paper on
modern nursing ethics, think of comparisons:

Two nurses whose ethics are different

Two situations that require different ethics

Nursing ethics of the last century compared with today's ethics

The contrast in ethics between doctors and nurses

Similarities between nursing ethics and those of another profession

You would then go on to explore *one* of these in depth, listing as many comparisons and contrasts as possible.

Making a list of similarities and differences takes the pressure off; you
can say, "I'm only listing things." But when done, you'll have some ideas
and details, as well as the basis for organizing your paper. Comparison and
contrast can open up almost any topic—but you must work hard to get
beyond superficial comparisons and contrasts.

■ *Practice 2-6:*

Think of three possible approaches using comparison and contrast to *one* of
these topics: manners, the criminal justice system, or Christmas shopping. Pick
your best and create a half-page list of specific points to support your idea.

6. Create Metaphors

A metaphor is a special comparison, not between things in the same category (two novels, for example), but between things in different categories
(a novel and a beverage):

Reading this book is like drinking a cool, clear glass of water.

Her party was like an insane asylum.

Old-age homes are like warehouses.

The city is wearing a veil of fog this morning.

Why make such comparisons? Because it's fun, and it stirs a reader's imagination and visualization. This brainteaser helps *you* because it suggests
many ideas.

Let's return to the topic of "Education" to show how you could use this
brainteaser to come up with ideas that did not appear when you used classification. Start by listing all the comparisons you can think of, not worrying if
some sound silly. Let's try "Colleges and universities."

A college or university is like:

a factory

the army

a farm or garden

a beehive or anthill

the ocean

a circus

a meal

a tree

This is, of course, a rough list. The next step is to glance over it, adding a few details to each item to see which ones have the most potential.

In comparing a college or university to a factory, I think of courses in which the same work is done in mass-production lecture halls, or of how breaks between classes resemble shift changes. The *idea* behind this metaphor suggests that school is routine, uncreative, time-serving. Someone who feels this way may have the concept for a paper here.

The circus metaphor works well, especially when applied to the last week of classes, when students are a bit wild—they dress outrageously, and the "clowns" try out their routines in class. The instructor becomes a ringmaster trying to keep the show going. Some students give beautiful performances, while that tiger in the front row is crouched to pounce if forced to write another paper. To explore this concept further, we could make a list of more circus things and try to find equivalents. See if you can add to the following list and make the metaphoric connections to your educational experience:

The three rings

Buying a ticket

The high-wire act

Elephants bellowing

The sideshow

Monkeys

Peanuts, popcorn, and cotton candy

The bleachers

The cages

The freak show

Cleaning up the elephants' mess

The whip and chair

The mood of a paper based on the circus metaphor would be light, unlike that of a paper based on the grim factory metaphor. The humour would be gentle yet sarcastic, poking fun at college or university as an entertaining game.

Following is a dialogue that occurred in a composition class. The students, working on a paper on teenage suicide, were trying to find metaphors to uncover the topic and reveal fresh approaches.

TEACHER: What can you compare suicide to?

STUDENT A: An ending.

TEACHER: Okay, what kinds of endings are there? Let's think of endings and then see if we can come back to suicide.

STUDENT B: A rear end.

STUDENT C: A cliff edge.

STUDENT D: A book ending.

STUDENT A: Like a book with the last pages ripped out—that's suicide.

STUDENT B: How about a dead-end road?

STUDENT A: Or a road that leads nowhere?

STUDENT E: Suicide's more an escape.

TEACHER: From what? Metaphors ought to be visual.

STUDENT F: An escape from prison. Life's like a jail to some people. They want to be free.

STUDENT E: Suicides like to control what happens to them. They feel like victims until they plan to kill themselves. Then they're in charge.

TEACHER: So what's that like?

STUDENT G: Like—writing a play. They make everything happen as they want—for once.

A metaphor can be the backbone of your essay, or it can simply help you to create a few details that will add sparkle to your paper. It's good for creativity, visual detail, and humour. In academic and business writing, though, you may want to keep metaphors on a short leash.

■ *Practice 2-7:* Pick one of the metaphors for college or university (or invent one of your own) and make a half-page list of specific equivalents.

7. LIST EXAMPLES

This brainteaser provides you with *details*. Simply list all the specific examples about the topic you can think of. If you're writing about abortion, for example, list all the cases you know: ones from the news, people you know, stories mentioned by friends or teachers. An example must be a *single*, concrete instance, never a generality. This brainteaser tells you quickly which topics you don't know enough about before it's too late. If it's an assigned topic, of course, you may need to do some research to get examples.

If you were going to write a paper on alcoholism, for instance, these examples might occur:

Matt—a gentle young man in your biology class, told you he was attending AA meetings. Several times his class comments were incoherent. He was quiet and lonely.

Rico—an older man in your English-composition class, wrote an essay describing his recovery from alcoholism, which the instructor read aloud. In this paper, he told about the hell of shakes and fits he used to go through and how desperate he was to make up for the time he was "dead" for his four children.

Jeanette—the mother of a teenage alcoholic. Her son ruined her family, almost bringing her to divorce. She threw him out of the house.

Ed—a 50-year-old man who stole money from his daughter for booze.

Once you start a list of examples, you will often realize you know far more stories than you thought. Catching one example often hooks more. To develop this list into a paper, you might narrow it to teenage alcoholism or the effects of alcoholism on families.

Examples are essential to support and make concrete most writing. This brainteaser is a good one to use early in writing a paper, but it will not help you to organize your details.

■ *Practice 2-8:* List half a page of your own examples for a paper on alcoholism or drug abuse. Fill out some of the examples with details. To move toward an idea, state a *point* the examples seem to suggest.

8. Make Bug Lists

One way to approach any topic is to criticize it or complain about it. You begin this brainteaser by saying, "What really bugs me about [topic] is [list of complaints]." A bug list helps you to formulate a problem, and solving a problem is a great topic for many papers.

Here is a good example. Christine, who worked at a nursing home, used a bug list to decide what she could write on. She listed dozens of complaints: about the old folks themselves, about the way the home was managed, about the families of the residents, and, most creatively, about her own flaws as an employee. She decided there was no easy way to make the home more humane and caring. She wasn't aware of this until she went through a pretty exhaustive list of complaints. Old Mr. Fitzwater was just a miserable grouch, and his bad humour couldn't be blamed on family or staff. And there was that gloppy unfood served each day—she'd spit it out too if someone tried to feed it to her. And while she understood why an orderly might feel irritated by continual messes, she didn't like the employees handling the old people as if they were machines to be oiled. She even found complaints about the building's design, which encouraged isolation; it was more tomb than home.

Christine, of course, could not cure all these ills, but by listing the problems, she saw how some things could be fixed, and she even brought them to the attention of her supervisor. And she found a new bug: he was afraid to do anything about her bugs.

Dissatisfaction has solved many problems, so put yourself in a sharp, critical mood for this brainteaser. Mention little things as well as large, abstract things so that you have both details and ideas. Be honest. In reviewing your brainteaser list later, you may decide to tackle a lot, as Christine did, or focus on just one criticism and seek an interesting and creative solution for it. Bug lists are excellent for career problem-solving and for argumentative papers. If not used with other brainteasers, however, they can lead to excessively negative writing.

■ *Practice 2-9:* Make a half-page bug list about public transportation or a fast-food restaurant.

9. ASK QUESTIONS

This brainteaser works especially well if you're confused about the topic or don't know much about an assigned topic. Ask all the hard questions that *you* want answered. You might begin by saying, "What is important to know about [your topic]?" Be a reporter; ask who, what, when, where, why, and how questions.

Let's try this approach with the topic "The Special Olympics":

Who runs the Special Olympics?

When did it first start, and who started it?

How do they pick the athletes?

What events or modified events are held?

What qualifies one as "special"?

How hard do the athletes train?

Where? With whom?

Where does the financing come from?

Why do the athletes participate?

How does the experience affect the athletes?

Asking questions takes some of the intimidation out of an unfamiliar topic and prods you in the right direction. You can be fairly sure your readers will want to ask the hard questions too, so your paper will move in a direction that will satisfy your audience. If your boss assigns you a task or report to complete, be sure to ask the hard questions yourself, early in the process, because bosses have a way of asking the really tough questions after tasks and reports are done.

After you finish your list, try to answer each question with all the ideas and details you can. If you can't answer some, you'll know where your research must begin. Use other brainteasers—examples, senses, alternative viewpoints—as you work to answer the questions. Sending the questions to your subconscious mind, of course, may also stimulate answers in the days or weeks ahead. Asking questions teaches you how to learn, helps you to write to an audience, and focuses you on key issues. It's good for research and problem-solving.

■ *Practice 2-10:* List half a page of questions about automobile engines or a career you're considering.

10. USE HUMOUR AND FANTASY

Go wacky and wild. Think of all kinds of fantasy situations for your topic and of the humorous side to it. This form of thinking is often downgraded because it sounds unintellectual or silly, but fantasy and humour have solved many personal and world problems. The German poet Goethe once said, "The intelligent man finds almost everything ridiculous." And Dorothy Parker, the great humourist, said, "Wit has truth in it." Think of how a grin or a joke can often end an argument. Think of all the comic movies, plays, and books that have changed people's ways of thinking. One of the greatest antiwar plays ever written is *Lysistrata,* a story about the women of two warring armies who go on a sex strike until their husbands agree to stop fighting. No sex for any man, the women on both sides vow. It's a hilarious fantasy that makes a serious point about the stupidity of war—that killing and lovemaking don't go together—and Aristophanes wrote it 2,400 years ago.

Some people will find this brainteaser hard. But anyone can develop this part of his or her thinking repertoire. Being able to let go, without prejudging dumb ideas, is the key. Following are a few ways to help loosen your imagination.

1. Reverse the normal rules of reality. Gary Larson, who created *The Far Side* cartoon, did so with deer who hunt people, salmon who wear tourist caps and carry cameras and who ride a boat upstream to the spawning grounds, and ants in lab coats who try to figure out how to get rid of their pests—humans.

2. Break a social, scientific, or mathematical law related to your topic and imagine the results. Do you hate speed limits? Imagine the results of having no speed limits. Do you hate high taxes, especially the GST? Imagine a Canada without them, or a Canada of 100% taxation, or a Canada without money.

3. Create a new rule or law and imagine its effects. Suppose library holdings could be recorded on microchips that could be implanted in the brain of each human being at the age of 10. What would happen? If you're

interested in world harmony, you might imagine a world government or the outlawing of foreign travel.

Using humour or fantasy jump-starts personal writing, fiction, and satire, and occasional flashes enliven professional writing. It's creative, but risky. Know your audience first.

■ *Practice 2-11:* Think of a fantastic or humorous way of ending war, preventing divorce, or reducing traffic deaths. Fill out your idea with a half-page list of details.

If you can remember only one thing from this chapter, remember this: the more brainteasers you devote to a topic, the wiser you'll be writing the paper. Your idea will be tougher, more resistant to attack, if you scrutinize it from many perspectives. The typical response to a problem such as writing a paper is to get *rid* of it; brainteasers help you to learn to embrace a problem and make something positive out of it.

Brainteasers should be fun—you are playing the mind's video game, punching all the buttons and switching electricity through the cobwebs of the skull. Enjoy it, relax, watch the show. There is no perfection, no rule for neatness or order.

Brainteasers give you control over your thinking. You can passively accept whatever ideas come to you, not knowing if they're the best or the most honest you have, or you can reject intellectual helplessness. Active use of your brain's capabilities leads to self-reliance and confidence. You edge a few centimetres closer to mental freedom when you can challenge an idea you find appealing.

Writing is about interesting ideas brought to life with vivid details. All the structure, word manipulation, and grammar in the world won't breathe life into a dead paper. Spend time creating lots of ideas, because good ideas make structure, word choice, and grammar easier. Content creates form.

While these 10 brainteasers can bounce you into any topic, there are many more. In fact, below are eight more you're smart enough to figure out on your own. Then there is a list of other brainteasers along with topics they're especially good for.

 # ADDITIONAL BRAINTEASERS

1. See the topic through an "ism": Feminism, Judaism, Buddhism, socialism, atheism, racism, capitalism. A variation on alternative viewpoints. Good for opening the topic to established philosophies.

2. Personalize, then depersonalize: Relate the topic to your experience; then see it completely apart from your involvement. Good for testing theories against your own life and for breaking your own prejudices.

3. Try on a new mood: See the topic from a variety of moods. Be paranoid, frivolous, serious, energetic, hopeful, generous, angry. Good for surveying your own feelings.

4. Vary your thinking style: Think verbally by using sentences; then think orally by speaking to a friend, peer group, or tape recorder; then think mathematically by listing statistics, percentages, and formulas about the topic; then think visually by drawing diagrams or clusters of ideas and details. Good for freshening your outlook.

5. Find paradoxes and seek opposites: If the topic is "A hard time in your life," turn it around to a hard time you are thankful for. "Your joy is your sorrow unmasked," Kahlil Gibran said. Good for developing honesty and creativity.

6. Be a devil's advocate: Take the unpopular side of an argument. Good for achieving freshness, but hard to support (if it were easy, it would be popular).

7. Predict the future: Why not? You've done everything else.

8. Bonus: Invent your own brainteaser.

OTHER BRAINTEASERS IN THIS BOOK

1. Bouncing between ideas and details (ch. 1): Good for all types of writing. Helps to focus and support writing.

2. Looping (ch. 4): Good for shaping freewriting toward a draft. Lacks overview of whole paper.

3. Clustering (ch. 4): Good for visually oriented people. Shows relationships between items so that outlining is easier.

4. Brainteasers for developing theses (ch. 4): Good for research and persuasive papers. Focuses your purpose before drafting. Weak for narrative and descriptive papers.

5. Iceberging and other eye-training brainteasers (ch. 8): Good for creating sharp detail and symbolism. Forces you to probe your topic physically.

6. Brainteasers for developing introductions (ch. 5): Good for focusing your idea as well as getting started.

7. People-describing brainteaser (ch. 9): Good for narratives and career writing (such as criminal justice or marketing) in which analysis of people is required.

8. Informative brainteasers (ch. 10): Process, cause, effect, and essentials. Good for organizing and focusing college and business writing.

9. Persuasive brainteasers (ch. 11): Facts, values, logic, and refutation. Good for supporting arguments and wringing ideas from a topic.

10. Literary-essay brainteasers (ch. 12): Gut reactions, critical perspectives, and explication. Good for any topic analysing a text. Forces you to look more closely at meaning. May require training in literary techniques.

11. Using library and non-library sources (ch. 13): Good for filling in missing material, surprising readers with facts, and feeling supported by others. Can control the paper or downgrade your own ideas if overused.

ROADBLOCKS TO GOOD IDEAS AND DETAILS

Despite all these brainteasers, there will be times when you will find yourself staring at a blank piece of paper at 2 a.m. or at a few sentences that are so bland and empty you can't build a thing on them. All writers have these awful moments, so nothing is wrong with you as a writer if you have dry spells. We'll discuss two common causes of such blank periods.

1. FEAR OF RISK

Despite the desire to do well, many people are just afraid to put anything on paper that is daring or a bit odd. They're afraid of being judged as weird or of revealing something secret about themselves. When they sit down to write, the flow of ideas is blocked by this internal censor. Sometimes your mind will let safe ideas through and you can manage to write something at least. At other times, the hold-back message shuts down the flow of *all* ideas; you want to write, but nothing comes.

Solutions
Tell yourself to write down the most outrageous things about your topic— the wildest, grossest, most absurd things. You reduce the fear of risk by telling yourself that this is a throw-away list no one else will see. If you are writing about pollution control, for instance, you can let loose the little demons to say all sorts of irresponsible, risky things on note paper:

1. Let's pollute faster so we kill off humanity—the world may be better off without us.

2. There ought to be pollution hit squads. Instead of taking polluters to court, these action groups could break polluters' windows or dump garbage, oil-killed animals, or chemical wastes on the lawns of company presidents. They could also picket their houses, churches, and clubs.

3. To cut down on garbage, we could forbid wrappers on all things that don't need to be sanitary, such as clothes.

4. Use big machines to crush garbage into blocks; then build houses with them.

Next, evaluate your absurd, secret list. The first point is just nastiness talking. The second is illegal and mean, but modified a bit, it might be usable. Perhaps we could pass laws to hold individual employees responsible for company pollution and to prosecute, fine, and jail them. The third point may also have merit if toned down a bit. The fourth sounds like a technological problem (to make odour-free garbage houses), but turning junk into treasure is viable with some items—such as automobile tires or bottles.

2. INSECURITY ABOUT YOUR ABILITY TO THINK

People with this block are amazed that anything at all appears on paper. When *any* idea appears, they are so thrilled they don't dare put it aside or try for another option. They feel compelled to accept any idea as a gift of the gods. These writers do not see writing as a skill to be learned; they think of it as a one-time miracle.

Solutions

Writing is a learnable and reliable skill, and a wealth of ideas exists in everyone's mind. In his book about human intelligence, *The Dragons of Eden*, Carl Sagan calculates that the human eye can absorb 5,000 bits of information per second and that all these data are stored in the brain, which recombines each bit many times with others, forming ideas and adding to them second by second. The average human brain contains an unimaginably large number of pieces of information and ideas—2×10^{13}—which is *far* greater than the total number of electrons, protons, and neutrons in the universe! Be impressed with your own brain power. Rely on it.

If you're a thank-God-I-have-an-idea person, you're too humble. Use brainteasers regularly for several months until you build up your confidence that you do have many ideas to choose from. You must demystify the creation of ideas. Having ideas is human nature; it comes with our genetic code.

Highlights of Chapter 2

1. Brainteasers are ways people think. They are learnable and can be used to teach yourself to think more clearly, creatively, and quickly. They will help not only in writing but also in academic and professional thinking tasks. Although brainteasers may seem artificial at first, they will become natural with use.

2. Use your subconscious mind for the incubation of ideas. Think early and often and take notes painlessly. Remember: ideas create inspirations, not the other way around.

3. Continue using a particular brainteaser until you either hit a dead end or catch fire. When you catch fire, follow the ideas and details until the heat dies down.

4. Trust yourself—you do have ideas.

5. Coming up with ideas regularly is a part of most jobs for which a degree is needed. You likely won't be asked to write a report for the boss until you have come up with good ideas.

6. Use these brainteasers any time you get stuck for ideas or details. They can help you to choose a topic, develop a topic, or jump start a stalled draft.

7. Brainteasers improve honesty. They are not formulas, because each person uses them differently. They help you to probe more deeply into your unique experiences and views. Risk letting your mind free. Be suspicious until you can see your topic from several angles.

Writing Suggestions and Class Discussions

1. Incubation Exercise: Your teacher will assign a paper. For each class, bring in a half-page list of new ideas and details for that paper.

2. Sensory Brainteaser:

   a. Fill one page listing sensory details about your first home. Try to include all five senses, being as specific as possible. Allow these details to bounce into ideas, but keep returning to the senses.

   b. Same as a., except list sensory details about the first time you saw death. Recall hidden details.

   c. Same as b. on any topic of your choice.

3. Alternative-Viewpoint Brainteaser:

   a. In a sentence or two, describe one failure you have had. Then list your feelings about its significance, causes, and effects. Now write out how two people close to you saw your failure differently. Try to think as they did.

   b. Take any controversial issue today and write half-page lists for the viewpoints of the parties involved. Concentrate on honestly seeing the issue as they do.

    c. Do an alternative-viewpoint list for any topic you choose.

4. Break Stereotypes, Unquestioned Ideas, and Slogans Brainteaser:

    a. Take some unquestioned idea (playing national anthems at sporting events, for instance) and see if you can expose some unreasonableness about it.

    b. In a paragraph, describe a situation in which someone stereotyped you because of your age, sex, race, physical appearance, or some other reason. Then list all the exceptions to this stereotype that you can think of—in yourself or others.

    c. Pick a popular slogan that bothers you and list five or six objections to it.

5. Classification Brainteaser:

    a. Classify types of students at your school and list a few details of each type. Try at least three different patterns before detailing the best one. Try to avoid falling into stereotypes.

    b. Classify a type of film into subcategories. For example, list three types of space films or four types of war films. List some examples under your best scheme.

    c. Classify reasons why people succeed in their careers (what qualities does it take?). Give details for each.

    d. Classify any topic of your choice. Give details for each category.

6. Comparison/Contrast Brainteaser:

    a. You are assigned to write on violence in hockey. Develop some ideas by comparing/contrasting it with violence in football, baseball, or any other professional sport. Fill a page with points of similarity/difference.

    b. Compare/contrast American and Canadian magazines of the same type (*Chatelaine* vs. *Mademoiselle* or *Time* vs. *Maclean's*, for instance).

    c. Use comparison/contrast for any topic of your choice.

7. Create Metaphors Brainteaser:

    a. Life is like.... List 10 possible metaphors to finish the sentence. Then pick the one you like best and fill the rest of the page with details that could develop it. No clichés.

    b. A teen's first sexual encounter is like.... List 10 possible metaphors. Star the two that seem the most original.

    c. Create a list of metaphors for any topic of your choice.

8. List Examples Brainteaser:

    a. You are assigned the topic "Computers and the average person" in your Introduction to Computers course. List at least 10 concrete examples you could use in your paper. Allow your mind to produce ideas as the examples come. Circle ideas that seem to tie the examples together.

    b. List 10 examples of teenage crime. As you review your list, add explanations of its causes or ideas on how to stop it.

    c. List 10 examples for any topic that interests you.

9. Make Bug Lists Brainteaser:

    a. Make a 15-item bug list for one of the following topics:

        Unemployment insurance

        Evangelists

        Television

        Your job

    Now circle the two or three items that have the most potential for a paper and try to probe more deeply into them by providing details and more explanation.

    b. Write a bug list for a topic of your choice.

10. Ask Questions Brainteaser:

    a. You are a reporter interviewing yourself about your future plans. Ask tough, honest questions. Ask follow-up questions if not enough is coming out. Don't settle for vague generalities.

    b. Pick an ethnic or cultural group you are curious about and ask questions about those things that puzzle you. Suggest some answers where you can and list sources you might try for additional information.

    c. Ask significant questions about any topic of your choice.

11. Use Humour and Fantasy Brainteaser:

    a. List all the humorous things you can about one of these topics:

        Blind dates

        Family holidays

        Funerals

    b. List a page of humorous or fantasy ideas about any topic of your choice.

12. Using any three brainteasers, develop two pages of ideas and details for one of these topics:

        Retirement

        Pornography

        City life

        A book you read recently

Country life

Vegetarianism

13. Using any three brainteasers, develop two pages of ideas and details for any topic of your choice. This can be a personal, academic, or career topic you care about.

14. You wake up one morning and discover one of three changes in your life:

   a. You have aged 25 years. If you're over 50, you have lost 25 years!

   b. Your sex has changed.

   c. Your species has changed.

   Thinking from alternative viewpoints, describe the next 20 minutes of your life accurately. These viewpoints may be read to peer groups and debated.

15. Your peer group's job is to write a bug list of what's wrong with high school, then to solve two or three of the problems.

16. Your peer group's job is to break television stereotypes of cowboys, businesspeople, one ethnic minority, teenagers, or police officers. Choose one, state the stereotype, then break it.

17. This is your fantasy: you are the director of community relations for a successful corporation. The company wants to donate one million dollars to your community for good will. You are to advise the company how best to donate the money. List various possibilities; then give reasons for your choices. A peer group may debate these lists.

Chapter 3

Paragraphs:

Little

Combinations of

Ideas and Details

*If design govern in a
thing so small...*
Robert Frost

*S*o far, this book has tried to open up your thinking process to create more and better ideas and details through the controlled chaos of brain-teasers. In chapters 3 and 4, we will begin shaping these creative lists into more finished writing. Paragraphs are good places to begin thinking about order, for like essays, they combine ideas and details. In an essay, the key idea is traditionally called a *thesis*, while in a paragraph, the key idea is traditionally called a *topic sentence*. The rest of an essay or paragraph consists of details that enliven or support the key idea. In theory, everything in an essay or paragraph must *relate* to the key idea; nothing should be *redundant*.

In actual writing, of course, paragraphing isn't so neat. Determining what fits together and what doesn't involves interpretation, and it may be tough to realize you are repeating yourself. It's also true that many paragraphs by reputable authors lack topic sentences, contain two ideas, or use repetition for effect. It's simply the nature of writing to break rules. *As long as your reader can follow you,* you'll get away with breaking rules. Yet most good writers *do* follow two guidelines most of the time:

1. Each paragraph should combine one idea with as much vivid detail as can reasonably be packed into it.
2. Each paragraph should stick to its key idea.

THREE WAYS TO BUILD PARAGRAPHS

Here's an example from a student essay on being a waitress:

> When you wait on tables, remember that people are unpredictable. With this in mind you won't get flustered, annoyed, or irritable when customers ask for margarine instead of butter, whole wheat instead of white, cottage cheese instead of coleslaw, and French fries instead of salad with their linguini alfredo. Nor will you think anything of it when a person orders pumpkin pie topped with chocolate ice cream or scrambled egg beaters (cholesterol-free powdered eggs) with greasy homefries and bacon.
>
> —Liza M. Agban

This paragraph states its key idea in the first sentence and then enlivens it with six compact examples of diners' unpredictability. This common paragraph pattern can be visualized in this way:

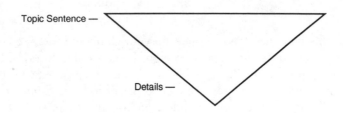

The "largest" part of this paragraph, its topic sentence, comes first, at the wide end of the inverted triangle; the "smaller" part, its details, comes next, toward the narrow end. A sentence about sore feet or about salary would simply not fit in this paragraph. But a sentence about the unpredictability of customer tips *would* fit.

The topic sentence-to-details paragraph is common because it makes sense; it's clear from the beginning where you're going, both to you and your reader. Here's another example of the same pattern from a student essay about the destruction of rainforests:

> Rainforests contain nearly half of all the plants and animals in the world—many of which have unique medical properties that humans must save from extinction. Some rainforest plants are used to treat Hodgkin's disease, multiple sclerosis, and Parkinson's disease. A delicate, tiny blue periwinkle flower found only in Madagascar, for example, is the key element in a drug used to treat leukemia. Ecologist Norman Myers estimates there are five million rainforest species found nowhere else in the world, and many are becoming extinct before we ever discover what wonder drugs they contain.
>
> —Sally Lujetic

While topic sentence-to-details paragraphs are the most common, good writers occasionally *start with details and build to their key idea,* as in this student essay about working in an insurance agency:

> The face of the clock, reflecting the cool, grey wall, reads 8:55. Outside the office, a face presses against the glass door—its nostrils flared, accusing like some grimacing, tribal mask. Do I look intimidating sitting amid disordered files, vagrant pens, computers, and fax machines, and muttering words like "subrogation" or "earned premium"? Inside the bright but still inaccessible office, I almost feel guilt for allowing this person to stand outside while I sit inside. Like a near-realized sneeze, the feeling passes, and I pretend nobody's waiting to get in. When the indifferent clock reads 5:05, similar masks reappear at the door, along with pummelling fists. Sorry! The office is closed.

"C-l-o-s-e-d," I mouth to the irate face outside. The clock's indifference has completely become mine.

—Irene Kuzel

This intimate, honest paragraph gains power by delaying its message; the sharp details of the author's thoughts, along with the descriptions of the customer, office, and clock, make us *want* a conclusion in the last sentence. If we were to visualize this paragraph, it would look like this:

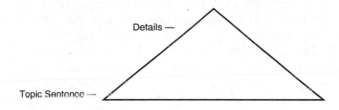

This shape works well to build up suspense in narrative paragraphs. Here's another example:

My first day of school, I wore a frilly pink dress with lacy crinoline puckering out around my bottom. The night before, Mom had to hide it so I wouldn't wear it to bed. I felt so pretty that day, as if I could stand on tippy toes forever like a ballerina. Mom held my hand, smiling. When the school bell rang, I thought everything was going to be okay, but Mom fainted with one of "her things." I tried to catch her, but she slipped through my small, helpless hands to the pavement. A trickle of blood ran down her sleepy face. Epilepsy, we'd been told. I knew she didn't *want* these things, but why did she have to have one *now*? A girl with pretty, carrot-coloured hair stared with sympathetic, mocking eyes and asked, "Is that *your* mommy?" So badly did I want to be accepted by the other children, I lied as I walked away. "Oh, no," I said, "That's not *my* mommy," words that haunted me for years afterward.

—Christine Bailey

This paragraph starts simply, then expands to larger issues. As an introductory paragraph to an essay, it tempts us to read on for more detail.

Informative or persuasive paragraphs can also use the details-to-topic sentence format, as in this one on legalized gambling in Canada:

Americans are streaming across the border by the tens of thousands to visit Canada. But wait—something has changed. They are not coming to visit our national parks or admire our clean cities. They are not coming to explore the Trans-Canada Highway or wonder at our vast open spaces and fresh air. These new visitors have greed in their hearts and dollar signs in their eyes. They gravitate to places such as Windsor, Montreal, and Winnipeg, but not to see the sights, sample the cuisine, or enjoy the culture. Instead, they enter dark, stale, smoky buildings with one intention: to gamble in the new casinos that many provinces have recently opened to help cover their crushing debts.

This paragraph teases the reader by establishing a paradox: Americans are visiting Canada, but with a new motivation. Only at the end is the key idea revealed: that some Americans are now visiting our country to gamble legally and that provincial governments are capitalizing on this new tourist attraction. The details-first paragraph makes sense because readers are more easily interested by stories and examples than by abstractions.

Later in the same essay, the writer relies on a third type of paragraph construction—one in which the topic sentence is surrounded by details:

After the first week of operation, the new Casino Windsor had attracted 100,000 people who spent almost $6.5 million. The provincial government is obviously smiling, because it stands to collect at least half of the money generated from the casino. And with annual gross revenues estimated at $300,000,000 at Windsor alone, it seems like a windfall that will immediately benefit everyone. But in our enthusiasm to offset the deficit, could we be overlooking the serious social consequences of gambling? Could the casinos put other businesses in jeopardy or become another tax on workers who cannot control themselves? What about the costs of treating compulsive gamblers or the morality of governments encouraging citizens to participate in games when the odds against winning are so enormous?

This paragraph begins with a series of impressive statistics that define some of the benefits of legal casinos, makes its main point in the middle by questioning these rosy assumptions, and then concludes with a series of parallel questions that support the topic sentence. It could be diagrammed in this way:

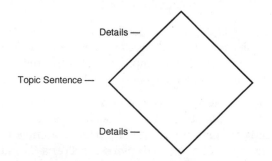

Some paragraphs may not need a definite topic sentence, and the three patterns only suggest options for arranging details and an idea. Most writers do not say to themselves, "Ah ha, now I'm going to write a details-to-topic sentence paragraph." But writers *do* sense the placement of details and an idea. You must always move your reader between the general and the specific.

■ *Practice 3-1:* Look at the paragraphs in an old essay and determine which of the three models of development you used. Try rewriting two or three paragraphs so that the order is altered. For example, turn a topic sentence-to-details paragraph into a details-first paragraph.

■ *Practice 3-2:* In *Roughing It in the Bush* (1852), Susanna Moodie describes the hardships of pioneer life in Canada. Examine the following paragraph and determine which of the three models she uses.

> The prospect from the windows of my sister's log hut was not very prepossessing. The small lake in front, which formed such a pretty object in summer, now looked like an extensive field covered with snow, hemmed in from the rest of the world by a dark belt of sombre pine-woods. The clearing round the house was very small, and only just reclaimed from the wilderness, and the greater part of it covered with piles of brushwood, to be burnt the first dry days of spring. The charred and blackened stumps on the few acres that had been cleared during the preceding year were everything but picturesque, and I concluded, as I turned, disgusted from the prospect before me, that there was very little beauty to be found in the backwoods. But I came to this decision during a Canadian thaw, be it remembered, when one is wont to view every object with jaundiced eyes.

 ## TRANSITIONS

Most sentences and paragraphs have a natural flow. But if you find the jump between two sentences difficult or awkward, try using transitions to connect them.

Repeat key words. Pick up a key word from the previous sentence. This word (in this sentence, it is "word") helps to sew sentences together. Alternatively, *use pronouns* to recall the previous sentence:

This is why we must...

Because of this man...

It is a problem...

Or, *use specific transitional expressions*:

For changes in time: now, then, meanwhile, before this happened, afterward

For changes in space: on the other side of the room, farther down the trail, nearby

To show contrast: however, despite this, although the police say, on the other hand

To provide evidence: for example, in fact, for instance, one case involves

To amplify a point: in addition to, besides, on top of this, also

To conclude (section or essay): thus, therefore, finally

To show sequence: second, next, last

These are key trail markers for readers. By numbering your points clearly, you prevent your readers from thinking you only have one mixed-up argument; transitions help them to see how things fit with each other. Transitions are "invisible"—like punctuation. Don't fear boring a reader with them. Many times you will use transitions naturally. On the other hand, if people seem confused about how your paragraphs and sentences connect, consciously include more transitional expressions. As an example, read the last three sentences of this paragraph without my two transitions, "on the other hand" and "as an example."

Highlights of Chapter 3

1. Each paragraph should combine one idea with vivid details.
2. If your paragraphs are skimpy—one or two sentences long—consider adding more detail.
3. If your paragraphs sprawl over a page or two, see if you have mixed two or more key ideas into one paragraph.
4. In revising, add transitions to show how the parts of paragraphs are related.
5. Vary your paragraph patterns by occasionally starting with details and building to the key idea.

Writing Suggestions and Class Discussions

1. Write a topic sentence-to-details paragraph on one of the following topics. Do a half-page brainteaser first and include at least four details in the paragraph. Be creative with your choice.

   Oil

   Your favourite television program

   Zoos

      Provincial politics

      High school dances

2. Write a details-to-topic sentence paragraph on one of the following topics. Do a half-page brainteaser first and include at least four details in the paragraph.

      Bridges

      Math teachers

      Men's hat styles

      One bigot you've met

      Holiday rituals

3. Write a topic sentence-surrounded-by-details paragraph on one of the following topics. Do a half-page brainteaser first and include at least four details in the paragraph.

      Halloween

      Garbage

      Laundromats

      Something in school that's hard to learn

      The human hand

4. Bring your best paragraph to class for a peer review, revise it, and turn in a finished copy.

5. Write a "paragraph anthology" paper of three paragraphs on unrelated topics. Each paragraph should have a title and be about half a page in length. Underline your key idea in each.

✔ **PEER-REVIEW CHECKLIST: PARAGRAPHS**

1. Underline the topic sentence. Does the rest of the paragraph stick to it? If not, suggest changes.

2. What is the most interesting part of the paragraph?

3. How well supported is the topic sentence? Suggest one more detail the author could include.

4. How could one of the details be made more vivid?

5. What is the "shape" of the paragraph?

6. Mark all transitions used. Where might others be used?

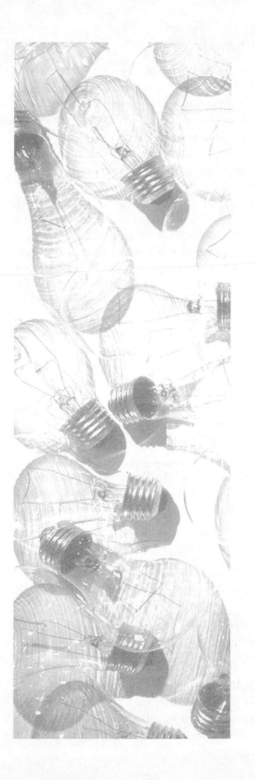

Chapter 4

Order from Chaos:

Thesis and

Outline

---

*A place for everything,
everything in its place.*

Benjamin Franklin

*T*he debate about organization breaks down into two main arguments. On the one hand, writing needs order. Ideas presented randomly as they flow from brains—or brainteaser lists—are often chaotic. On the other hand, overorganization can kill the very truth a writer hopes to convey, for truth has a nasty habit of resisting preplanned schemes. This chapter seeks a reasonable middle ground between these extremes: the minimum organization needed to focus your writing. Why "minimum"? Because—except in rare cases—no one ever exclaims, "Your organization really grabbed me!" Fresh ideas and vivid details do that. That's why brainteasers are crucial. Nothing makes organization easier than creative, vivid brainteasers; nothing makes organization harder than vague, skimpy lists of preliminary ideas.

Let's start with an attitude. Organization must come from you. Don't cram your ideas into somebody else's box. And don't ignore organization, for it rarely occurs magically without conscious effort. The writer who plans how the essay will be structured and who studies a draft's structure will discover incomplete ideas, unbalanced emphasis, and redundancy. The writer who plans will discover these things—before the reader does! In other words, developing a thesis and outlining should not only refine existing ideas but also create new ideas and details: *planning structure is a brainteaser too.*

 ## A WORKING THESIS

A thesis is the key point your essay makes—the assertion, message, core idea, or purpose the rest of your essay illustrates or proves. This is where conscious organizing usually begins, because a thesis creates the relationship between a paper's parts. Here are some sample thesis sentences:

1. Fathers and mothers who try to fulfil their lost chances through their children often crush the children's personalities.
2. The Canadian military's United Nations peacekeeping forces have played a vital role in helping to stabilize dangerous situations throughout the world.
3. The abstract-painting exhibit on campus is awful.
4. Brian Mulroney was our worst prime minister since Mackenzie King.
5. My room-mate models her life on a TV soap opera.

Some of these are personal topics, some informative, some argumentative, but as theses, they share two qualities. First, they give the essay a flag to rally around. They lead a reader and writer to anticipate and visualize the essay to come. Second, they are assertions—complete statements.

■ ***Practice 4-1:*** What do the five theses (above) promise a reader?

Statements such as "My essay is about welfare" or "Welfare is an important topic of concern today" fail as theses. What *about* it? There's no flag. Is the writer really going to tell us welfare is important? That's obvious. The real message hasn't emerged yet. A thesis asserts a viewpoint: "Two approaches look more promising than others in solving our welfare mess: workfare and entrepreneurism."

Not all types of writing need a working thesis. Narratives usually *imply* their messages, and simple reports don't need formal theses. In "How to Repair Your Bike," or "A Summary of the Minutes of the Students' Association Meeting," the thesis is obvious. However, almost all analytical, persuasive, and informative writing does require a thesis.

Try to develop a working thesis sentence during or after your brainteasers, but before beginning your first draft. You will probably modify it several times during writing. This is a good sign that your thinking is not too rigid; until final revisions, you should always be developing the ideas.

A thesis develops in two stages:

1. Narrow the original topic until it is vivid and small enough to handle in your allotted space.

2. Make an assertion or express a viewpoint about this narrowed topic.

SAMPLE: A WORKING THESIS

Suppose the professor for your psychology course assigns an essay on love. The topic makes you panic. Thousands of books, poems, and articles have been written on the subject. How can you say anything significant in four or five pages? Well, you can, and here's how.

First, *narrow the topic before doing brainteasers*. Love? What kind? Sexual? Brotherly? Romantic? Love of country? Can you list three other kinds? Your brain teaser will be hopelessly vague unless you're more specific than "love." To narrow, think a bit about the *circumstances* of the paper:

For whom am I writing? (audience)

Why am I writing this? (purpose)

What obvious topics should I avoid? (freshness)

These three questions apply to most writing tasks, and asking them will save you wasted work on doomed topics. In this case, your psychology professor is the audience. You might grab an uninformed audience with a general topic, but not her! Your purpose is to show you've learned something; you can't just throw back her lectures. You decide to try the topic of romantic love.

To narrow it more for vividness, do some brainteasing—*asking questions:*

Why are the words "I love you" so important?

What are the symptoms of romantic love?

What chemicals are secreted when we are in love?

How long does the "being in love" stage last?

How important are looks and personality?

Why is romantic love so compelling?

Is romantic love culturally determined?

Does it exist as an ideal in all cultures?

This brainteaser will help you to understand what's involved in this topic—
to *learn* more.

Here is another attempt to find a new angle on the topic by listing examples:

Love and obsession: stalking.

All the people I know who are newly in love: staring at each other across
a table, holding hands, thinking about the other all the time.

Arranged marriages in India: romance is not an issue (or is it?).

For most people, does sex lead to romantic infatuation, or is it the other
way around?

All the songs on the radio, the ads in magazines, the movies our children
watch (*The Little Mermaid, Snow White, Beauty and the Beast*): it's impossible to resist the message about the prince and princess who find each other.

Going to a friend's wedding and having the marriage end six months
later: how fragile is the illusion of love?

The same friend swears he is in love a few weeks later.

From this brainteaser list, you decide to narrow your topic to the contrasts
between arranged marriages and those based on romantic love.

Now you're ready for the second step in creating a thesis: *to make an
assertion.* Because you've decided to write a contrast paper, you should do a
contrast brainteaser for more detail. Here's a start on it:

Arranged Marriages	*Romantic Marriages*
Limited freedom	Complete freedom
Compatibility is the main criterion	Being in love is the main criterion
Parents help to arrange, some-times with intermediary	Individuals choose without help
Finances, caste, and class are crucial	Romance often overcomes class and financial considerations
Few expectations of partner: love may grow over time	Partner is idealized: greater chance of disappointment
Little contact with future spouse	Unlimited possibilities

In these three steps, we have moved from a series of spontaneous questions and examples to a more limited list of contrasts. We have moved from the general notion of love, to romantic love, and finally to the differences between arranged and romantic marriages. If we were to generate a thesis statement from the list of contrasts, it might read something like this: "Arranged and romantic marriages differ because individuals and their associated cultures have different expectations and values about love and freedom."

This section is pretty much as it might come out of your head; it *is* sloppy, and it has no sense of thesis in the early stages. If you had taken a different path (for instance, developing the notion of love as an illusion), your thesis would likely be radically different. The connections between topic choice, brainteasers, and thesis formulation are crucial, but unpredictable. You must make the unseen jumps of thought on your own and give them your stamp. To develop a good thesis, you must play back and forth between topic narrowing and brainteasing.

Here's another suggestion to help you narrow a topic and conjure up the thesis lurking in your early thoughts. Write out half a dozen sentences like the ones below, finishing the incomplete idea. Do this after reading your brainteasers:

What I really want to say is…

The most gripping part of my topic is…

The key question about my topic a reader would want answered is…

What interests me most about my topic is…

If you're still stuck, back up. Make a short list of key words from your brainteaser lists and formulate a thesis sentence from them.

 ## LOOPING

Some students skip a working thesis, saying, "I'll just write a draft and fix it later." A few people can do this—but if you question them closely, virtually all really have done brainteasing and thesis work in their heads beforehand. Most writers who skip thesis preparation start confidently for a sentence or two. Then the next paragraphs fumble into new ideas and repetition, trying to tie things together without direction. About halfway through the paper, the writer realizes what the thesis might be, and the paper smooths out a bit near the end. Revision of this tangled stuff is torture; the ideas are smeared together, and the details are skimpy. It's almost a sure route to a poor grade. In effect, the writer is using the draft to generate ideas, organize them, and convey them through the right words. It's too much to ask of one sitting.

You *can* freewrite to generate ideas and structure, however, by looping. To loop, write freely for 10 minutes, without censoring ideas, much as you do during a brainteaser, except that instead of listing, you write full sentences, letting one flow to the next. You then *extract* the key sentence or concept from this freewriting and copy it on another sheet of paper. You write for another 10 minutes using the extracted sentence as a guide, then extract the best sentence from *that* freewriting until you formulate a thesis. Looping works well for people who like writing connected sentences rather than the helter-skelter of brainteasers.

In either case, you should rethink your thesis at all stages of writing a paper, except when revising mechanics and grammar. A thesis that never changes during drafts is a red flag. You may be grinding down the truth for the sake of the system. Play around with the topic before settling on a working thesis. Find out what's there, pile up some building blocks, and—with a *working* thesis—have a rough plan before constructing the essay. But be prepared to do some fine-tuning along the way.

■ *Practice 4-2:* Create a working thesis for one of the following topics. First, list three to five potential narrow topics within the general one; then choose the one you think will be the freshest. Do a half-page brainteaser. Finally, write a working thesis. Show your work on paper.

Or, try looping; write three free-form paragraphs, extracting a key sentence from the first to start the second, and from the second to start the third. Your thesis must still be narrow and stated as an assertion.

Freedom of the press

Tourism

Underwear ads in newspapers and magazines

Single mothers

 ## OUTLINES

Writers debate endlessly about the usefulness of outlines. Students say of former high school teachers, "My God! She said we had to have fifty three-by-five index cards and a two-page outline. The outline had to have five divisions, and each division had to have at least two subheads, and *they* had to have two subheads, and they...." However, there are other voices: "My teacher said not to worry about an outline: just write what we feel, and it'll be true. Just be loose. Well, I'm real loose—I'm totally disorganized. I need help." Perhaps a middle ground is best.

In skeletal form, the multiple-level outline looks like this:

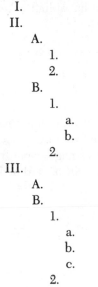

I.
II.
    A.
        1.
        2.
    B.
        1.
            a.
            b.
        2.
III.
    A.
    B.
        1.
            a.
            b.
            c.
        2.

Its relentless order seems as inevitable as fate. It gives writers who mould ideas and details to it a false sense of security—just because they're organized doesn't mean they've said anything worthwhile. It may also paralyse writers who assume their ideas are bad because they don't easily adapt to the outline.

And it may kill spontaneity in the drafts. Advocates of outlines *want* to eliminate the dangers of spontaneity—disorganization, uncertainty about what to say in the next sentence, redundancy. But they kill spontaneity's virtues too—coherence of mood, surprise, discovery. Overoutlining often creates dead, lifeless drafts. The writer simply colours inside lines already drawn.

Finally, meticulously detailed outlines create unnecessary labour, because they're seldom used in practice. As philosopher Søren Kierkegaard once commented, "Most systematizers are like a man who builds an enormous castle but lives in a shack nearby." Most advocates of intricate outlines don't even use them; instead, they write from humbler, shacklike outlines. We get hung up on detailed outlines because we like abstract order and want to believe that creativity can be planned perfectly. It can't. Writing based on a minutely detailed outline is usually dull. Most good writing by scientists, businesspeople, and essayists fails to meet the standards of a multidivisional outline.

The other extreme, starting without any outline, may work for some people, but it too is flawed. Without any plan, you *are* going to stumble, wander around, repeat yourself. If you want to do a good job, you'll need to do heavy rewriting to separate the brilliant tidbits from the garbage—and simply to see what you've said. This path, of course, is the one writers must take when composing at the last minute. It gives them the illusion that a draft is being produced, because pages fill up.

THE SCRATCH OUTLINE

The scratch outline is a single-level outline that only shows main headings (the I, II, and III in the example above). For a two- or three-page paper, three or four headings will do; for a four- or five-page paper, five headings will do. An essay on the dangers of seatbelts might be outlined in this way:

Introduction

Pregnant women

Fire during an accident

Drowning during an accident

Back problems

The writer then assigns details from brainteaser lists to the appropriate heading and starts drafting. The scratch outline *does* offer direction, but it *does not* stifle creativity. Within each section, *details are fluid*, so you can be spontaneously creative and still know where you're going next. A scratch outline can be seen as a whole; headings can be easily added or rearranged. Most professional writers use this kind of bare-bones outline.

FROM BRAINTEASERS TO OUTLINE

Some brainteasers *have built-in outlines*. Classifying, comparing/contrasting, alternating viewpoints, and asking questions create structure by their nature. You may have to consolidate or rearrange a bit, but they point you toward a narrow thesis and an outline. For example, if you do a classification brainteaser on death, you may classify the ways people behave while dying:

Calm—death is natural, a part of life

Patient—to make up for wrongs

Humorous—playing a joke

Philosophical—the "famous last words" death

Religious—death leads to afterlife

This is already an outline. You need to make a thesis assertion—for instance, about which approach to death makes the most sense—and perhaps do an examples brainteaser for details to illustrate each heading, and you're ready to write. As examples, you might use deaths you've witnessed or those of famous people. A humorous example is the death of comedian W.C. Fields, a lifelong atheist, who was found on his deathbed reading a Bible.

"What are you doing?" a friend asked Fields.

"Looking for loopholes," Fields answered.

In another example, the dying words of Crowfoot, chief of the Blackfoot Indians, could fit into the "Philosophical" category: "What is life? It is a flash of a firefly in the night. It is a breath of a buffalo in the winter time. It is as the little shadow that runs across the grass and loses itself in the sunset."

Distribute your examples to the headings. If you have headings with no examples, drop them. If you have interesting examples, but no heading, try to invent one.

A scratch outline for an alternate-viewpoints brainteaser uses competing views as headings. In asking questions, the key questions become headings. In comparison or contrast, the major similarities or differences are headings.

■ *Practice 4-3:* Make a scratch outline on interracial dating or athletes as role models, using any of the brainteasers as an organizing pattern.

One danger of using brainteasers with built-in outlines is falling into a cookie-cutter approach: stamping out outlines without thinking of your message first. *Never let a pattern interfere with what you think is true.* For most brainteaser lists, you must create original outlines. You may have a technique that works for you. But if you don't, or just want to try something else, here are three ideas.

1. Start by reading your brainteasers slowly, and on a separate sheet of paper, rewrite key items—potential outline headings. You'll probably copy too many at this point—they'll overlap and need to be combined later. Key ideas should be ones that run deepest in you, have strong visual impact, or offer the most conflict.

2. Or, start by reading over the brainteasers, but instead of working immediately for outline headings, simply draw lines between items that seem closely related. Your brainteaser pages will resemble spider webs when you're done, but then you can study each set of connected items to decide what heading would unite them. Write these headings on a separate sheet of paper, as with the first method. Likewise, assign each worthwhile item in your brainteasers to a heading, crossing out irrelevant or dumb stuff you encouraged while brainteasing. Or, label a heading beside each worthwhile item on your brainteaser pages.

3. Use clustering, which is essentially a diagram. Write your topic in the centre of a clean page and then draw lines out, like spokes radiating from a

wheel hub, to related ideas. Clustering stimulates ideas (as does a brain-teaser) yet keeps your topic literally at the centre of focus. Each item must connect to another by a line—either to the central topic or to any radiating heading. Try connecting each item to a heading first. If it doesn't belong, connect it to the topic. When done, you'll have a visual representation of your ideas—where you have the most ideas, what fits with what.

SAMPLES: THREE SCRATCH OUTLINES

 To illustrate these three options, let's try to organize an essay on the subject of death using classification. We begin by listing the types of responses to death:

Acceptance

Humour

Religion

Philosophy

Then we label our examples brainteaser with these classifications:

(ACCEPTANCE)

Psychologist Carl Jung's last words: "Quick, help me out of bed.... I want to look at the sunset."

(RELIGION)

Surgeon Wilder Penfield: "when I operate and the patient dies, I know exactly when the soul leaves the body."

(HUMOUR)

Dylan Thomas's last words: "I've just drunk eighteen straight whiskies—that's a new record."

(PHILOSOPHY)

Queen Elizabeth I's last words: "All my possessions for a moment of time!"

(PHILOSOPHY)

Crowfoot's words about life as a shadow moving into the sunset.

(HUMOUR)

W.C. Fields looking for biblical loopholes.

(ACCEPTANCE)

Sir Walter Raleigh's words to his executioner, who was concerned about the manner of his death: "It matters little how the head lieth."

(HUMOUR)

Oscar Wilde's purported last words: "Either this wallpaper goes, or I do."

(RELIGION)

Cotton Mather's last words: "Is this dying? Is this all? Is this what I feared when I prayed against a hard death? Oh, I can bear this! I can bear it!"

An outline that *rewrites the brainteaser list* would look like this:

(ACCEPTANCE)

Carl Jung and Sir Walter Raleigh

(HUMOUR)

Dylan Thomas, W.C. Fields, and Oscar Wilde

(RELIGION)

Wilder Penfield and Cotton Mather

(PHILOSOPHY)

Queen Elizabeth I and Chief Crowfoot

An outline developed from clustering would look like this:

Our last step is to decide what order the headings should follow. We needn't worry about the order of details. We rearrange the headings a few times to see how they'll flow when we write the first draft. Do some headings have to go before or after others? Most writers save their most creative idea for last.

Outlines are like bones. Nobody sees bones, but a person would sag into a baggy lump without them. You need a skeleton to help your essay stand up. And you need a thesis to help your essay walk straight instead of reeling and wobbling. How do you know if you're organizing too much or too little? Show your professor your work. If you feel lost during drafts, try greater organization. If you feel bored and confined, try more brainteasers and maybe looser organization. The one thing you can't do is write the way you always have if it's not working. The writer who really wants to improve can do so at *every* stage of writing: thinking of fresher ideas and details, making theses and outlines, writing the draft, and revising.

Highlights of Chapter 4

1. Good organization balances spontaneity and control. You can kill thinking with a stranglehold outline, and you can become hopelessly lost without some plan.

2. Using brainteasers to generate plenty of ideas and details will do more to solve your organizational problems than any organizing formula.

3. Developing a thesis is the first step in organizing many papers. This sentence states your paper's key idea. Consider audience, purpose, and freshness when you shape this sentence. After you have a working thesis, read over your brainteaser notes to make sure it fits what you have. This sentence may become the most revised one in your paper.

4. A scratch outline works well, but you have to be comfortable with your method. To be honest, however, try a variety of methods during this course. You may have been using a method wrong for you. Some types of writing are better with more outlining (persuasion and research, for example) and some better with less (narration and description, for instance). Try looping, clustering, labelling, and drawing lines if you never have before. Give yourself a lot of options.

Writing Suggestions and Class Discussions

1. Narrow three of the following topics into ones you can handle in two or three pages. Concentrate on freshness—anticipate the obvious things others might say. Some topics may seem boring; you must make them interesting. Prepare brainteasers for each as you work. Alternative approach: try looping to narrow your chosen topics.

    Road construction

    Nuclear power plants

    Television shows

    Courage that's overlooked

    A book you've read or movie you've seen

    Prejudice you've suffered

    Open topic

2. Now write a working thesis for each of your three narrowed topics. Be sure it's a complete sentence and makes an assertion the rest of the essay can relate to. Alternative approach: use looping to arrive at your three working theses.

3. For your best two thesis sentences, write scratch outlines. Aim for three or four headings and assign your best brainteaser material to them. Use any outlining method discussed, but tell which kind. Bring all work to class.

4. Write a draft based on one of the outlines.

5. Find an interesting, fresh topic lurking inside the following unpromising ones. Do so by narrowing each to three options. Then formulate a working thesis for the best of each narrowed topic.

   High school versus college or university

   Truck drivers

   TV violence

   Libraries

6. Evaluate the following as potential theses. What strengths and weaknesses does each have? Imagine what you'd have to do as a writer to fulfil reader expectations for each.

   Pets bring out the worst in their owners.

   Japanese cars have been extremely successful in Canada.

   Noise pollution is bad.

   Statistics on teenage pregnancy don't tell how it hurts one young woman at a time.

   Chevrolets are better than Fords.

   I'm going to write about my first love and my latest love.

   The Maple Leafs and the Canadiens are rivals.

   Vancouver is the most beautiful city in Canada.

   We ought to extend mandatory recycling to tires.

7. Write a brief, tactful letter of complaint to a company or organization that has mistreated you. Make a half-page list of ideas and details, formulate a thesis that specifies what you want from the company/organization, then outline your letter. Consider your reader's viewpoint.

8. Use the techniques discussed in this chapter to develop a paper you must write for another course. Bring a thesis and outline to class for a peer-group discussion.

✔ PROCESS CHECKLIST

A Working Thesis

First, narrow the topic during and after brainteasers.

(Narrow according to audience, purpose, and freshness.)

Second, make an assertion about the topic in a complete sentence.

Looping option—create a thesis through freewriting.

The Scratch Outline

Use only main headings—no subdivisions.

Find main headings:

> by using brainteasers with built-in outlines;
>
> by rereading brainteasers and notetaking;
>
> by drawing connecting lines in brainteasers;
>
> by clustering ideas.

Assign items from brainteasers to headings.

Decide on the best order of the headings.

✔ PEER-REVIEW CHECKLIST: THESES AND OUTLINES

1. Is the thesis as narrow and clear as the samples in this chapter? If not, suggest other angles.

2. Does the thesis have spark? Freshness? Suggest how to improve it.

3. What promises does the thesis make for the coming essay?

4. Does the outline make sense? Try rearranging the main headings. Try adding or combining headings.

5. Are there enough details for a vivid essay? Sharpen some and add others by asking the author to explain what will be said about a heading or two.

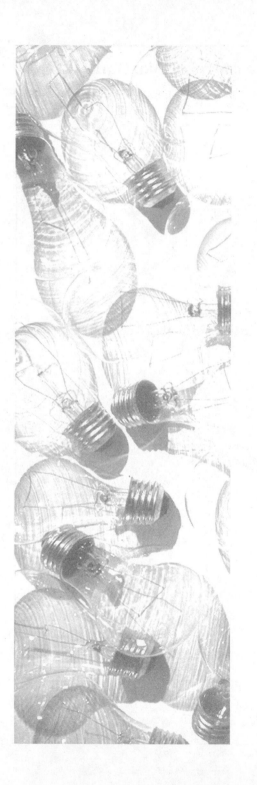

Chapter 5

The Draft:

That Frenzy

Near Madness

---

*A journey of a thousand
miles begins with the
first step.*

Lao-Tze

"*W*hy is it that I can never get a paper going! I thought I was into the topic—I did some brainteasers and made an outline. Yet my pen just wants to doodle when I sit down to write the draft. Everything I start to write looks awful—if anything comes at all." We've all felt this block at one time or another when trying to begin a project. Most writers sometimes experience choking uncertainty when starting a draft. It may be caused by fear of commitment to one idea or of switching from thinking in notes to thinking in sentences. Whatever the reasons, here are a few ideas to make the draft go easier.

THE CONCRETE INTRODUCTION

The introduction can be particularly hard because most people don't put much prior thought into it. A typical outline just says "Introduction." Yet we instinctively know that the introduction will set the tone for the whole paper, will grab or sedate a reader, and will either point us in the right direction or bog us down in swampy confusion. So as our first task in the draft, we must write a key paragraph without the prewriting help the rest of the paper will have. No wonder writers hesitate at that first sentence.

Many introductions are "warm-ups": the writer is groping for the right tone, the properly phrased thesis, and the interesting lead-in. When students are told that their introductions are too long or vague, that they should get to the point more quickly, they sometimes respond that their readers have to get used to them. But what's really happening is that the *writer* is getting used to the topic. Nothing gets a reader used to you faster than a sharp opening; nothing makes a reader feel uneasy sooner than an introduction that mushes around a topic. How does the following one make you feel?

> Homelessness is a very important topic today. The future of our society depends on solving this problem. So many people are suffering, and homelessness is different than it was 10 years ago. It's time we did something to cure this blot on society.

This introduction evaporates if you try to squeeze a specific idea out of it and does not give you a clear picture of what's ahead.

To avoid initial paralysis, start your paper not by warming up but by being already hot. Warming up is for leftovers; an introduction should set a fresh appetizer before your reader.

One strategy is simply *don't write the introduction first*. Start by drafting the first heading in your scratch outline, and write the introduction after the rest of the draft is done. This way you'll have plenty of prewriting ideas and details for the first paragraph to start the momentum rolling. As your draft evolves, the introduction you write later will fit the paper better. The weakness of this approach is that you may miss the self-guidance the introduction provides. You can compromise by starting the paper with this simple working sentence: "The purpose of this paper is...." Obviously, you'll have to improve this bland opening during revision.

Many professional writers try another method for the first paragraph. Their first few sentences attract and stimulate the reader's *interest*. Once interested, a reader is ready for the thesis, so a good introduction frequently starts with several concrete, perhaps puzzling details, then presents the paper's main idea in the last sentence. All six of the types of introduction below share this principle.

One technique is to *start with an anecdote*—a short story related to your main idea. It can be personal, researched, or fictional. Here's an example that could substitute for the vague introduction above:

> Hattie McBride's dress is torn and dirty. She pushes her shopping cart into an alley, pulls out the folded cardboard from the lower rack, and spreads it under a fire escape. She rummages among the wadded clothes and utensils on top until she pulls out a bottle of cheap wine. After settling down on the cardboard, she sighs. She is a grandmother, and she once owned her own home. Now, like thousands of other street people, she's become a social problem. Let's look at one solution for people like Hattie.

These details should make a reader hungry for the idea that would explain them—the thesis sentence, which comes next.

Another approach is to *start by asking a good question*. That's the trick— a *good* question. Obvious questions or those needing only yes/no responses don't arouse our interest. Examples of bad questions: "Would you like to be a street person?" "Are most homeless people happy?" They instil mild interest, but they don't push the reader toward a theme, just a yes or no response. A better question is one with open-ended answers, such as:

> Every time I walk downtown and see men and women shuffling around in rags and scavenging like stray dogs, I wonder why. Why would a person choose to grub in garbage dumpsters, sleep in abandoned cars, and huddle around wine bottles? What can be done to help reclaim these people into society? After talking to some of them and reading about the topic, I think that there are three main reasons why people end up on the street and that there is hope for some of them.

These questions are specific and involve readers by *asking them to account for a situation, not simply respond to a question like a test*. Whether readers think of an explanation or are simply puzzled, they will be primed to listen to what you have to offer, and that's the introduction's job. Notice also how concrete details hold our attention as these questions develop.

A third technique is to *start with a striking fact or facts*:

> Nearly two-thirds of all homeless people once held responsible jobs, and one-quarter are employed; one-tenth hold university degrees; over half have families, most of whom know about their present condition. Homeless people should bother us not because they've degraded themselves but because they point out how industry, education, and family have failed.

The same pattern holds here: vivid details followed by the thesis. A striking fact must be something unexpected. The following doesn't qualify: "Many automobiles produced in our high-tech society continue to be unsafe." But this one does: "Twenty percent of the cars we drive today have life-threatening flaws in their construction." Always remember the power of the specific.

A fourth technique is to *start with a quotation that leads to your thesis*:

> "For God's sake, get them off the beach!" said the disgruntled director. "Get the security people— now!" During the taping of a TV commercial at a Vancouver beach, several homeless men crawled out from under a lifeboat the actors were using as a prop. The men had slept all night under the boat. Police escorted them off so the photos of Lotusland would be undisturbed. Cruel as the director's words sound, they may reflect a typical Canadian attitude toward the homeless: we don't want to think about you.

A strong quotation dramatizes an idea—it interests readers by creating conflict or mystery. They read on to find out why the person said it or what the author of the paper will say about the quote. The quotation leads them to the thesis.

Fifth, *open with a problem or dilemma*—viewpoints that contradict each other. Present several sides of a controversial situation before working toward your solution in the thesis:

> Being homeless means being powerless. Such people have no money, no stake in society, and no knowledge of how to escape. Without an address, they may not be enumerated for local, provincial, and federal elections, and in some cases may even be unable to receive social assistance. How do we empower those who have no addresses? Some advocates of the homeless suggest that we could invent a new system, whereby social insurance numbers alone could be used by some people to vote or apply for welfare.

Using a problem/dilemma in your introduction helps you to clarify issues for both yourself and your reader.

Sixth, ask yourself, *"What will people first think of this topic?"* Speak directly to your readers' concerns. First, closely identify with their viewpoint(s), then lead them toward considering a new idea:

> Perhaps you've seen the wino who curls on the warm grate in the middle of winter or the man who emerges from a doorway to ask for a loonie you're too afraid not to give him. Perhaps you want to shout at them in disgust, "You shouldn't live this way! No human being has to accept this!" I felt this way too, until I met Robert Cole, the philosopher of the homeless.

A final point: your introduction hooks the reader, but it also *promises* the reader what will come. As in the striking-fact example, you may even list the main points to be covered. But be careful not to promise what you can't deliver—the essay will be like a flashy car that gets repossessed during a big date.

■ *Practice 5-1:* Write a series of six introductory paragraphs on one of the following topics using each of the techniques: (1) starting with an anecdote, (2) asking a good question, (3) beginning with a striking fact, (4) starting with a quotation, (5) opening with a problem, and (6) speaking to readers' concerns.

Cutting social programs to balance the budget

Funding of education

Alternative music

Legalization of marijuana

 # WHAT TO FOCUS ON DURING COMPOSITION

Once you get past the introduction (or postpone it), you may be fortunate enough to experience that frenzy near madness—the compelling rush of energy and insightful concentration that carries writers along. You may only need to refer briefly to your notes to start another cascade of sentences. If this happens, and the draft still sparkles in the cold light of the next morning, consider yourself lucky.

But the frenzy of inspiration has a way of not showing up or of teasing a writer with a two- or three-sentence burst and then vanishing. The writer who depends on inspiration will have some lucky, effortless compositions, but much more despair and frustration. Most writing—just like most living—is done at an ordinary pitch of mental excitement and in a professional manner. Fine frenzies are memorable and cherished because they are not everyday happenings. All writers must learn to write without them. Ironically, it's when you are plugging away at an ordinary pitch of concentration that inspiration sneaks into your fingers and brain. While the fickle muse will not always carry you off, you can improve the odds of inspiration through concentrated prewriting and a proper focus during the writing of your draft. Following are four suggestions.

1. *Most importantly, concentrate on the logical, smooth flow of ideas and details.* Think visually as you bounce between ideas and details. As you clarify a generalization, supply details so your reader can visualize it. As you give examples, think of the conclusion you can draw to round out the paragraph.

2. *Use your outline intelligently.* Your scratch-outline headings should become topic sentences for paragraphs most of the time, and your listed details should fill out paragraphs. But don't think of your essay as a colouring book in which you're simply filling in spaces. You can and should think of new examples and recast ideas as you write. Don't let an outline chain you. On the other hand, don't run off in totally new directions for long sections without referring back to the outline—you could end up confused or with what should be two papers. If you really see a new direction for the paper as you draft, take a few minutes to throw together another scratch outline, scrap the old draft, and chase after your new thoughts.

3. *Move fairly quickly as you write the draft.* Doing so helps things to stick together. If your mood changes between writing parts of the draft, the tone may change. Ideas that you mean to bring up later (but haven't written down) tend to be forgotten during interruptions. Ernest Hemingway believed the best place to interrupt the draft for the day was at a spot where he knew exactly what the next sentence would say. That way, the following day, it would be easy to start up again. Other writers tend to stop at a tough spot, hoping incubation will solve the problem for them overnight. There are some writers who work slowly. The French writer Gustave Flaubert was known for drafting only one paragraph per day during the composition of *Madame Bovary.* But for almost all writers, I'd recommend a fast pace—a two- or three-page paper should be drafted in one sitting if you've done good prewriting, and a four- to six-page paper should be no more than a two-sitting effort. It takes sustained effort to engage your mind in the topic. The speed record may be held by Isaac Asimov, who claimed he could draft a nonfiction book in 70 hours. That's hot!

4. To facilitate the flow of words, *imagine speaking your draft to some- one as you compose.* If it's a personal essay, imagine the person to be a friend. If it's an argumentative or informative essay, imagine speaking to your intended audience. If you don't remind yourself in this way that you're writing for people, you may treat writing as a mechanical process, and the sparkle of a human voice will evaporate from the draft. Visualizing your

audience helps you to fill in gaps, keep a consistent tone, and even generate new ideas as you compose. Some writers say their sentences aloud and then type them. Others compose aloud from the outline into a tape recorder and then transcribe to paper, just to get this effect of speaking to an audience. As you "talk" to your readers, imagine them saying, "What does that word mean?" "Get to your point!" "How does all this relate to me?" "Keep my interest—give me a story or a wild fact." "Give me an example." Or "Where did you get that fact?"

WHAT NOT TO FOCUS ON IN THE DRAFT

1. Do not be overly concerned with mechanics, spelling, or sentence structure.
2. Do not get caught up in word use and style.

Why not? Because secondary matters bog down a writer during the draft and interrupt the smooth flow of ideas and details. If a great metaphor or vivid verb comes to you, fine. Take it. But don't spend five minutes during the draft searching for one. Save this effort for revision.

WHEN YOU GET STUCK

Notice it's not "if" you get stuck. All writers occasionally spin their wheels in the mud of a draft. You can continue to gun the engine and splatter goo hoping you'll wiggle loose, or you can try alternative strategies to get to the dry land of the next sentence. Following are some tips to use when in a rut.

1. Use brainteasers (discussed in chapter 2):

   Use your senses to visualize the topic.

   Imagine an alternative viewpoint to your last sentence.

   Classify or compare/contrast the last point you made.

   Think of a metaphor for your last or next point.

   Ask a reporter's questions about your next point.

   Break stereotypes you've just stated.

   Try a humorous or fantastical touch.

   Give an example.

   Think about what bugs you about what you're saying.

   See the topic through an "ism."

   Personalize/depersonalize.

Find a paradox.

Be a devil's advocate.

Predict the future.

Try on a new mood.

2. Study your scratch outline and think of a transitional phrase to move you to the next point:

On the other hand...

The next reason to support this proposal is...

Second...

However...

Despite this fact...

The next morning...

When I saw Bill again...

3. Reread the last page you wrote. When you reach the blank space, you may have built up enough momentum to leap across it.

4. Reread your thesis and ask how the next point should relate back to it.

5. Ask what your reader would want to know at this point. Would he or she have a question to ask? Would he or she be confused or want to protest? Use the responses as a cue.

6. Skip the tough section and move to the next one. Fill it in later. If it's really hard to complete, it may be illogical or inappropriate in the paper.

7. Write several alternative sentences to see which one sounds the best.

 ## BLOCKS DURING DRAFTING

Fear of risk and insecurity about your ability to think can disable you as a writer. You suddenly fear you're going to say something really dumb or embarrassing, and your pen quivers in hesitation. You think: "What will my professor think if I say I've used cocaine? Or that my uncle abused his children? Is my idea juvenile? Maybe I should be safer, hide more. Maybe I should just scrap it all and start over."

These are common fears. You must risk sounding silly to get anything drafted. The fact is, no first draft sounds polished. And dealing with embarrassing facts forces you to be more honest about the topic. In any case, there's time to reconsider in revision. At the draft stage, trust yourself and keep moving.

FEAR OF MESSINESS

We've heard it so often: "Neatness counts." And neatness does count in writing, but *only in the final draft*. Many people want to write drafts logically, grammatically, progressing word by word to a perfect conclusion. They're doomed. Within a few sentences, they see the imperfections, the ideas that contradict each other, the detail that doesn't fit exactly, the awkward sentence. "All right," they say to themselves, "I'll write more slowly, more carefully." Before long they're up to their hips in quicksand, and the writing stops. Why? Because they're asking too much of themselves. Even a genius cannot think, organize, draft, and fine-tune at the same time. Shakespeare and Mozart may have churned out masterpieces with little revision, but the history of literature is one of messy cross-outs, redrafts, thrown-away pieces, and ink spots. If ideas, details, honesty, organization, brilliant word choices, and grammar could come at once, we'd all be best-selling authors.

Solutions

Go play in the mud. Relax and enjoy the surprises and messiness of thinking. Most ideas creep out of dark and sometimes dirty places. When these misshapen creatures peek out, you'll drive them back inside your brain if you demand perfection. New ones will be slow to emerge. Accept the fact that writing emerges incomplete. If you write with a computer, you already know how fluid the text can be. Let the messy first draft flow out, and later you will be able to start shaping the essay into a finished piece.

POOR WORK ENVIRONMENT

Your sister is playing loud head-banger music. Your desk is too low and makes your back ache. The room is stiflingly hot. You just ate and feel sleepy. Your paper's going nowhere. Anything relating to your physical environment can affect your ability to write. Some people like to be comfortable and cosy. Some must turn on music or the television; others can't concentrate through such distractions. Some people require absolute silence and privacy; others like to sense people moving around them because utter silence is intimidating. Some are morning people, some evening people. And so on.

Solutions

People serious about thinking and writing give their minds the best environments they can. Control the things you *can* control. Manipulate your environment so it helps instead of hinders you. Put books under your desk legs (or saw them down a few centimetres) so you're comfortable. Work at the time of day you're at your best. Don't kid yourself—maybe you really *are* watching the television. Try writing in silence. Also note that almost all professional writers use computers with word-processing programs, and most students who have access to a computer for a semester never want to go back to pen and paper. The reasons are obvious and have already been described. For some students, the work environment improves remarkably when the text is suddenly neat and tidy on the screen and easily revised there. If you have never used a computer, give it a try.

■ *Practice 5-2:* Make a list of your most frequent writing blocks. Come to class prepared to discuss how you have resolved them in the past and what new strategies you might employ in the future.

 # CONCLUSIONS

Don't dawdle. A murky, wordy ending hides your message. You want a sharp, crystalline sentence or two to highlight your key idea. Specific suggestions for conclusions to narrative, persuasive, and research papers will be discussed in later chapters, but one all-purpose approach is simply to return to a concrete example, fact, anecdote, question, or dilemma from your introduction. An essay on the homeless might conclude in this way:

> Hattie McBride died of malnutrition on her cardboard mat under the fire escape. If the work-for-shelter program and the building-rehabilitation plan I have proposed were enacted, there might be fewer Hatties dead on cold winter nights in alleys.

Highlights of Chapter 5

1. An introduction should interest a reader with details, then present the thesis that leads a reader to the main body. You can do this by telling a story, asking a good question, presenting a striking fact, quoting someone else, opening with a problem, or addressing your reader's concerns.

2. While drafting, focus on the logical, smooth flow of ideas and details, moving quickly (without getting bogged down in minor matters) and addressing your intended audience.

3. While drafting, do not focus on style, words, mechanics, or spelling.

4. When you're stuck, use the brainteasers from chapter 2, refer to your outline and thesis, reread the last page you wrote, ask what your reader would want to know next, or search for a transitional word to the next point.

5. Two common blocks while drafting are fear of messiness and a poor work environment. Tell yourself not to be afraid of a little dirt (all drafts have it), and change your work environment if it's hampering your writing.

6. Consider using a computer for easy drafting and revising.

Writing Suggestions and Class Discussions

1. Evaluate the following introductions. How does each try to grab your attention? What technique(s) does it use? Does the thesis lead you into the paper? What do you expect to follow? Is there any room for improvement?

   As Sir Walter Raleigh stepped up to the executioner's block, he ran his finger along the axe blade. "This is sharp medicine," he said, "but a sound cure for all diseases." Raleigh, most historians now agree, was innocent of conspiring to kill Queen Elizabeth, but capital punishment prevented his being discovered innocent. I think we ought to have capital punishment today, but there ought to be a two-year delay to allow other evidence to turn up.

   While sitting in the university library on a warm spring day, you fantasize about graduation and how proud you and your parents will feel when you go up on the stage to receive your degree. Suddenly your stomach ties up in knots, and you feel yourself break into a sweat. After years of hard work, you will have a degree in hand, but what comes next? You anticipate long days filling out applications, reading the want-ads, knocking on doors, writing letters and getting rejections. You remember the statistics on youth unemployment in Canada, even for people with postsecondary education, and you cringe at the thought of settling for a mindless job in the service industry.

   The program W5 showed a four-year-old boy who'd been abused by his mother's boyfriend. Beatings with a heavy object had caused permanent brain damage. His back had four-centimetre-deep whip marks from a leather belt. And the abuser had carved his initials into the boy's backside. This boy will never ride a bike, walk, or even talk. He is fed intravenously and must urinate through a tube in his penis. He received a lifetime of retardation and pain. Yet his abuser received 15–20 years in prison, and his mother, who let this happen, received five years. Another child, just a baby, burned to death after kerosene was poured over him. The only two people in the house were never even put on trial. Beyond how they could do this, and what we can do to help, the question we must ask is: what is wrong with our judicial system?

2. Find two magazine articles that strike you as having strong introductions. Bring them to class and be able to explain why they work well.

3. List five aspects of your work environment that encourage your thinking/writing. List two things that hinder your thinking/writing. Discuss how to change the poor conditions and create or maintain the good ones.

4. For your next paper, bring to class two alternative opening paragraphs, using two of the six methods suggested in this chapter. Both introductions should be on the same topic, but do not rephrase the same introduction.

5. Suppose you have to write a paper on family stress for a sociology class. Write three trial introductions, using a different technique in each. For the last sentence of the paragraph, formulate a thesis or main idea that leads from the details to the body of the paper.

6. Write introductions for two of the following topics. Try to hook the reader's interest, then move toward a thesis the paper will develop.

   Men's or women's hairstyles

   2 a.m.

   Animal experimentation

   Dates who drink

   Birthdays

7. Write an introductory paragraph and have another student assess its effectiveness by filling out the peer-review checklist.

✔ **PEER-REVIEW CHECKLIST: INTRODUCTIONS**

Author: _____

List three possible titles for your paper:

Reviewer: _____

1. Which title do you find the most intriguing? Why?

2. How does the introduction grab your attention? Is it effective?

3. What promises or expectations does this introduction give for the coming essay? Suggest issues or questions the author should cover.

4. Make suggestions to improve the wording of the introduction. Also mark them on the draft itself.

5. Which detail draws your eye into the introduction? If you think the introduction needs better detail, suggest what might be done.

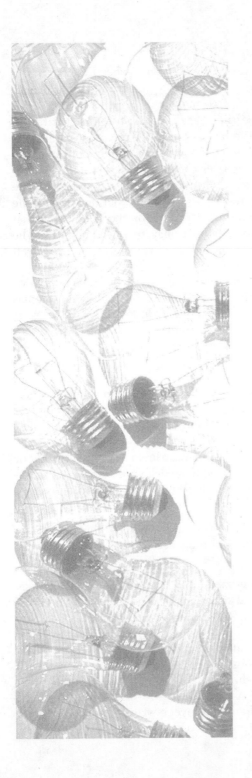

Chapter 6

Revising Drafts:

Writing Is

Revising

The manuscript revealed the usual signs of struggle—bloodstains, teethmarks, gashes and burns.

Annie Dillard

The secret of good writing is to strip every sentence to its cleanest components.

William Zinsser

*M*any people assume a writer's job is 95% done when the first draft is complete. Now, they think, we'll correct spelling and typos, read it over to see how it flows, and then crank out a clean copy.

It would be great if it were that easy. But experienced writers— whether they publish essays, write business reports, or compose theses— know that "revising" means "reseeing." A writer is simply not doing the job if reseeing is limited to fussing over spelling and a few surface blemishes. That's an amateur approach. You must try to resee and refeel the entire paper, back down to its roots. Novelists, nonfiction writers, the person who writes a company's annual report, or the committee that writes your college or university catalogue may revise for months. The inspired genius who whisks out immortal masterpieces on the first draft is 99.99% myth.

For virtually all writers, up to and including Nobel Prize winners, revision means a total, word-by-word reseeing of the draft. Revision means rewriting the good parts as well as the bad. Only during revision does most writing move from poor to acceptable or from acceptable to good or outstanding. Your professor does not expect from you the fanatical dedication of published writers such as Ernest Hemingway, who revised the last paragraph of his great World War I novel, *A Farewell to Arms,* 39 times. But your professor *does* want you to revise more than just the surface, to take the manuscript through at least one complete revision. Your writing *will improve* through honest, close revision, and only then will you know how good you are as a writer.

Revising draws from a different part of your brain than brainteasing or drafting. Creating is self-centred, accepting, and sloppy; revising is reader-centred, judgmental, and orderly. Although most people find one easier than the other, we're all capable of both.

■ *Practice 6-1:* Think back to a time you said something that hurt someone or caused you trouble. If you had a chance to revise what you said, what would you say differently?

The lonely writer tapping away in solitary confinement is also largely myth. Most writers in professional situations depend on advice and criticism from others during revision. Alternate viewpoints give us perspective on what we are too close to notice; they remind us what we have forgotten to mention or point out what might confuse a reader. Even Shakespeare had help. His acting company commonly deleted scenes and suggested changes during rehearsals for such classics as *Hamlet* and *Romeo and Juliet.* Most bosses will ask to see drafts of proposals, reports, or significant letters their employees write—and will suggest changes. Or they may ask employees for suggestions on their own drafts.

Grant writers, legislators, and scholars all ask peers for criticism before the public sees the final document. The word "criticize" in this sense does not mean to rip the writing apart but to highlight weaknesses *and* strengths and to make *positive* suggestions.

An important part of your education is to learn how to handle both kinds of revision—on your own, and with the help of others. Following are some things to look for and a process to follow when revising first drafts.

ON YOUR OWN

Try this five-step guide to revision, but keep in mind that it is an *ideal process that rarely if ever can be followed exactly.* Like thinking, revising is often sloppy. Remember to consult the revision-process checklist on the inside covers of this book. This should be considered another brainteasing list that will remind you to think in all the ways you should during revision.

Begin by revising major things—the ideas and details—and then work on secondary items such as organization and diction. Correct punctuation and spelling last. Why? So you don't waste time correcting spelling if you later decide you need a better word or waste time thinking of a great adjective if you later throw out the entire sentence. Imagine a draft as a building to be rehabilitated. Painting can't begin until the walls are in place, and that can't begin until the supporting girders are square and plumb. Occasionally, changing a word or phrase can clarify a main idea, and if doing so seems important, go ahead. But don't spend your early time tinkering.

You may want to read your draft over once or twice for general flow, but if you focus on one thing during each reading, you'll do more real thinking and less falling in love with what's already there. Writers often get "sick" of drafts because they're following them instead of demanding specific things of them. If you keep rereading and waiting for a "bump" to jolt you, you'll fall asleep. I recommend reading through and revising the draft once for each of the following aspects.

1. Ideas
2. Details
3. Order
4. Words
5. Mechanics

A two- or three-page paper can be revised for all of these in an hour, and careful revision is almost sure to raise your grade one level.

1. Revise Ideas

Honesty, Freshness, Coherence

Clarify the main idea. First, read through your draft quickly. Now, without referring back to the essay, try to state your main point or purpose. Write it out in one sentence. You may be surprised that you'll be able to say it more sharply after reading the paper. Compare it to the initial thesis sentence and substitute the new one if it's better, or revise the old if necessary. If you had trouble writing a statement of purpose, your paper may ooze in several directions.

If your paper lacks a sharp focus, try this technique: read through it again, copying down sentences that seem to state purpose. Try to combine them into one statement. If this works, great. Replace the wobbly thesis. If you can't combine the sentences, you'll have to accept the fact that you mixed two or three main ideas together. You must then divide your essay into parts, some of which will become your new version, the rest of which will leave the house in a brown bag.

Second, when revising for ideas, test your main idea for *honesty* and *freshness*. Be ruthlessly honest to see if you've slipped into superficial thinking or oversimplification. Qualify or moderate extreme sentences. Be particularly alert for contradictions or potential rebuttals to your arguments. Don't ignore them. Your paper will be stronger and more honest if you confront and respond to them (see "refutation" in chapter 11). Techniques cannot substitute for your intense concentration or involvement in your ideas. A checklist is only a reminder of things to look for.

Third, read through the draft as your reader will. If you have a particular reader in mind, *be* that person. What will confuse him? What points will she deny or contradict? What have you left out that will be important to them? This is a wonderful brainteaser for revision.

■ *Practice 6-2:* Reread your last paper and (1) underline key sentences that reveal purpose; (2) combine them into a one-sentence statement of purpose; and (3) find two places you could have raised an objection or modified an idea for more honesty or freshness. Make the revisions.

2. Revise Details

Visualize and Support

Read the draft again, honestly evaluating the details. Are they vivid and convincing? Support each major generalization by adding examples, sensory details, descriptions, and facts. Suppose you have written the following in a draft of a paper on Tennessee Williams's play *The Glass Menagerie:*

Laura lives in a fantasy world in this play. For instance, there's her glass menagerie, the old phonograph records she plays, and her visits to the greenhouse. She can't even attend business college.

The right information is here, but it's not vivid enough to make us see Laura's fantasy world. Let's expand just *one* of the details:

Laura lives in a fantasy world. The greenhouse she visits is full of exotic flowers—tropical plants that can't exist in the cold world where she lives. Their fantasy world is protected from reality by artificial heat and fragile glass, just as Laura can go on living only because her mother and brother protect her from the cold reality of the Depression.

In revising for detail, remind yourself that readers are hungry for facts, quotes, pictures, and examples. Feed them details; save corrections of grammar for later.

■ *Practice 6-3:* Find three places in your last paper that could have used more details. Write them in.

3. REVISE ORDER

MAKE IT EASY ON THE READER

Check the essay's *overall organization.* You don't have to read in the normal sense—just skim the main sentences. If your paper is more than five pages long, take notes on a separate page by jotting down a heading for each paragraph or section. Doing so can help you to see if you are repeating yourself or if you should combine two sections. Now's the time to cut redundant paragraphs or draw arrows to move things around.

Next, check to see that each *paragraph* sticks to one idea. Are the *transitions* smooth between them? (If not, add key markers such as "On the other hand," "Another reason to support this proposal is…," or "Once outside, Ferguson saw….") If you see a lot of one- and two-sentence paragraphs, or if you notice that one paragraph runs over a page, a red light should flash. These paragraphs may indicate that as you motored through the first draft, your thinking became scattered. You may be able to join the skimpy paragraphs or insert breaks into the elephant-sized ones. Make sure every sentence in a paragraph points at the same target.

Finally, flip directly from your introduction to your conclusion. Do they match? If not, scream, and then revise.

■ *Practice 6-4:* Revise your last paper for organization. Outline the paper, check paragraph unity, and add transitions where needed.

4. REVISE DICTION

WAXED WORDS SPARKLE

At this point, you should know which sentences and paragraphs will be in the final paper. Now focus on words. Tinker. Wax and polish. Do you repeat the same words or challenge the reader with a few exotic *palabras*? Be ruthless with clichés—they are corpses in your living essay. Do you define key terms? Be more concise. Punch up bland verbs. Substitute slashing, red-eyed adjectives for dull ones. Create a metaphor to make a boring paragraph crackle with lightning. New words can improve ideas. Consider sentence variety. Unlike the previous sentence, which is a short, imperative one, this complex sentence delays the main subject and verb with an introductory phrase. Both kinds snap the reader to attention. (Chapter 7 is devoted entirely to polishing words.)

■ *Practice 6-5:* Pick any paragraph from a previous paper; improve three word choices and perk up a vague or dull spot with a metaphor.

5. REVISE MECHANICS

By reading through the paper lightly for mechanics, you'll only catch the errors you don't normally make. But the deadly ones are those you make regularly and don't see. Go through the paper once searching just for the errors teachers repeatedly mark on your papers. This must be a conscious effort, or you won't improve. If your vices are sentence fragments and apostrophes, search only for these little vermin. Work with the handbook section of this book; don't guess. If you're a weak speller, check any word you wouldn't risk in a $1,000 bet. After two or three papers, they won't be *your* errors any longer.

■ *Practice 6-6:* List your three most common errors in grammar, punctuation, and spelling. If you don't *know* what they are, examine your last few papers. Use this as a personal checklist. Write it in your notebook.

HELP FROM OTHERS: PEER EDITING AND TEACHER CONFERENCES

By this time, you should have exhausted your own resources. Your draft should be scratched up with improvements. Now you may be asked to print a clean, revised copy to give to other students to read (peer editing) or to discuss with your professor in a conference. These can be your most valuable opportunities to learn to write well. You'll write for a real reader, not a cardboard one. You'll see how others write, and you'll learn from them.

PEER EDITING: HOW TO GIVE AND RECEIVE HELPFUL CRITICISM

When called on to critique another student's paper, your goal should be to help the writer create better ideas, sharper details, smoother organization, and more vivid diction. You may also repair punctuation and spelling.

The reviewer/editor must be honest. The person who writes on your paper "I love it!" or "I wouldn't change a thing!" may flatter you momentarily, but doesn't help you one bit. You may feel shy about fooling with someone's ideas or unqualified to criticize, but making an honest effort to help someone else improve a paper will teach you to revise better yourself. You'll learn to see some of the hidden possibilities behind your own words, to see your own drafts more objectively. Teachers who encourage peer editing expect *both* parties to learn.

You must be tactful, of course. The person who scrawls changes all over the paper and says, in effect, "Revise everything!" is just as dishonest as the person who wants to award the Nobel Prize. Help the writer to reach his or her destination.

Because most writers need help recognizing what they have written and understanding how an audience will react, it's probably best to start your comments simply by mirroring back to the writer the message or feeling the essay gave you. You can do this with one or two of these lines: "What I remember best about your essay is…" or "The main point I get from this is…" or "The most visual part of your essay is…." After the author lets you know you're aboard the same spaceship, you can move on to suggestions for ideas, details, organization, and wording. Work together. If you were confused at a certain point, for instance, brainstorm with the author for several possible clarifications. Note: writing comments forces you to be concrete and to wrestle with the author's problems in words. But it's crucial to talk to the writer as well. Your suggestions may need explanation and revision too.

MISCELLANEOUS

Mark any confusing passages and discuss them with the writer. Whatever you react to strongly in any way should be discussed. Try to *enjoy* peer editing; allow yourself the pleasure of inhabiting someone else's mind for a while.

RECEIVING PEER-EDITOR COMMENTS

Remember, your peer editors try to be honest. If they feel confused, you can try to clarify the point, but you can't tell them they're not confused. What peer editors tell you is something you can never see for yourself: how another person receives your communication. You can never be your own reader.

Strike a balance between total acceptance and total rejection. If you're too pliable, you may accept changes you shouldn't. It's *your* paper; don't let a strong personality dominate it. On the other hand, a close-minded writer may say, "It's written this way because that's the way I wanted it. It's my paper, isn't it?" This person supposes the paper is perfect because it came out exactly as intended. Papers *shouldn't* come out as intended; that's a sign you haven't *learned* as you moved through the stages of writing. Your paper is not a monument to what you thought at one moment but an attempt to communicate an idea as freshly and vividly as possible to someone else. Listen to what your readers say. Before rejecting changes, ask the reviewer, "Why do you say that?" A little probing can help you to open up an idea you thought of as canned and shelved. You don't have to follow slavishly each suggestion, but do welcome new possibilities as potential friends.

Bring questions to a peer-editing session. Ask about things you've wrestled with or wondered about. For example, "Is this a corny sentence?" or "It seems too long. If you had to cut one section, which would it be?" or "I'm worried I sound too harsh. What do you think?" Only by showing yourself eager to find weak spots will reviewers really open up to you.

Below is the opening paragraph of a letter written as a class paper. First is the rough draft as brought to a peer-review session:

Dean H. Bukpass
Faculty of Academic Services
Cascadia University
575 Molroney Rd.
Lotusland, B.C.
V3E 6K6

Dear Mr. Bukpass,

As you probably are already aware of there is a major problem with student parking at our school. At the end of every class one can be sure to find a line of students in their cars waiting for people to leave so they can park. Not only is this an inconvenience, but it causes arguments among students racing for empty spots, and it makes us late for class. You should consider building parking garages or consider some other possible solutions to this problem.

The reviewer thought the thesis was clear, but suggested that the author "put in a story, and more details," to catch the reader's eye. She also pointed out a few flaws in the format, the choppiness of the first sentence, and the exaggeration in the third line ("every" and "be sure").

Here is the same text with the author's revisions penned in:

JULY 14, 1995

Dean H. Bu[c]kpass

Faculty of Academic Services

Cascadia University

575 M[u]lroney Rd.

*Looking at their watches every 30 sec.,
they wonder just how late they will be
to class today. Teachers are not
sympathetic and some threaten to
penalize tardy students by reducing their
grades. What can we students do?*

Lotusland, B.C.

V3E 6K6

Dear Mr. Bukpass,

As you probably are already aware of there is *exists* a major problem with student parking at our school. At the end of every class *almost* one can *almost* be sure to find a line of students in their cars waiting for people to leave so they can park. N[o]t only is this an inconvenience, but it *making us late for class,* causes arguments among students racing for empty spots, ~~and it makes us late for class.~~ You should consider building parking garages or consider some other possible solutions to this problem.

Notice that the author revised additional items beyond those suggested.

Next is the final draft, with even more improvements. The new visual details certainly help, as do the ironed-out sentences and "little" corrections (including the reader's name!).

July 14, 1995

Dean H. Buckpass
Faculty of Academic Services
Cascadia University
575 Mulroney Rd.
Lotusland, B.C.
V3E 6K6

Dear Mr. Buckpass:

As you probably are already aware, a major problem exists with student parking at our school. Following most classes, one can almost be sure to find a line of students in cars waiting for people to leave so they can park. Looking at their watches every thirty seconds, they wonder just how late they will be today.

Most teachers are not sympathetic, and some threaten to penalize tardy students with reduced grades. What can students do to make class on time when we drive? Besides being an inconvenience and making us late, it causes arguments between students racing for an empty spot. Please consider building parking garages to solve this problem.

TEACHER CONFERENCES/TEACHER COMMENTS

Your teacher will probably be the most attentive reader you'll ever have. If you write a boring or confusing letter to customers or supervisors, they'll stop paying attention. Your professor will persevere and mark the rough, confusing, or vague spots. *Improvement* is the point of this effort. Therefore, the most important marks on your papers are not the grades but the comments. They are guides for future papers. Study each comment on returned papers carefully. If you don't see where you went wrong, or how you could improve a section marked "awkward" or "vague," or why a teacher wrote "good" somewhere, find out. Ask. Be hungry for feedback; that's how you move forward. If you think of comments as simple test scoring, you've thrown away a road map. Take the time to figure out the symbols and abbreviations your teacher uses.

If your teacher has conferences about rough drafts, think of them as opportunities. Come prepared with questions. "Why does my opening sound flat?" or "Did I overdo the facts on the dangers of nuclear waste?" *Take notes* and mark sections your teacher discusses so you can work on them later. As with peer editors, be open to suggestions and try to resee your work objectively through your professor's eyes. However, if your professor seems to have the wrong idea about where you want to go with the essay, make clear what you really want to accomplish and ask for suggestions on how to get there.

THE FINAL DRAFT

After you finish revising, there are just a few final touches to prepare a hand-in copy.

1. Title the paper. Make the title work for both you and your reader. The best titles convey information and also a concrete image to hold the eye. Which of the following titles promise boredom, and which promise an experience?

   English Paper #2

   Air Pollution

   Whose Poisonous Gas Is It?

   Death Stalks Your Home

2. Format. Write your name and class in a corner. Centre the title and place it a quarter of the way down the page. (It should be capitalized but not underlined or in quotation marks.) Type your papers or use a computer even if it isn't required. Typed communication is professional. It'll make you feel prouder of your work. A word processor will also help you to see your writing more objectively than your friendly, familiar handwriting (see below). Number the pages. Double space and use only one side of the sheet. Leave one-inch margins.

3. Proofread after typing and make corrections—that's what professionals do. Here again is where a computer comes in handy—if you have a lot of mistakes, you don't have to retype the whole thing (see below). Here are some sample proofreader's marks:

   ¶   New paragraph

No ¶   No paragraph

   ⊔⊓   Reverse order of items enclosed

   ∧   Insert mark (write new items above line)

   ℓ   Delete mark (can be used for one letter or one line)

   ≡   Capitalize letter

   lc   Lowercase letter

   #   Space needed

4. Paper clip your essay.

REVISING ON A WORD PROCESSOR/COMPUTER

You are a writer, not a typist, and are likely to revise more if you don't have to retype everything or decipher your messy notations on paper. The steps in writing and revising with a word processor/computer are just like those in writing by hand, only more efficient. (And this will be the communication tool you'll be expected to command in many careers. It will be well worth your time to learn to use one.)

Try saving each revision with a new name. For example, call each subsequent draft essay1, essay2, essay3, et cetera. This way you have a current record of each draft and the revisions you made. Some instructors may want to see the process you worked through in moving from the first brainteasers to the final paper.

There are some drawbacks to writing with a computer that you should be aware of. First, because small changes are easy to make, you'll be tempted to focus on small items. This is why a full screen is important. Five- to eight-line screens prevent you from seeing larger blocks of an essay and pretty much require you to run off a hard copy. Second, because a word processor gives a neat surface appearance of finished work, you may be deceived into not really studying the logic and sentences. You've got to dig it up, no matter how polished the work *appears*. Third, word processors with spell checkers may give you the illusion that your spelling is okay. However, if you type "affect" where "effect" belongs, or "kiss" instead of "kill," the machine recognizes a legitimate word and won't alert you to your contextual error. Rely on your own knowledge—and on dictionaries.

Highlights of Chapter 6

1. A writer must welcome revision, not fear it. It may be tough to believe that your essay will survive being picked apart and glued together in little pieces. But that is how ideas are made better, and that is how professional writers—whether they write memos or publish books—operate.

2. Peer criticism requires both honesty and tact. Use the suggestions in this chapter to get started. When you receive peer or teacher suggestions, welcome them as helpers.

3. Revise with specific things in mind, not just for general flow. Revise your papers one time each for ideas, details, order, words, and mechanics. Use the specifics in this chapter as a checklist. But remember: no checklist or process for revision can substitute for your intense concentration and involvement in your subject.

Writing Suggestions and Class Discussions

1. Make up three questions about the draft of an essay you're working on. Leave room for responses and attach them to your rough draft for your peer editor or professor. Try for a mix of broad questions about thesis or organization and specific questions about particular words or sentences.

2. To practise revision, write a half-page paragraph on one of these topics:
   Adult toys
   Children and toys
   Wise elders
   What I don't like about my present job
   "[Your choice]" is a great song because...
   Open topic

3. Revise your paragraph on your own:
   a. Rewrite the main idea/topic sentence without looking at the original; then compare it to the original. Use the clearest one or make changes.
   b. Sharpen the details—make at least two points more specific.

    c. Circle all transitions and improve them if necessary.

    d. Improve three word choices (verbs, adjectives, metaphors) and rewrite any clichés. Then find two or three needless words and cut them.

    e. Check all spelling and grammar.

4. Bring your revised, retyped paragraph to class for a peer-editing session. Attach two questions about the paragraph for the reviewers. Using peer suggestions, revise the paragraph and submit a finished version.

5. Read the following student essay and consider what you would say to help the writer revise it.

    State what you think the main point is.

    What is most appealing about this draft?

    What details are best?

    Are any parts incomplete or confusing? Point out a place where more detail or more vivid detail could help to clarify.

    Indicate two or three particularly strong words.

    Indicate several weak or vague words and suggest alternatives.

    Correct the few mechanical errors.

BASTARD

Miguel Martinez

I have always been awed by the strange bonds fathers are supposed to have with their sons. Literature, television, and film have shown these relationships to be complex and intense. Even my friends in school would relate stories of massive power struggles. The part about love they left out but I knew it was there.

I grew up believing my father to be dead. At least that's what my mother told me when I asked her. I know the only reason I did ask was I had just entered kindergarten and my classmates were always talking about this strange being, a sort of god, they called Daddy. Contrary to popular belief, those of us having only one parent do not feel that anything is missing. At least I didn't until I found out I was an oddity. There is no biological instinct inside us saying that there should be someone else. There was just me and my mother. Period.

Off I went through school. My mother was involved with other men, and we lived with two of them. They were never "Dad," just "Uncle." These relationships didn't work out, and when I was six, my mother gave up on men entirely. We moved to another city, and she started working. For the next 10 years, my mother and I didn't see much of each other. She was a waitress, keeping odd hours, and I was in school or playing. She did make a big point of eating together, even if it was in the greasy spoons she worked in.

When she was able to spend more time with me, I was sixteen, and pretty set in my ways. I suppose I should have let her have her way, but the arrogance of youth took hold again. I left. I didn't have anywhere to go, I just wanted to travel. I spent the next 8 months travelling the country. I did return eventually, only to find my mother filled with a sense of failure. It hurt knowing I had caused someone such hard feelings. She begged me to enter the Armed Forces, and while I wasn't a big fan of the military, I went. The night before I was to leave, my mother sat me down and asked if I ever wondered who my father was. I told her, quite honestly, that I didn't, that she had said he was dead. Well, she gave me his name and told me he was living in Saskatchewan. She told me he didn't care about me, as he had always known who I was, but never made any attempt to contact me.

The news didn't faze me. Friends will ask if I have any urge to find him. I get satisfaction from their expressions when I tell them I have his address and phone number. But just as they can't understand my apathy toward him, I can't understand their reliance on fathers.

Below are comments on the draft by the writer, peer editors, and professor.

The Writer's Concerns

1. I didn't explore the aspect I wanted to—it seemed too general and jumpy what I was trying to get at.
2. One sentence that drove me crazy was "Off I went through school" (third paragraph). It just didn't flow.

The Peer Editors' Comments

1. The only "jumpy" part was the fourth paragraph. Time seemed too compressed. You were six and then entered the forces.
2. You need more detail on growing up without a father. The most vivid detail was your not asking about your father. The least was why your mother wanted you to join the military. I'd like to see more about why you didn't miss or need a father.
3. Third paragraph—for 10 years you didn't see much of your mom?
4. First paragraph needs more detail.

The Teacher's Comments

1. It's strong in honesty. Daring. Potentially a powerful paper.
2. But it doesn't follow its nose to the end of the idea. Your purpose is unclear, as you suspect. Are you dealing with (1) the mother-son relationship, (2) the life of a single mother, (3) the social problems of bastards, (4) your lack of a need for a father, or...? All these are here, but you need to decide what main point the others will support. Conclusion is inconclusive.
3. First and second paragraphs are good—a snappy start.
4. Fourth paragraph needs more detail—it's abrupt, seems to start a new idea.
5. Last sentence of fourth paragraph is awkward.

Your Comments

1. Add three more suggestions to the list—where do you think the writer needs to concentrate?
2. Revise this essay as if you were the writer, incorporating all the comments made by the writer, peer editors, and teacher.

✔ **PEER-REVIEW CHECKLIST: DRAFTING AND REVISING**

Author: _____

Reviewer: _____

Instructions:
1. Read the paper slowly and carefully.
2. Mark parts that were confusing or problematic with a "?"
3. Mark strong sections with a "G" or "°".
4. Check the appropriate boxes and write out comments.
5. Return this sheet to the author and discuss your reaction.
6. Do not mark small things such as spelling yet.
7. This sheet should be attached to the final draft.

	STRONG	AVERAGE	WEAK
AUDIENCE: well targeted?			
IDEAS: original/fresh?			
deep/complex?			
DETAILS: sufficient number?			
vivid enough?			
ORGANIZATION: main point clear?			
smooth flow of ideas?			
WORDS: concise and vivid?			
MECHANICS: correct?			

What is the strongest part of the paper?

What would you like to know more about?

Give two suggestions for improving the paper.
1.

2.

✔ **PEER-REVIEW QUESTIONS: DRAFTING AND REVISING**

Author: _____

One question or problem I want the reviewer to help me with is:

One sentence I'm not satisfied with is (mark it and explain why it bothers you):

Reviewer: _____

My response to the author's first concern is (discuss and brainstorm with the author):

Provide a possible rewriting of the weak sentence.

What is the purpose (thesis) of the essay?

Note one section that could use more detail or support.

What idea could be added or cut to enhance the paper's purpose?

Find a paragraph needing a smoother transition and suggest one.

Suggest three changes in wording or sentence structure that will enhance the paper.

1.

2.

3.

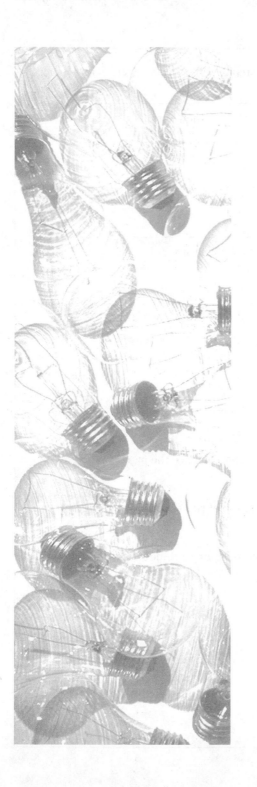

Chapter 7

Writing with Style

To improve one's style means to improve one's thoughts.

Friedrich Nietzsche

The language must be careful and appear effortless. It must not sweat.

Toni Morrison

Figures of speech are not the ornaments of language, but the elements of both language and thought.

Northrop Frye

$\mathcal{A}$fter revising your draft for ideas, details, and organization, comb through your words. Words make ideas croak or sing, convey an authoritative or awkward tone, and arouse or sedate readers. A smooth, graceful, clean style proves a writer sweats the words.

It isn't luck. Instead, it's a skill that can be learned over time, by training yourself to pay attention to the subtle sound of your text: the pitch of words—the way they combine and harmonize—and the tempo—the way words move forward, impelled by the combined energy of vowels, consonants, clauses, and phrases in varying combinations.

This chapter outlines an *honest, vivid* style for college, university, professional, and personal writing. It will help you to find a voice that is clear, precise, compelling, and, above all, attentive to the needs of your audience. At the heart of stylish writing, there is always a point, and all the glittering words cannot brush fancy makeup over a bad or nonexistent idea. Style begins with brainteasers—when you work up a topic with interesting ideas and details. Revising words means revising ideas, for words and ideas are inseparable and together create "style." Ironically, as we struggle for style, we must make it look smooth and effortless, sweeping away any signs of that struggle.

 ## HONESTY

VOCABULARY

Some writers think big words sound more sophisticated or intellectual. Flipping through a thesaurus or dictionary for fancy synonyms, they might revise this sentence in this way: "They inaugurate a scrutinization of a thesaurus in diligent quest for ostentatious synonyms." An expanded vocabulary does create options, but the big-word approach usually doesn't work. First, if the writer doesn't really know his or her words, they tend to confuse a reader or show the writer's *un*sophistication. Second, big words rarely impress good readers, who want a smooth journey, not a sojourn over gargantuan, albeit splendiferous, boulders. Usually, the simplest, most direct word is best; the fanciest draws attention to itself. Use the occasional fancy word or technical term when you need to; don't sprinkle them like salt over the entire paper. Write within yourself.

This does not mean you can get away with dull words. Your vocabulary should be colourful and vivid, but that rarely requires the use of big words.

ACCURACY

Honest writing demands accuracy, and this means revising the sloppy word choices we *all* make during composition. If you don't find three or four inaccurate words in each paragraph of a draft, you're either a genius or not searching hard enough. Ask if each word presents exactly the tone or picture you want. It's obviously wrong to misstate a fact or statistic, but it's also dishonest to exaggerate or use absolutes:

Al *always* arrives late.

Marcie's *never* had a sick day in her life.

You'll *love* the new Ford carburetors.

Drug dealers are murderers, *pure and simple*.

Absolutes are words such as "always," "never," "all," "every," or "none." Leaving no room for exceptions, they sound dramatic and make writers feel forceful, but they are often (not always) dishonest. On the other hand, some absolutes are true: *all* humans die. Ask yourself during revision if an "often" or "usually" might better describe Al's lateness or if a "hardly ever" or "as long as I've known her" might more accurately describe Marcie's health. To say someone will "love" a carburetor will probably be an exaggeration for all but the most fanatical car owner. It might be more accurate simply to describe its outstanding features. Why is it an exaggeration to say drug dealing is murder, "pure and simple"? Because it's neither pure nor simple, but requires distinctions—drug dealing differs from, say, strangling someone, or from selling an automobile that may end up killing the user—and you must show *how*.

Being tough with words will make your ideas tougher too. Question key words ruthlessly. Hunt for "weasels": words that seem to say something, but weasel out of it. (For example, "Computers *may* help you to write one or two grades better." Bananas *may* help you to write two grades better too.) Inaccurate language makes you appear an unreliable and sloppy thinker.

EUPHEMISMS AND CRUDE LANGUAGE

Euphemisms are expressions that make things sound nicer or grander than they are. When a used car is called "pre-owned" or "pre-enjoyed," a trucker "a commodity relocation engineer," or a garbage collector "a sanitary engineer," the writer is prettying up the truth. Notice that many euphemisms hide behind the crooked use of big words. In a famous letter released during the Vietnam War, orders were given to assassinate a secret agent, but the words "assassinate" and "kill" never appeared. The agent was to be "terminated with extreme prejudice."

Euphemisms have their place in conversation. If your friend Bob is fired, you may choose to say he "lost" his job, was "laid off," or "furloughed" to spare his feelings. But unless you need to spare your *audience's* feelings, writing demands a stricter standard of honesty. If Bob was fired, say he was fired. Consider whether it's more accurate to describe an agent as "shot," "murdered," "assassinated," "blown away," "offed," or "eliminated." Each term has a different implication. At a funeral, the dead person may be euphemistically referred to as "the dearly departed" or "the late Bertha Smith," certainly not as "the stiff" or "the corpse." The dead are "conveyed to their final resting places," not "hauled to the worm farm."

Notice that some alternatives to the euphemisms here are unnecessarily brutal. Crude expressions, like euphemisms, give you power over, or distance from, unpleasant facts: euphemisms deny them; crude words exaggerate them so they can be laughed at. In revising for honesty, ask if your words are *appropriate to the subject*—not sickeningly sweet, not unnecessarily crude. Obscenities, therefore, should only be used to duplicate the way a person speaks; the drama they create is usually dishonest—a cheap way to shock the reader.

CLICHÉS

Clichés are dead places in your essay. Like all inaccurate word choices, they come more easily than the perfect word and have a way of nesting in rough drafts until revision. Then you must root them out and plant live words in the holes.

Some writers may defend clichés by saying, "Everyone knows what a cliché means." But this is not always true. For example, is the expression "toe the line" or "tow the line"? Visualize it and you'll see the different images for each spelling. A student who described a nasty woman as "an old batilacks" obviously had no idea the original expression referred to a weapon, "a battle axe." Nor do readers pay close attention to clichés. They know there's no new idea, no new, interesting word that requires attention. Do you really want your readers to drift away? Complete these images:

Hungry as a _____

Gentle as a _____

Quiet as a _____

Eats like a _____

Busy as a _____

Slippery as _____

Most people will complete these images with the same one or two words; the expressions are that predictable. Clichés slide easily in *and out* of readers' minds. If you want to show how slippery a political issue is, for instance, don't compare it to a greased pig or an eel. Compare it to a wet gangplank, a slimy creek bed, an icy wheelchair ramp, or a sales-person asked for a refund. Try this approach with the examples above; invent two creative alternatives for each clichéd expression. Start by pic-turing what you're describing. Feel, see, hear, taste, or smell it as a *thing*, not as a word.

SEXIST LANGUAGE

Aside from the ethical argument that sexist language is wrong—that it con-tributes to bias against women—it can alienate readers (both male and female) who find it offensive. You may also create a picture of yourself as a sloppy thinker who stereotypes and generalizes without much thought. If you always refer to lawyers or scientists as men, for instance, you should know that 50% of all current law students and 20% of all advanced-degree science students are women. Following are three options for dealing with the "she-he" problem.

Option A: When sex is irrelevant, use "he or she" or a sexless pronoun (plurals almost always work well). "A student should prepare his schedule" could be "Students should prepare their schedules" or "A student should prepare his or her schedule."

Option B: You may sometimes use "he" and sometimes "she" for exam-ples, as this book does occasionally. Just remember, some nurses are male; some mechanics are female.

Option C: Use a gender-neutral term instead. "Chairman" can be "chair-person"; "postman" can be "letter carrier."

Do these little variations matter? Some people might claim we know that "mankind" includes both males and females, as do jobs that end in "man." But even though we "know" it if we think about it, hearing "man" used thousands of times in our lives to describe the species, respected positions, and important activities has probably hammered values into all of us. Many researchers believe these small messages affect our self-image, confidence, dreams, and goals. Whether you agree with this view or not, it's undeniable that most educated people, businesses, and public institutions are sensitive to sexist language. The penalties far outweigh the rewards for using such language today.

■ *Practice 7-1:* Revise the following sentences for better honesty in word use.

1. My antagonist inaugurated a campaign to terminate my presidency of the club.

2. Last but not least, we must work our buns off if this new business is to prosper.

3. Lucien Bouchard is a traitor.

4. If you show your true colours, you'll get your just desserts.

5. When buying a reconditioned car, delve into mechanical functioning as well as the amenities, or you may end up with a less than wonderful vehicle.

6. The North American Free Trade Agreement between Canada, the United States, and Mexico is not worth the paper it is written on.

7. The anti-abortionists never consider the lives of pregnant teenagers.

8. Canada has been completely humiliated by its ineffective immigration laws.

9. An athlete must accept his responsibility as a role model.

10. My grandfather passed away of a heart attack.

VIVIDNESS

Someone might ask, "If I weed out big words, extreme words, clichés, sexist language, and euphemisms, won't my style be dull?" No. You're cleaning away the debris to make room for real style. Honesty and vividness come from concreteness and from improving key words—especially verbs, modifiers, and metaphors.

CONCRETENESS

During revision, replace general or vague words with those that are specific or appeal to the reader's senses. This is the difference between pretend meaning and real meaning. If you can't pin a sentence down to specifics, cross it out. You haven't lost a sentence—you've *gained* clarity. Notice how wimpy the following sentences are.

The Neon is a good car.

We had an exciting time!

Abused children suffer mentally as well as physically.

The words needing pep are so general that a reader gets no specific image from them. In revising, choose words that relate to specific details:

The Neon is a sporty, economical, reliable car.

Our blood pressure blasted off, and we screamed ourselves hoarse.

We see the scars and burn marks on abused children, but a mother screaming "I wish you were never born!" scars them too.

Here's a brief list of vague words to watch out for:

good	bad	great
nice	fantastic	beautiful
ugly	cute	sad
happy	success	awesome
awful	terrible	big/little

Their hazy generality poisons vividness. If you try to improve these words with a thesaurus, you may substitute "salubrious" or "benevolent" for "good," or "deplorable" or "grievous" for "sad." Although slightly more specific than the originals, they still don't *define* or *make visual*. In revising for concreteness, resee the thing described; *think in pictures, not in words.* Replacing vague words with specific ones will do more than any other technique to make your writing tangible and clear.

■ *Practice 7-2:* Rewrite the following sentences for more concreteness. You'll need to interpret the writer's purpose, because the sentences are vague.

The GST is a bad tax and should be replaced.

What an ugly sight a garbage dump is.

He is really a great friend.

VERBS

One key word to examine is the verb, the strongest word in any sentence because it conveys action. Yet when students are asked to underline all verbs in their papers, 80% turn out to be forms of "to be": "was," "were," "are," "is," "am." "To be" is the dullest English verb. Other colourless, bland verbs include "go," "have," "get," "do," and "become." Some vivid verbs of action are "hack," "spring," "peel," "plow," "flick," "gobble," and "rip."

Study this sample sentence: "As the rush of people walk through the downtown area, the clanking and shaking of the old train is heard." The sentence buries its vivid words "clanking" and "shaking." Make them the main verbs and scratch out the weak "is heard" at the end. Also, "walk" is a weak verb when the writer has "rush." Here's how the writer's peers revised it: "As the people rush downtown, the old train clanks and shakes past."

In the next sample sentence, "is" saps potentially stronger verbs: "To many people, an education is a burning desire." Better: "Many people burn for education."

■ *Practice 7-3:* In the next two sentences, first locate strong and weak words and then restructure the sentence around a stronger verb.

1. The question often asked by apartment dwellers is, "How am I going to furnish this place?"

2. There was a clashing of negative events that helped me to find myself.

Some verbs, such as "look" or "walk," are often too general; try to substitute more specific ones. "She looked at me." Boring. Did she stare, peer, leer, ogle, scrutinize, examine, study, peek, glance, or glare? Notice how the substitutes are more specific and visual than "look." Each adds tone and attitude. Many flat sentences spring off the page with new verbs.

■ *Practice 7-4:* List 10 substitute words for "walk" that are more visual and specific.

ADJECTIVES AND ADVERBS

Many writers have been told adjectives and adverbs describe. True. But adverbs (which modify or describe verbs) and adjectives (which modify or describe nouns) are *helpers*. Rely on better nouns and verbs first. Which is the sharpest in each example?

1. Janet walked very, very slowly.
   Janet dawdled.
2. The car moved quickly away.
   The car sped away.
3. Jack was an extremely big man.
   Jack was a Goliath.

In each case, the second is more precise and visual because a weak adjective-noun or adverb-verb gives way to a strong noun or verb.

One particularly flat type of adjective or adverb is the *intensifier*: a word that says, "Yeah, well, even more than the next word." These are the most common:

very	extremely
so	definitely
too	excessively
extra-	least
-est (ending)	most

Here are a few in inaction:

He was the happiest man alive.

It was an extra-easy assignment.

The oil spill was extremely bad.

Laws for handicapped rights are so very hard to pass.

Intensifiers remind me a little bit of shouting arguments between children: the louder the better. This sentence beats its chest: "It was an extremely, definitely, extra-important, most so very needed event." The problem is, there's no chest to beat, no concrete noun or strong verb to accentuate. Replace intensifiers with more concrete nouns or verbs. For example:

He was ecstatic.

The oil spill covered 300 square kilometres.

■ *Practice 7-5:* Revise the other two examples.

METAPHORS

Vivid writing often relies on metaphors. Einstein used the metaphor of riding a light beam to help explain his theory of relativity, and scientists Crick and Watson used the metaphor of two snakes wrapped around each other to describe the structure of the DNA molecule. In chapter 2, you learned to use metaphors as a thinking strategy. In revising, sharpen metaphors for *compactness, coherence,* and *concreteness.*

Metaphors should be *compact.* Their power comes partly from suggesting a lot in a small space. Don't explain yourself away:

> Cameron is very tall and very thin and has often been compared to Ichabod Crane. His most distinguishing feature is his long fingers. If you've ever been to a costume shop and put on a pair of phony fingers, you'll know what his look like. Well, maybe not that long, but they are longer than yours and mine.

This writer had an interesting, vivid comparison, but he diluted it into a thin tea. Revised:

> Tall, thin Cameron has been compared to Ichabod Crane. His fingers are like the scrawny, phony fingers in a costume shop.

You can suggest metaphors sometimes with just one word—the ultimate in compactness. Here are some from student papers:

> Sandy chirped a reply.
>
> This popcorn kernel of a man was a wrestler?
>
> Bill's cabbage brain couldn't understand.

■ *Practice 7-6:* Write out a one- or two-sentence metaphor and then rewrite it compactly with one star verb or adjective. For example, "Our economics course is like a maze in which we cannot find our way out, like experimental rats in a psychology experiment" could be reduced to: "We groped through the maze of economics all semester."

Metaphors should be *coherent*—everything in the picture should fit together. The following metaphors pull the reader in several directions. The first:

Our household was emotionally barren, much like the deserts of loneliness people create to save themselves from being bruised or hurt by someone else.

The writer creates an effective desert image, but then stirs in a new or mixed metaphor with "bruised." He or she needs to continue the desert image, perhaps with a reference to being lost, thirsty, or victimized by the sun or desert predators. The second:

Even though Neil Young possessed extraordinary potential as a musician, his motivation was like an abrupt red light that faded in and slithered out periodically.

Another good metaphor derailed. Using "slithered" switches images. Red lights can fade, but they can't slither. The writer should stick with the traffic-light imagery.

■ *Practice 7-7:* Revise the Neil Young sentence.

Finally, metaphors must be *concrete.* They should appeal to our senses with sharp sights, smells, sounds, tastes, or touches. Notice how the following improves with more specific visualizing:

Original: Her dreams were ruined by fear, like the presence of an ugly pollutant in a clean body of water.

Revised: Her dreams were ruined by fear, like chemicals seeping into a pristine pond.

■ *Practice 7-8:* Rewrite these sentences for sharper metaphors:

1. Terry Fox was a tower of strength.
2. We are at a crossroads where we must sink or swim.
3. The mast of the ship towered upward like a candle on a dining room table.
4. His voice was like a lion's. It made a lot of noise, and it felt like it was coming after you down a hallway if you tried to get away.
5. Peace comes like rain.

STYLISH SENTENCE STRUCTURE

VARIETY

Glance at your sentences. Do they all follow a subject-verb-modifier format? Are most stubby, or are they long, twisted snakes? Readers like variety.

Reading many short, choppy sentences is like picking up a handful of beads; help the reader to string them together. A page of long sentences is like a jungle to hack through—you want more air and light. Break up a series of straight statements with an occasional question. Mix simple, compound, and complex sentences (see chapter 14).

■ *Practice 7-9:* Find a place in your last paper where three sentences in a row are nearly the same length or use almost the same structure. (Hint: look for ones using a subject-verb-modifier pattern.) Change the length or pattern for variety.

■ *Practice 7-10:* Just to see what your sentence lengths are, count the number of words in each sentence of your last paper. What is the shortest? What is the longest? What is the average length? In class, compare with your classmates.

PARALLEL STRUCTURE

Parallel structure means matching words or groups of words in a series or on each side of a conjunction:

Correct: The general ordered troops, ships, and planes overseas. (Troops, ships, and planes are all nouns.)

Correct: She wanted to stop the clear-cut logging, preserve the old-growth forest, and still not destroy the local economy. (Three verbs with modifiers.)

Wrong: The general ordered troops, ships, and bombed the airfield. (The last item is a mismatch.)

Wrong: She wanted to stop the clear-cut logging, the old-growth forest, and still not destroy the local economy. (The second item, a noun, mismatches.)

You might consider one other aspect of parallel structure when working on a particularly important sentence: the items should build to a climax.

Good: His childhood days were filled with fear, cruelty, and a concealed love. (Because the student contrasts love with negative things, it springs up at the end like a surprise blossom; in the middle of the list, it would lack emphasis.)

Weak: The proposal backfired; the workers staged a huge demonstration, the legislature was recalled for an extra session, and the plan cost $100,000 more than expected. (The workers' demonstration is most important and therefore belongs last.)

■ *Practice 7-11:* Write a sentence that lists parallel items in a series. Each item must be a phrase or clause of at least three words.

CONCISENESS

Essayist and children's book author E.B. White recalled his former writing professor, William Strunk, leaning on the lectern in class, peering over his wire-rimmed spectacles, and barking, "Avoid unnecessary words! Avoid unnecessary words! Avoid unnecessary words!"

Concise writing says *as much as possible in as few words as possible.* This means keeping a reader interested, supplying vivid supporting detail, and emphasizing key points. Many brief papers state a thesis without bringing it to life. They may be wordy or vague or simply cover less than a longer yet more concise paper.

We all talk around our ideas most of the time. But in revising, cut the fluff and highlight the important. On average, most writers can trim 20 to 30% of their draft during revision. Much small-scale wordiness takes up space but contributes nothing:

Wordy	*Better*
He went on to say…	He added…
The hat was red in colour.	The red hat…
We proceeded to depart.	We departed.
In my opinion it seems to me…	I believe…
Ken was slugged by Joe.	Joe slugged Ken.

Here's an introduction that amounts to cotton candy:

Weak: It is very interesting to compare what different essay writers have to say about writing essays. In our book, we have different essays on writing by Margaret Atwood, Rudy Wiebe, and David Suzuki, who are all famous Canadian authors.

Notice the repetition and the lack of a clear, vivid thesis.

Improved: Margaret Atwood, Rudy Wiebe, and David Suzuki present three different views on writing essays.

Nothing important is lost. The sentence improves by being direct. Readers expect a certain density of information per paragraph. A concentrated style means not only using concrete and vivid words but also removing needless words.

A hat that is "red in colour" says it twice; red cannot be a shape or a smell, only a colour. Is "the honest truth" more true than just "the truth"? Chop redundancy to strengthen the following sentences.

The constitution was totally demolished.

He is a completely unique artist.

The railroad was extended a distance of 60 kilometres.

I plan to enter the field of nursing.

In the fall of the year, school once again reopens.

At that point in time, we faced a serious job crisis.

All writers puff up drafts; *good* writers condense them. Concentration and practise, not talent, will make your writing concise.

Connecting words such as prepositions, "that," or "which," or anything not carrying the main weight of a sentence, may be fluff. Cutting two verbs to one strengthens sentences, especially if you exterminate a "to be" verb:

Wordy: The bureaucrats avoided some of the work they were assigned.

Concise: The bureaucrats avoided some assigned work.

Wordy: The catalytic converter is used for the purpose of reducing air pollution.

Concise: The catalytic converter reduces air pollution.

■ *Practice 7-12:* Make each following sentence more concise. Save vivid words and convert passive verbs into active ones.

1. At that point in time, the Blue Jays went to bat for the purpose of getting some desperately needed runs.
2. The old Parliament buildings were entirely destroyed by fire.
3. He had a long grey beard that had not been trimmed very recently.
4. He brought tears of laughter to a great number of people with his jokes.
5. Those who commit murder are not deserving of the people's mercy.

Highlights of Chapter 7

1. Revise your draft for diction and style by going over it once for each aspect listed. Reading with focus is more likely to pinpoint problems than just riding the flow to find bumps.
2. Revising for honest word use means using a vocabulary you control, testing the accuracy of your words, avoiding weasels and absolutes, and getting rid of euphemisms, crude language, and clichés.
3. To make your style more vivid, revise for more concrete and visual words, replace "to be" and other dull verbs with action verbs, replace some weak modifier-subject combinations with stronger nouns and verbs, eliminate intensifiers, and flash an occasional metaphor.
4. Revising sentence structure can improve style too. Vary your sentence lengths and format and revise for tight, climactic parallel construction.
5. Concise writing has more impact. Ruthlessly cut redundancy and wordiness.

6. As you read over your draft, anytime something confuses or bores you or causes you to daydream or skim, stop! Go back. Reread the last few sentences as if through a microscope. A reader's attention will be two or three times more fragile than yours. A sharper verb, a less wordy phrase, or a more concrete noun may keep that reader with you for the rest of the ride.

Writing Suggestions and Class Discussions

Revise the following for honest word use, vividness, parallel structure, and conciseness.

1. It was a blistering June day; the heat could be seen radiating from the pavement.
2. Pete is definitely one of a kind.
3. We must grab the bull by the tail and face the situation.
4. The first time I encountered Jose, it was in a foreign country.
5. The war in Rwanda was filled with a great many human atrocities.
6. Dr. Baikman is a short, dark man who looks as if he's beginning to get old.
7. She has a way of making people feel very special.
8. Alan's superficialities were especially on my bug list.
9. Queen Morena dumped on the count. She declined his matrimonial proposal.
10. A garden is in her face where roses and white lilies grow.
11. Canadian students must give up drugs if they want to escape the prison of this filthy crutch they use to bury their weaknesses.
12. After returning from the little girls' room, I proceeded to expostulate on the numerous beneficial phenomena of mixed-gender lavatories.
13. When I was at the age of 12, my mom started to become a little better, treating us more like human beings, although the discipline was still there.
14. Upon my arrival, I quickly apprehended the culture change and beheld the Newfoundland accent and idioms embellished by the McCormack family.
15. After the whistle, Sam attacks his opponent with a killer instinct, driving him to the mat and gratifying what he sets out to accomplish.
16. There was a fear of anyone approaching him.
17. His right eye was dangling out of its socket, his lower lip was stretched under his chin, his nose was almost completely torn from his face, and hanging facial skin.

18. Her medication was putting weight on her that was visibly noticeable within a few days after it was prescribed.

19. Carolyn's life was like water, moving and shifting with no anchor.

20. It's always too late to straighten a kid out after he's been in jail.

21. There are many different variations in colour.

22. Janet lacked a confidence factor.

23. Negotiations will either grind to a halt or be hammered out.

24. At 7 a.m. in the morning, the weatherman predicted major thunderstorm activity.

25. Evaluate the overall sexist slant of the first 24 sentences.

More Exercises

1. Exchange rough drafts with another student. Each of you should ask for help with words/style in one troublesome paragraph. Do all you can to help each other with honest word choices, vividness, sharp sentences, and conciseness.

2. Your professor will mark one paragraph in your draft or paper needing stylistic pruning and pep. Revise it thoroughly.

✔ PEER-REVIEW CHECKLIST: STYLE

Author: _____

Reviewer: _____

Read through the author's rough draft only for style. Suggest changes on the draft itself, but leave it legible for the author.

1. Find a weak verb (is, are, has, get) and suggest a more visual action verb to replace it.

2. Find an exaggeration or absolute that ought to be modified. Suggest a revision.

3. Look for a cliché that needs a fresher image or a generalization that needs more detail. Suggest a revision.

4. Find an intensifier and suggest a stronger noun or verb to replace the weak one the intensifier tried to build up.

5. Look for an example of sexist language or stereotyping and suggest a revision.

6. Pick one paragraph and suggest ways to eliminate redundant or empty words.

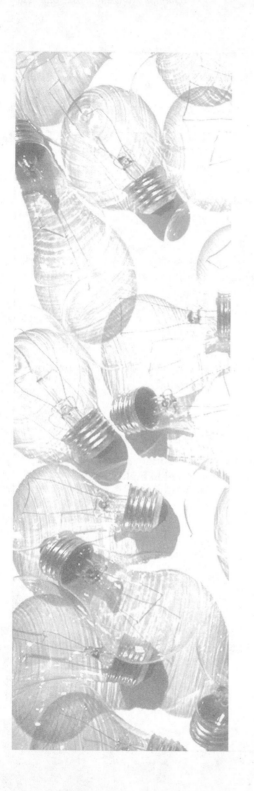

Chapter 8

Description:

Making Your Audience See

[The writer must] venture into the finer labyrinths opened by…senses, touch, to learn the texture of leather, of earth; smell, the tinct of sweetgrass and urine; taste, the golden poplar sap or the hot, raw buffalo liver dipped in gall.

Rudy Wiebe

To see takes time—like to have a friend takes time.

Georgia O'Keefe

*W*hich of these statements are true?

1. Description is flowery and poetic.
2. Description bogs down writing.
3. Description belongs in creative essays, not in persuasive or informative writing.

None. Each one distorts the real nature of description. Fancy, gooey descriptive passages can smother ideas and are unacceptable as professional communication. Such passages give description a bad reputation. Good description doesn't need to be overly dense or luxurious. For example, the following passage describes a seizure a student's infant daughter suffered as a result of a DPT vaccine for pertussis:

> Lying in a puddle of vomit, Katelyn's head tilted to her shoulder, her eyes fixated left, looking like quarter moons. When I picked her up, I realized her head was locked to her shoulder. "Katie!" I yelled. She didn't hear me. Once in her father's arms, her legs locked straight out. Her tiny arms pulled tight against her chest, and her head shot back. My husband held down her tongue just as her jaw locked shut. Her eyes rolled upward, then they were gone.

At the hospital, the child's condition was stabilized, and the author goes on to describe her condition:

> There, lying in a crib resembling a cage, clad only in her diaper, was our baby daughter. Her chest was covered with leads monitoring her heart. Her arms, braced with tongue depressors, were violated with tubes and needles. Inches from her body was a "crash kit" equipped with electric paddles should they be needed.

> —Alana J. Lockwood

This vivid, factual description draws readers into the author's informative critique of the DPT vaccine, which each year causes seizures in thousands of normal children.

Description breathes life into writing—transforms typed words into pictures, sounds, and ideas. *Good* description makes the writer's idea dance in readers' heads, so they forget they're reading words. *Bad* description, by trying to impress readers with lush words, distracts from the idea.

Good description is essential for *all* writing, from business reports to personal letters to poems to persuasive essays. Description commits writers to honesty by pinning down vague statements with concrete details. Honest description challenges everyday experience by scrutinizing the world to reveal what's really there.

Here's an example of good description:

The fish are not biting this evening. I row myself to the centre of the glassy lake, and as I wait, I accept that there is nowhere to go and nothing to do. I listen to the bird song that surrounds me and realize that I have been tuning out a symphony. I wish that I were a naturalist who could recognize each whistle: the low hums, the sweetly repeated chirps, the little flute notes that sail on the quiet air. I close my eyes and lose myself in the gentle rocking of the boat, notice the evening temperature just beginning to cool. And it doesn't matter that I have not had a nibble on my line or that I will have to break open a can of beans later. I realize that I didn't come here to fish, but to catch a glimpse of myself in the night.

This passage makes us *see* as well as understand, which is description's great virtue.

In persuasive or research papers, powerful description, in combination with statistics and other facts, can support a thesis. In a paper arguing for strong penalties for pregnant women who use drugs, a student's research describes the effects of cocaine on newborns:

Because cocaine causes fetal malnutrition, when the baby is born, its dry, cracked skin resembles the cover of an old, leather-bound book (Fulroth 70). Cocaine babies are almost always underweight. Their heads are 20% smaller than average. Their limbs jerk and jitter constantly, and their hands fly period- ically to the sides of their heads, eyes startled wide in terror. Cocaine babies' heartbeats soar, and their lungs pump like hyperactive bellows. They cry inconsolably, a creepy, catlike wail that can last hours and that indicates severe neurological damage (Knight 71).

—Heidi Daniels

This chapter discusses ways of developing a better eye for description, so you too can make readers experience words, not just read them. The first part concentrates on thinking, the second on revising.

 # A WRITER'S EYE: SIX WAYS TO VISUALIZE IDEAS

1. EXPERIENCE THE SUBJECT: DON'T THINK IN WORDS

Suppose you were asked to describe your room. Your first attempt might look like this: "My room is three metres by four metres and painted blue.

I have a bed, a dresser, a stereo, a chair...." There is obviously no life to this minimal description. Some students who realize it's flat might attempt to enliven it with so-called descriptive words: "My room is robin-egg blue with beige accents. I have an antique maple dresser, an enormous bed, a four-speaker, dolby-sound stereo cassette player...." There is a little more life to this one, but it still does not engage the reader. Both examples fail because of mistaken goals.

1. Description is not a catalogue of everything present.
2. Description is not created by thinking of picturesque words.

Description *is* created by mentally reexperiencing what you hope to describe. A catalogue may help as a brainteaser, but it won't create *quality description*. For that, you must create an *idea* on which the description hangs, and you must concentrate on seeing and feeling your subject, not on choosing descriptive words. Evoke it inside yourself, and only *then* describe it in words. Reexperiencing often leads to vivid words naturally *and* ties description together.

Suppose you are writing about access for the disabled in public buildings. Your first brainteaser list of descriptive details might include wide stalls in washrooms, interpreters for the deaf in schools, low water fountains with large handles, wheelchair lifts on buses, and perhaps several disabled people you have known (an examples brainteaser). You could use this list to compose an essay, perhaps entitling it "Improvements in Public Access in Recent Years," but these descriptive details aren't sharp enough yet. You haven't "reexperienced" them vividly.

Let's take the bathroom stall as an example. Imagine yourself entering it in a wheelchair. Experience the bodily movements you need to make to accomplish this simple act. Go slowly; see or feel each moment clearly before going on. Could you do it during 10 minutes between classes? Picture yourself rolling amid the waists of walking people, bumping open the washroom door and scraping past, rocking and turning several times to shut and lock the stall. Your books and papers fall off the wheelchair tray when you hoist yourself with the cold bar, your chair sliding nearly out of reach. After, you contort to push the handle behind your back, and then you speed to class late, bumping cluttered chairs aside to make a space.

This description shows a train of thought, roughly as it came out. It's a brainteaser in paragraph form, not finished writing, but it shows more life, more tense description, than the first list. If you want your essay to inform people about barriers the handicapped face, visualizing details will give you—and your readers—a clearer sense of what's involved.

We accomplish this by thinking, not just in words, but in pictures, touches, and sounds—just as we experience things in real life. Feel the subject from *inside*, not from outside. Allow yourself to become your subject, and let it speak through you; don't treat it as an object. At its extreme, this is the experience of poets and fiction writers, when they swear a piece "wrote itself." But even a menu writer must see, taste, and smell dishes to describe them well. Business reports and academic papers require this approach too. The more you refeel or visualize your topic, the easier vivid description will be.

Some writers can type or write *as* they reexperience, but many can't. If words block experiencing, try this: sit back, *pen or computer out of reach*, and picture your subject, imagining new details as you explore it. Relax. Let the topic talk. Release your subconscious—censor nothing; accept everything. Concentrate on seeing more sharply as you go on. Push your memory, recall facts, use *all* your senses, daydream. Most people stop when the first shadowy pictures appear. You should continue, going slowly, probing deeply. After a vivid experience gels, record your sensations, still not paying attention to words. Simply record vivid images, allowing new descriptions to flow too. *Later* you will take control and fine-tune the picture. As W.E.B. DuBois said, "Produce beautiful things, but stress the things rather than the beauty."

■ *Practice 8-1:* After fully "experiencing" two of the following, record your descriptions.

Your room

A machine or tool

Teenage alcoholism

Senior citizens

An encounter with the police

2. USE BRAINTEASERS TO TRAIN YOUR EYE

Experiencing concentrates on unrestricted seeing. Brainteasers prod your eye in a more organized way. The two most important brainteasers I've already mentioned: using your senses and listing examples. As you experience your topic, if you only see obvious things, switch senses. Concentrate on hearing, smelling, or touching it. Or list examples for your topic. Then experience it.

Suppose you're describing to your boss flaws in the design of the store you work in. Be a customer. Walk through the door. Wait! How does the door open? Is it a pull door people always push because it has a horizontal, long handle, not a small grabber? *Feel* yourself jolt as the door bounces loose from many bumps. *Feel* the customers' anger. It angers people. How about the entrance way cluttered with gumball machines and a kiddie ride? *Hear* the whirring, whumpy-whump of the horse ride and the whining of kids begging mothers for quarters. Angry mothers, worn-down mothers.

Nickle-dime robbery. Now move into the store. *See* the line of people and the cash registers, instead of a pretty dress or glittering jewellery. *Smell* the seafood section. Walk through other stores with your senses for *comparison.* Now you're ready to write.

To describe something more freshly, push past the obvious with a break-stereotypes brainteaser. Describe the obvious; then puncture it. Suppose you're describing the wonderful vacation cottage your family rented last year. There's the breathtaking view of lake and mountain, the fish that beg to be caught, the clean country air. Stop! Be critical. Didn't you see beer cans in the stream leading to the lake? Weren't trucks hauling building supplies up that pristine mountain? Didn't motorboats roar past at midnight?

Making comparisons, alternating viewpoints, and drawing analogies can also stimulate your descriptive eye. If you're describing a local park, for instance, think of alternative viewpoints. Some people might only see a rolling hill, some obnoxious children playing, and mosquitoes biting every few seconds. Others might remember the place in winter, kids flying down the same hill in toboggans, the bitter cold, and the snow-covered trees. Still others might see the park as it was years ago, before the picnic tables, bicycle paths, and joggers. Allowing yourself to *experience* these other viewpoints helps you to see more. The more you see, the more powerful and alive your description will be.

■ *Practice 8-2:* Do a senses brainteaser and one other brainteaser to gather sharp descriptions for the following topics. *Experience* them for five minutes before you focus on words.

A childhood place

An eyesore local authorities should fix or remove

A commercial product about which you have strong feelings

Student housing

3. Use the Iceberg Principle

The iceberg principle, as its name implies, is based on the idea that powerful writing only shows the tip of the iceberg, nine-tenths of which exists under water. In essence, less description is sometimes more, because it can suggest what is not visible. When faced with describing a complex or huge topic, *don't feel obligated to cover everything!* You may end up with a shapeless catalogue. Instead, search for small, key details that capture the essence of the larger picture—like a camera close-up.

In describing a new word processor, for instance, you'd probably confuse and bore readers by detailing all its features. But you might best illustrate its accessibility by describing one or two functions, such as moving a sentence from one spot to another or reformatting.

The iceberg principle forces readers to pay attention by drawing them in close. That perspective creates surprise and drama. It also requires you to *trust your reader.* By relying on a small, intimate detail, you hope your reader will *infer* the larger picture by actively imagining along with you. (If someone writes, "Ralph set fire to the child's kite," there's no need to add, "I think it was cruel.")

Describing a red-veined, bulbous nose and a sleek, powdered nose will suggest quite different things about their owners. Description can thus carry the idea of an essay through symbolism or representation. To describe a group, you don't have to describe every member of the group. Pick *typical* members to symbolize the whole. For example, an essay on student fashion could centre around a few clear snapshots: baseball caps, pierced noses, "jock chic" (T-shirts, shorts, and running shoes). Keep in mind that the iceberg principle is just a metaphor to remind you to focus on the most significant detail—it's a way of capturing a potent image that concentrates the idea you want to communicate to your reader.

■ *Practice 8-3:* Take an iceberg approach to two of the following topics. Find two details that capture the essence of the general example.

"Older" men in college or university

Suburban houses or city apartments

Local election campaigns

Local weather

4. Other Eye-Training Tricks

1. Describe your topic as if to an audience unfamiliar with it. For example, you might try to describe a ballpoint pen and its use (or any other object of modern civilization) to a Tibetan hermit-monk. If you imagine your audience knows nothing, you must see freshly.

2. Think of your topic as part of a process—not as a thing. A static thing invites dullness, but few things are truly static. The earth rockets through space about 1.6 million kilometres per day and rotates about 1,600 kilometres per hour; its crust rises and falls about half a metre each day. Everything has an origin and an end, and is recycled into new life. Open your mind to see your topic as a process in time and space. A simple description of your room, then, connects to all the people who lived in it before, how it came to be, and what will happen to it after you're gone. If you're writing about handling customer complaints at work, make your audience picture the process all parties go through before and after confrontations.

3. Describe what's not there. A person who doesn't smile, cry, or become embarrassed may be interesting for that. That my word processor can't combine single and double spacing is a major drawback. The lack of student housing shapes the atmosphere at many schools.

■ *Practice 8-4:* Look closely at a small natural object, such as a moth's antennae, an ant's face, or a bit of soil. Try using two of the "other" techniques to think descriptively. Pull your details together with an idea. Do the same for some overlooked part of your anatomy.

 ## REVISING FOR VIVID DESCRIPTION

To this point, we've experimented with ways to *think* descriptively. Now, here are a few tips to sharpen description when *revising* your *wording*. Be open to change, *All words describe*, you want your descriptions to be the kind you can rap your knuckles against.

1. THE SENSES TEST

Ask if your descriptive passages pass the senses test—can you see, smell, taste, touch, or hear something in every passage?

Original: The accounting procedure is awkward to use.

Revised: The accounting procedure requires flipping back and forth among three pages.

"Awkward" is an abstract word readers can understand intellectually, but they cannot experience it with their senses. "Flipping back and forth" suggests awkwardness and helps them to experience the procedure more fully, with sound, sight, and touch.

Original: The apartment smelled dirty and rotten.

Revised: The apartment smelled like mildewed shoes.

The apartment smelled of urine and beer.

The revisions create different images, but both are sharp. "Dirty" and "rotten" are not sense-oriented.

2. THE SPECIFICITY TEST

In revising, ask if descriptions can be more specific. Test your honesty—how concrete and exact can you be? The broader a description is, the vaguer it reads; the narrower it is, the sharper. Try *several* options for unspecific words before deciding.

Example: Heather walked into the room.

Specify "room" as "lecture hall," "kitchen," or "men's room" and the sentence focuses for readers; specify "walk" as "strutted," "dashed," or "limped" and the sentence leaps at readers.

Example: Ordinary lawn chemicals cause harmful side effects on a human being's health, including respiratory, skin, and neurological problems. They can also seriously pollute and deteriorate the quality of nearby watersheds.

Here's how a student made this topic more specific and tangible:

> Lawn chemicals cause headaches, runny noses, rashes, and nausea. Other symptoms may include vomiting, heavy sweating, dizziness, and disorientation. Their nitrogen seeps into groundwater, ending up in streams and ponds. This causes algae buildup, reduction of oxygen, and eventually dead water.
>
> —Jeanette Crouse

Specificity enhances meaning as well as visual appeal.
Scan the following phrases:

A beggar with a cup

A beggar with a Burger King cup

Why describe the cup? It is more visual, but it also pinches us with the contrast of "king" and "beggar." Try new descriptive adjectives, but slash those that don't carry meaning as well as visual appeal. Don't describe just to get more words.

■ *Practice 8-5:* In the following sentences, first mark words that could be more specific and then suggest three alternatives for each. Don't limit yourself to one-word replacements.

Bill ate his lunch noisily.

The union leadership called for a protest.

The summer breeze off the water is lovely at night.

3. The Freshness Test

These techniques create fresher descriptions:

1. Replace clichés with original expressions.

   Cliché: The 30-metre canyon walls stood over us.

   Fresher: The canyon thrust out its 30-metre chest.

2. Create metaphors for dull descriptions.

   Original: He had scary eyes.

   Revised: He had eyes like half-peeled grapes.

   His eyes tightened around my neck.

3. Cut flat details. If you can't improve a dull spot, leave it out—see if anything's really lost. If you want to sell a head of lettuce, would you leave on the brown, wilted leaves?

4. Do a mini-brainteaser for weak descriptions. Freewrite until something vivid emerges. Select the best for the revised description.

Highlights of Chapter 8

1. All writing improves with vivid description—whether it's a business report, technical manual, paper on global poverty, or letter telling Uncle Moneybags about the poverty of modern students. Description breathes life into your words—helps readers to experience, not just understand, your idea.

2. Beyond this, a sharp descriptive eye helps writers to appreciate and understand life more intensely, for description is really the art of experiencing the world honestly. It is not the art of fancy word painting.

3. The most important part of writing good description is to experience your subject.

4. You can also use brainteasers to stimulate concrete thinking or use the iceberg principle to find the representative detail.

5. Other eye-training tricks are to describe your topic to a naïve audience, see your topic as a process, or describe what's missing.

Writing Suggestions and Class Discussions

1. Write a long descriptive sentence about your favourite piece of clothing. Use as many senses as you can. Pack in details without writing a general inventory.

2. Write your own abstract, dictionary-like definition of love, hate, or madness. In a separate paragraph, show the word in action. Experience an incident or example. Use pictorial words, not abstractions.

3. Find a dull, three- to five-sentence printed description. Reimagine it honestly; then rewrite it more vividly.

4. Describe a hospital room. Find four overlooked details that, like the tip of an iceberg, represent the hospital experience.

5. Bring a music recording, photograph, or reproduction of an artwork to class. Before playing or showing it, read aloud a one-paragraph description you wrote of it. Use experiencing, brainteasers, and the iceberg theory to write your description.

6. Blind writers, such as Homer, Jorge Luis Borges, John Milton, and Helen Keller, have relied on senses other than sight. Sit in an unfamiliar setting, such as a bus stop or mall, close your eyes, and experience

only through your other senses. Spend 15 to 20 minutes doing this. Then write a vivid description.

7. Describe a technical process you know better than most people (developing photographs, tuning a car, or doing a company payroll, for example). Describe this process clearly and vividly for a reader with average knowledge of it. Use experiencing, brainteasers, and the iceberg theory to start.

8. Describe a common object, such as a button, key, or can opener. Discover details others might overlook. Write one paragraph.

9. I Spy Assignment: To develop your descriptive eye, discreetly observe a stranger for 10 to 15 minutes, learning all you can. Open up to clothes, habits, quirks, speech patterns, as well as physical features. Write several paragraphs. (Don't intrude on the person; do this in a public place.)

10. Write a descriptive paper on a place. Vivid detail should support a theme or idea. Write two or three pages. Use experiencing, brainteasers, and the iceberg theory to start.

11. Describe a group you belong to—a company, church, club, team, or clique. Describe it vividly and develop a theme. Use experiencing, brainteasers, and the iceberg theory to start.

12. Your teacher will ask peer groups to reexperience areas of the campus they're familiar with (bookstore, library, or cafeteria, for example). They should come up with creative, vivid descriptions, not through using fancy words but by discovering sharp, perhaps overlooked, details. The groups should spend part of the period observing and writing, then reassemble to share their notes.

13. Expand an exercise that turned out well into a two- or three-page paper.

✔ **PEER-REVIEW WORKSHOP: DRAFTS**

Author: _____

Reviewer: _____

Answer the questions as specifically as possible and discuss the essay with the author before doing part 2.

PART 1

Ideas: What point do you think the essay makes?

Are there any symbolic messages here? Explain.

Organization: Describe the essay's organization. Highlight the main pattern, but don't evaluate.

Would the essay be improved by rearranging, combining, or cutting some sections? Which ones? Why? Is anything important missing?

Descriptive details: Give the essay the senses test. Where does it do the best, where the poorest?

Which section(s) could be more specific?

Find a description that could be fresher. Suggest a revision.

PART 2

Peer partners should collaborate on three of the following six brain-teasers for each essay. First, talk through them. Then the author should take notes for revision. Work on sections the reviewer or author wants improved.

1. Experience the section by talking through it.

2. Use two brainteasers (bug lists, alternate viewpoints, etc.) to draw out more details.

3. Use the iceberg principle to find symbolic value in a detail in the paper or on these lists.

4. If you were writing for a naïve audience, what new descriptions might you add?

5. See the topic as a process—move backward and forward in time and list new details.

6. Describe what the topic does not have.

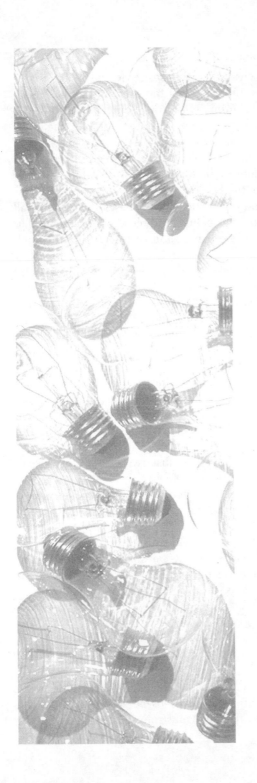

Chapter 9

Narration:

Telling Your
Audience a Story

*Words, sentences, books:
so much more than
simple pleasure, so much
the very heart of life
itself.*

Neil Bissoondath

*T*he earliest writers in every civilization told stories to convey their messages. Homer's tales of Cyclops, the one-eyed monster, and Circe, whose spells transformed humans into animals, not only entertained but also informed and persuaded the ancient Greeks about geography, the gods, humanity's place in the universe, and other things as Homer knew them. The ancient myth of Sisyphus, for example, tells of a greedy king who is condemned in hell to roll a boulder to the top of a hill. Just before Sisyphus reaches the peak, the gods make the boulder roll back down, and Sisyphus must start all over again. Up and down the hill he chases the rock for all time. Over the centuries, the story has been a parable about greed and has appealed to people as a memorable expression of the futility of much human effort.

Jesus frequently told stories to make his messages stronger. "The Good Samaritan" and "The Prodigal Son" seem to stick in our minds much better than, say, a typical sermon on charity. When Jesus told a crowd, "Love thy neighbour," a lawyer asked, "Who is my neighbour?" Jesus, realizing the man wanted to put a limit on whom he was required to love, did not directly define the word "neighbour." Instead, he told the story of a man beaten and robbed by thieves in his own country. The victim's neighbours, a priest and a local official, walked by without helping. Then a Samaritan, a stranger in the victim's country, stopped, washed the man's wounds, took him to an inn, and paid for his lodging. When Jesus finished, the lawyer knew the meaning of "neighbour," not from definition, but from the actions in the story.

Why have these stories lasted so long? Because stories are more visual, more easily remembered than abstractions. When we recall Sisyphus groaning behind his boulder or the supposedly good men passing the injured man before the Samaritan stops to help, the abstract message flows along with the story.

Successful speakers know that telling a vivid story can be more effective than using facts alone. A good storyteller creates a warm, appealing image; people view the teller as creative and smart, as one who commands attention with powerful images: in short, as someone worth listening to.

CONFLICT

The heart of a good story is conflict: forces in tension with each other. The four common types are person versus person, person against society, person versus nature, and person against himself/herself. A person struggling against an employer who cheats clients is person versus person;

someone battling the city to hire more disabled people is person against society; someone struggling to find the ski lodge after a sudden squall separates him from the group is person versus nature; a woman trying to decide whether she should have an abortion is person against herself.

■ *Practice 9-1:* Take a moment to recall examples from your own life to illustrate each of these conflicts. One of them may become your next paper. Write a few lines for each.

You vs. another person

You vs. society

You vs. nature

You vs. yourself

Let's look more closely at what makes a good conflict and why it helps your story to absorb readers' attention. First, only real sparks make real fires. Superficial conflicts—ones that come and go without deeply affecting us—won't make strong stories. A story about a mother forbidding her daughter to date a certain boy does not sound very promising, no matter how much the episode upset the writer. However, if the daughter learns that her mother has deeper motives—if, for instance, the boy reminds the mother of a boy who jilted her or of one she always wished she'd married instead of her daughter's father—then we have more hope for this conflict. Or perhaps we'll discover the mother is envious of her daughter's social success. Or perhaps the daughter wants to date a wild boy because she doesn't like the relationship her parents have. Here we have something more meaningful than a typical parent-child argument. The best conflicts draw out some deeper significance in the characters or the action. Readers want conflict so they can care about the outcome, so they can cheer or fear or doubt with the narrator. They also want conflicts that are *difficult* to solve. Wrong versus right or strong versus weak doesn't grip readers as much as conflicts in which wrong and right are murky or the forces opposed are equal.

Our lives are full of both inner and outer conflicts, but sometimes we don't recognize them. Following are three almost sure ways to find a strong conflict to write about.

1. Think about *the most intense moments of growth in your life.* They have changed not only the *outer* course of your life but the *inner* course as well by developing your philosophy or marking a turning point in who you are. Readers want a story to matter to the writer, or it won't matter to them. For this reason, it is sometimes harder to write about a personal triumph—winning the big race or being elected to a public office—than about a defeat or tragedy. Winning tends to keep our beliefs intact; we often learn more in losing. Nor do big tragedies necessarily mean a person has grown.

As Isaac Bashevis Singer said, "A wise man gets wiser by suffering. A person without wisdom may suffer 100 years and die a fool." The moments that make us grow, that tear away the familiar boundaries of our lives, are the ones that make good papers.

■ *Practice 9-2:* List three intense moments of growth in your life. In a few words, describe how each changed your outlook.

2. Look for good conflicts by thinking about an interesting person you've known: the rebel in the family or town, the eccentric uncle, the boyfriend or girlfriend you loved once and later hated, the "respectable" neighbour who abuses his children. You may side with or against the rebel. You may stir up vivid memories if you consider the things that attracted you to your friend and those that later drove you apart. Or, as an honest, intense observer, you may simply report the conflict you see.

■ *Practice 9-3:* Describe one of the most interesting people you've known and sketch out a conflict that focuses on this person.

3. Brainteasers can suggest strong conflicts for narrative essays. A bug list will surely turn up areas of conflict in your life. You can do a general list first and then pursue the conflict that most intrigues you. Dig to the depth of your dissatisfaction. The alternate-viewpoints brainteaser will help you to tell an honest story. Look at it from the viewpoints of the other people involved to discover your weaknesses and their strengths. Doing so allows you to make *real* opponents in the story, not just cardboard cutouts. Because a major aspect of storytelling is making readers visualize the story, sensory brainteasers will help you in your final draft. Remembering with your senses will stimulate your imagination too.

 ## COMPLICATION

After finding a powerful conflict, you must make it more complicated as the story continues. The novelist E.M. Forster said he always imagined one of his readers to be a person who only cared about what happened next, who wanted to be surprised by new twists, angles, or insights in each paragraph. If the story stagnates, it's usually because it has ceased to convey *new information*. This does not mean you must have continuous action, as many television shows do. Moving forward can be a matter of mental twists and insights as well:

> The new doctor doesn't seem to care about my infected ear. He makes me do all the talking, stares at me when he thinks I'm not looking. Is he nervous? His hand seems to shake a lot. Is that

booze I smell on his breath? Or just medicine? He leaves the room and returns after a long time. Maybe I have some horrible sickness that he's afraid to tell me about. He even sends the nurse in at the end to tell me I can go.

As I leave, I notice a photograph of the doctor and a girl who looks like me—we could be sisters. "His daughter died last month," the receptionist whispers.

What gives this little story some life is not the surprise ending—that's always too late to interest the reader. What gets it going is the initial conflict—the doctor is uneasy with the narrator (person vs. person)—and what keeps it going are the *competing explanations* for this unease that flash through the narrator's mind. Each sentence searches for facts and ideas to explain this behaviour; each complicates the story. Without them, the ending would be flat.

The most interesting conflicts involve people in difficult personal choices. It's always tempting to make things look black and white, right or wrong, or to depict a clash between the forces of good and evil, but such a polarized approach may lack subtlety.

Consider the example of a student who wrote a gruesome narrative about what happened to his wife when they decided to commit her temporarily to a mental hospital. Once she was signed in, the authorities could keep her there until *they* thought she was cured. They began chemical and electric-shock treatments that hurt and scared her. She begged to be released. The man began to doubt his wife and to believe the medical authorities that she was far gone, because each time he visited her, she was wilder, more rumpled, more "crazy looking." Friends and family advised him to "detach" himself from his wife. But something deeper in their relationship drew him back. He believed the authorities were more disturbed than his wife, and he eventually fought in court to release her.

This powerful conflict has a number of twists that keep a reader involved. The most interesting is the inner conflict in the man—whether to believe the "sane experts" or the "crazy" wife he loves. In the rough draft, the student portrayed the orderlies and nurses as snarling sadists with dripping fangs. It's easy to see why he felt this way, but the descriptions and the dialogue didn't work—they were too exaggerated. Later, he realized that most of the employees simply wanted to slide through tough days a little more easily; he'd asked too many questions and been deemed a "troublemaker." The workers were not devils, but people who'd grown calluses over their feelings. He didn't release them from their responsibility for his wife's pain, but in looking more closely at them, he discovered the real problem in his wife's mental health care. He believed the employees inflicted pain on patients to make them act more deranged and therefore less human. If they felt they were dealing with crazy people, it made their disturbing job easier. It's a powerful, honest insight because it's not oversimplified, and the essay gained complexity and depth because the writer looked beyond the obvious poles of conflict. The lesson: be sceptical of any angels or devils you create.

■ *Practice 9-4:* Using one of your practice conflicts, list some complications in it.

 # HOW TO RUIN A STORY

Teachers and textbooks don't often advise students how to mess up; but if you're interested in ruining a story, following are three ways to do it.

The first way is to start the story too early. If you're going to tell the story of your great fishing adventure, start with getting ready the night before, your restless sleep, waking, breakfast, packing the car, driving to the dock, and casting off. This is boring in one sentence. Imagine how boring it would be stretched to a full page! On the other hand, if you want an exciting start, begin at this moment: "I was rebaiting my hook when I realized that a squall had blocked out the sun and was heading straight for our boat." Or start at night after the first day, when your buddy spills the lantern fuel onto the campfire. If your story is about meeting a wonderful person during a vacation, start with the moment he bumps into you with his cotton candy and tangles it in your hair. *Don't* start with packing, travelling, unpacking, and setting up on the beach.

The ancient Greeks used the expression *in medias res* ("into the middle") to describe starting where real conflict begins. Have your characters begin *in motion,* not preparing to move. Do this and you'll be surprised how busy you'll be telling the real story and how little time you'll need to spend on that story-killer—background.

Following are some openings from student papers that hook a reader.

I was hunched over my crying baby brother when I heard Joe's footsteps behind me. "He fell," I tried to explain, "he was on the bed but he rolled and I... I...." Pain shot through my spine like a freight train had burst through the floor straight into my rear end. As he cocked his boot again, my mother dashed into the room and screamed.

—Raquel E. Torres

Night falls by the time we reach the inn. The crisp, country air, 10 degrees colder than the city, makes us shiver. Moths flutter around the lanterns that light our passage, and the only sound

is the crunching of gravel beneath our feet. Sumie hurries
ahead, sliding open the heavy wooden door.

—Bernadette Verrone

She was gone—again. I watched her red Trans Am disappear up
the gradual grade, then turned to see my bus round the corner,
creeping toward me like a bug in the cool, moist dawn. The
breeze was cold, and far away thunder drummed summer out of
service. The bus groaned to a halt in a diesel haze. The driver
opened the door, and I was sucked off the street.

—James Babcock

A second way to ruin a story is to give away the ending. If the following
sentence began a story, reading the rest of it would seem unnecessary:
"Little did I know the first time Bob approached me before class to borrow
a pen that in seven months we'd be married." It's dramatic, but it kills the
rest of the story. Compare it to this opening: "There was nothing special
about Bob that first day he approached me before class to borrow a pen. I
would have forgotten it except the next day he handed me a dozen pens
with a bow around them. Now I've got a nerd after me, I thought." The second version lets us know something is going to happen, but not what.

Giving away the ending applies not only to events but also to themes.
Good readers enjoy figuring out the significance of what's happening in a
narrative, and an opening sentence like the following can ruin that: "I don't
know if I'll ever marry again, but if I do, I'll put my wife ahead of my
friends." The writer of narratives must tease readers a bit, give them new
events and ideas, but also leave them a bit unsatisfied so they'll keep reading.

Tease them until the climax, that is. The third story-killer is drawing out
the climax, explaining too much. The climax should hit hard and then end.

■ *Practice 9-5:* Pick two places where you could begin one of the narrative
conflicts you developed earlier in this chapter. Which place seems best? Why?

 # DESCRIBING PEOPLE

If conflict is the heart of a narrative, its body is the characters—the
physical presence that moves the conflict. This is where your descriptions
must be sharpest, to make the people in your story jump off the page. Yet
as Virginia Woolf said, "This is the most difficult part of writing: I do not
know how far I differ from other people." We tend to make people in our
stories reflect our own ideas, habits, and values instead of presenting them
as *they* are. Using an alternate-viewpoint brainteaser is the best way to

overcome this problem. Give your main characters—*especially those with whom you disagree*—a few minutes of rough notes. Think as they think. See as they see. What motivates them? What do they care about? This identifying is essential for *honest, vivid conflict.* Suppose you've been cheated by a salesperson; you must try to convey what she believes, perhaps her anxiousness to succeed, or you'll create her as a fake, cardboard figure.

In addition to understanding how your characters think, you must help the reader to *see* them. Here are some things that create a picture of a person in words:

Physical description

Habits

Speech

Possessions

Others' opinions

Gestures

The man who empties an ashtray three times during an evening communicates character through this habit. If he also picks threads from his sleeve and rearranges the couch pillow continually, his character will be dominated by neatness in a reader's eyes. Gestures—such as poking a listener with a forefinger while speaking, or wrapping a sweaty arm around a shoulder— also create character. In preparing to describe people, use the above list as a brainteaser. Make a list of details for each item.

How do you know which details to include in the draft? Let's take physical description as an example. Simple, factual description adds detail, but will rarely light up a page. The following is accurate and specific: "Gregory Bates has brown hair and brown eyes, is 5'10" tall, and weighs 165 lbs." But this description does not bring Mr. Bates to life; these details should stay on the brainteaser page. They're vague, general details. A reader *assumes* a character is of average build unless told otherwise. Brown hair and eyes are so common they only narrow Bates down to several billion people. Instead, search for and choose the details that distinguish him from others: his mohawk haircut, the wart on his chin, his gangly arms. The reader will automatically fill in the rest as "average."

Here's another trick to describe people: when choosing details from your brainteaser lists, pick those that suggest deeper aspects of the person, *those that capture personality or beliefs.* Take eyes as an example. No other part of the human body is described as often. Yet "the windows of the soul" attract more flies than fresh air, more clichés than fresh descriptions. Light-brown eyes, sky-blue eyes, and sparkling eyes are dead eyes. A writer needs to find a twist: cow-brown eyes, winter-blue eyes, eyes sparkling like razors. Or are those eyes dung brown, milk-chocolate brown, or peanut-butter brown? Sooty, muddy, or walnut? Make a list of all the shades of brown you can think of and then choose the best one for your character's eyes. This shade will give the reader something specific for *better visualization.* It will *also convey more of the person's character.* Muddy eyes, for example, suggest vagueness, confusion, or even a dirty personality. All of these browns are equally suggestive.

■ *Practice 9-6:* What do the following descriptors say about the person?

lizard-green eyes

moss-green eyes

faded green eyes

■ *Practice 9-7:* List several vivid substitutes for these bland descriptors:

sparkling teeth

rosy cheeks

dark hair

Possessions reveal character because they represent choices we make. True, most of us buy many things unthinkingly—toothbrushes, pens, underwear. But our unique possessions represent conscious choices—the 20 boxes full of baseball cards or the chest of grandmother's lace doilies, the pink flamingo or the religious shrine in the front yard, the Harley or the Honda in the driveway. Gestures, habits, and what others say about someone also reveal character. A one-page brainteaser listing details should result in plenty you can use to bring a person to life in words. If you can't fill a page with notes, you don't know enough about the person to write him or her into the story.

Following is part of a student's narrative essay that describes a person.

THE RED HEART

Lisa Neal

I first saw Lish on the first day of classes. Her parents dumped her at the back door of the brick dormitory like a bag of garbage and then roared off in a black Cadillac.

I was shocked that the left side of her head was shaved and displayed a small tattoo of a black heart. Her hair on the other side was carrot-coloured and braided with beads. With her head held high, she sauntered in with two leopard-skin bags.

Her arrival sent shock waves throughout the dorm. I'm not sure if Lish felt the rocky movement or just ignored it, for minutes after arriving she invaded the bathroom with an old green toothbrush with yellowed bristles and a worn box of Cow

Brand Baking Soda. I was dismayed she was living in the single room across the hall from me. She left her door wide open as she unpacked her sparse belongings, which included posters of puppies and a Paddington Bear with matted fur and a tattered blue coat. Her night table and dresser were left empty except for a glass incense candle and a fluorescent-pink tape recorder.

As the days passed, I deliberately ignored Lish, but her presence oozed under my closed door, and I soon watched her with the curiosity of a child at the circus. At first, though, I only noticed her hair changing from carrot to watermelon pink, the way she dragged hard on her Export A cigarettes, and the addition of a ring in her nose.

Her parents whizzed in once more that semester, this time in a grey Rolls Royce, to bring her winter clothes. For the 15 minutes they stayed, the entire hall was pierced by yelling. I heard a few snatches of her father's growled words, calling Lish a "humiliation" and a "disgrace to the family." Her mother whined how Lish should be more like her older sister, who was going to become a "respectable and wealthy lawyer" instead of a social worker. The barrage of voices ceased with the sound of shattering glass, and her parents burst out of the room like two tourists fleeing a bear's cave. After a few moments, Lish emerged wearing her usual crooked smile. I was amazed! I would have been in tears. The only reminder that her parents had come was the disappearance of the incense candle holder—reduced to glass shards—and the lingering stench of perfume.

The next night, while I lay on my pink comforter watching Seinfeld, my phone buzzed. It was my parents giving me the usual razor-sharp threats to do well in my classes. After our yelling match, I slammed the phone down, pounced on my bed, and smothered my face in my pillow.

Immediately there was a timid knock, and I was amazed and a bit frightened to see Lish. She wore Mickey Mouse slippers and a pink flannel nightgown as she shuffled onto my robin-egg-blue carpet.

The story goes on to tell how these two very different young women established a relationship. Notice how Lisa has been able to compress so much about Lish into this section, as well as to suggest some contrasts with her own habits, values, possessions, and gestures.

■ *Practice 9-8:* Write a descriptive brainteaser for one person in the story you've been developing during this chapter.

DIALOGUE

Like other aspects of describing people, dialogue must be distinctive—your characters should sound not like *you* but like *themselves*. If you use real people in your story, listen for their unique speech patterns and quirks of language: the person who says "hey" or "ain't" or "prevarication," or who addresses people as "honey" or "pal" or "sir." Levels of education show up in dialogue too. "You ain't putting nothing over on me, eh" and "I'm inclined to disbelieve that assertion" come from two different people saying the same thing. Age, environment, and hobbies influence our choice of words. People who are into computers, cars, television, or the military will use vocabulary that reflects their interest, no matter what they talk about. Take a minute to think of a friend or relative who has a unique vocabulary or style of speaking.

Someone once said, "Dialogue is what people *do* to each other." In stories, your characters shouldn't spend time in small talk. Skip introductions, goodbyes, and "Please pass the butter" talk. Concentrate on the meaningful scenes. Each piece of dialogue must move the story along. Dialogue can carry scenes in which important revelations are made about a character, the action, or the theme. For example:

> The father rumbled into my office. "Why the hell didn't you put her on the goddamned bus if she ain't sick? I got work."
>
> "Your daughter has several bruises on her lower rib cage," I said, "and I suspect she may also suffer—"
>
> "I feel fine, Daddy," Rachel whispered.
>
> The man stared at her, his thumb working in his belt loop. "Yeah," he said. "You look awright."

How does the dialogue reveal all three characters in a short time?

HOW TO SAY SOMETHING WORTH SAYING

How can you make a story convey a good theme?

Tell the truth. Does your theme sound too simple because you've given yourself a candy-coated cliché or a safe, predictable message? You must *reexperience* the events, ask yourself at every turn if you missed something or closed your eyes to something. Use the brainteasers on unquestioned ideas and clichés and alternate viewpoints to break into new truths. But don't worry at the outline stage if your theme isn't outstanding. Themes require drafting and revision to emerge.

Question your own motives along with everyone else's. Be honest about aspects of the story that contradict your main idea. If the ending is basically good or optimistic, look for darker meanings lurking there. If it's a sad ending, look for positive aspects. Doing this will separate the superficial paper from the one that's probing. The poet Samuel Taylor Coleridge once said, "No man does anything from a single motive." Look for multiple causes of both your actions and the actions of others.

■ **Practice 9-9:** Make a rough statement of what you learned from one conflict you've had. Now look for an opposite message you could have drawn from the same experience.

Highlights of Chapter 9

1. Telling a story is a powerfully visual way of conveying a point, and successful people in all fields have therefore used stories to present their ideas. It is also a way of exploring personal experiences more deeply.
2. Conflict is the heart of narration; it focuses your story and makes readers turn the page.
3. Stories are most often spoiled by not getting to the conflict soon enough, by giving away the outcome too soon, or by continuing after the conflict has ended.
4. Stories are more likely to succeed when they begin in the middle of the conflict, when there are continuing complications to the initial conflict, and when the characters are forced to make tough decisions.
5. Create breathing, walking people in stories through their physical appearance, habits, dialogue, possessions, and gestures. Details that symbolize beliefs or personality will be the most powerful.
6. As with all other types of writing, a questioning attitude will lead to a theme that tells the truth about some segment of life and will guard you from predictable clichés.

Writing Suggestions and Class Discussions

1. Tell your best family story.
2. Tell a story of a run-in you had with a relative, but tell it with the relative as the narrator and you as his/her antagonist.
3. Write a narrative essay about an event in your life that changed your philosophy or way of seeing the world. Be honest.
4. Dialogue Practice: Write how you would ask where the washroom is at a restaurant. Now, ask as an Englishman, an elderly schoolteacher, a street kid, and a construction worker might ask. Choose words and style carefully.

5. You are 85 years old, and your friends are gathered around your hospital bed. Before you die, you want to tell them a story that will reveal who you really were and what your life meant. Tell that story. (It should be something that has not yet happened to you.)

6. Description Practice: Describe the eyes, mouth, and one other feature of someone close to you. Make a list of potential details; then choose the most revealing of character. Turn in one finished paragraph; also turn in your brainteaser.

7. You are a rehabilitation counsellor and have been asked to address a group of high school students on the dangers of drug and alcohol abuse. You're afraid they'll be bored if you start out preaching, so you decide to tell a dramatic story to lead into your points. Write this story.

8. Tell a story that brings an abstract idea to life. It may be true or fictional. Use one of these topics:

   Courage

   Prejudice

   Failure

   Cheating

9. Alternate-Viewpoint Practice: A mother (or father) aged 39, daughter (or son) aged 18, and grandmother (or grandfather)—age unknown—live together. The grandparent wants to remarry. Break the class into groups of four—one for each part and one to record notes. Have the groups present possible ideas/reactions each character would have.

10. Describing People Practice: Use the list of character features found earlier in this chapter to create a page of details to describe either yourself or a close friend. Go beyond the obvious.

11. List five conflicts in your life that could be potential subjects for narrative essays. In each case, specify the opposing forces and mention a key incident in which the conflict came to a head. Example: My conflict with my sister-in-law (person vs. person); we battle over the best way to raise children: the argument over kids smoking or the argument over attendance at their grandfather's funeral.

12. Do several brainteasers on the best conflict in 11 and write a two- or three-page essay.

✔ **PEER-REVIEW CHECKLIST: NARRATION**

Author: _____

A question I have for the reviewer is:

Reviewer: _____

	STRONG	AVERAGE	WEAK
OPENING: first sentence grabs?			
conflict established?			
IDEAS: complications of conflict?			
honesty/depth of theme?			
DETAILS: people vividly described?			
actions vividly described?			
DIALOGUE: realistic and sharp?			
punctuation, paragraphing good?			
ENDING: ends with a punch?			

What is the most vivid aspect of the story?

Respond to the author's question (offer several suggestions if possible).

Make another two or three suggestions about the story and discuss them with the author.

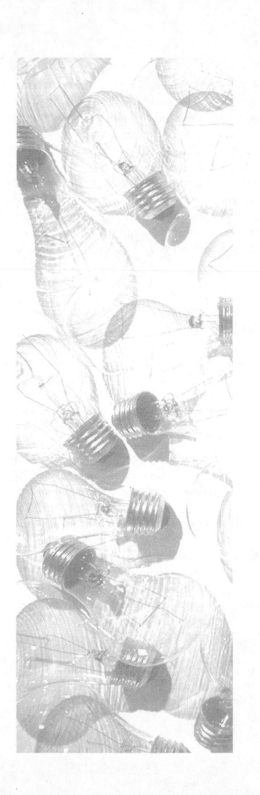

Chapter 10

Informative Writing:

Telling Your Audience What It Doesn't Know

Nothing can be loved or hated until it is first known.

Leonardo Da Vinci

$\mathcal{M}$ost graduates are surprised by how much writing is required in their careers. Nurses, social workers, police officers, and businesspeople discover writing fills far more job time than they ever anticipated. One engineer recently estimated that she spends 50% of her office time writing, not calculating or sketching plans. And of the writing you will do in the workplace, most of it will be informative: technical and business reports, memos, brochures, summaries of meetings, letters, speeches, and perhaps research projects or articles for professional journals or newsletters in your field. The last decades of the twentieth century have been known as "the information age." The person who can convey instructions, facts, summaries, and analyses *concisely, clearly,* and *vividly* will have an edge in becoming a valued employee or leader.

 ## AUDIENCE AND TONE

Informative writing strives for *objectivity*. This does not mean that you must exclude all feelings, but that feelings emerge from *information, not from opinions*. Using facts to support personal opinions is persuasive writing—discussed in the next chapter. In informative writing, your tone should be unbiased; you should think of yourself not as converting your audience but as educating it. But don't think of informative writing as boring, a mere reciting of facts. The writer's job—*always*—is to keep the reader awake, no matter what the topic. Unless your audience requires stiff formality—as in a lab or business report, for instance—occasional humour, vivid anecdotes, and lively words are usually welcome.

You do need to adjust your tone in informative writing for your audience. The amount and kind of information you might use writing about an archaeological dig will vary greatly depending on whether you write a paper for your anthropology professor, a letter to your mother, or a section of a job application. The professor will want more technical and interpretive information; your mother may find the experience of the trip and your reactions to the artifacts more important; a potential employer may be most interested in information on the skills you learned and how well you meshed with the rest of the team.

Suppose you're writing an informative paper on "The Gift of Life"—donating your organs to sick people when you die. How would your tone and information differ for the following audiences?

A sociology professor

Transplant surgeons

The family of the dying person

The general public

Following are some details about the procedure. Decide if particular audiences would or would not want to know them.

1. In a way, organ donation allows the dying person to continue living.

2. The donor is usually brain dead (a flat EEG line), but the heart is still beating and a ventilator keeps the person breathing during the removal of transplant organs (they deteriorate quickly without blood and oxygen).

3. A neurologist is consulted to declare the person brain dead.

4. The transplant doctor does not decide when it's time to save the organs.

5. The hospital does notify transplant doctors of likely cases so they can prepare ahead of time. They contact the receiving family and wait anxiously with equipment ready.

6. The hospital seeks permission (through the donor card) and consults the donor's family.

7. It is a rapid operation without anesthetics. The body is simply sliced open—"peeled back" as one doctor said in a professional journal—to save time. The desired organs are removed as quickly as possible. Then the breathing machine is turned off and the person dies.

8. The body cavity can be packed and stitched up for a funeral.

As you can see from the above facts, an informative writer must be sensitive to the intended audience. In this list, there is already an obvious slanting of the facts. They're aimed at a general audience: the language is not very technical and is presented without much sensitivity to the emotional needs of a grieving family. They probably wouldn't want to hear the anatomical details of organ removal.

Failure to consider the intended audience has led to some absurd "informative" writing. In 1919, British Prime Minister Lloyd George wrote a report to the Italian government on the economics of growing bananas, concluding by advising government officials to plant great banana plantations to reduce their trade deficits. He forgot that bananas can't grow in Italy.

 ## PACKING IN DETAILS

Here we are again. There's no way to write well without details, and the informative essay should bristle with them. During the prewriting stage, tease your brain by asking reporters' questions. You might start with this overall one: "What would *I* want to know about this topic if I could ask any expert?"

Suppose your topic is the effects of a nuclear war. *Ask personal questions.* What would happen to *me* if a nuclear bomb struck half a kilometre away, a kilometre away, five kilometres, 50 kilometres? Ask for graphic details. What would happen to my skin, bones, hair, eyes, sexual functioning, and digestion? How would it affect me if I survived? How would I eat? Whom would I live with? What would be the odds of finding friends or family? What aspects of society would remain?

Ask less personal questions. How would the living deal with all the dead and dying? Would society revert to a primitive cave culture, as some people predict? Would the survivors be inspired to deeper camaraderie? Would there be just a few bombs, or would the warring countries let loose hundreds? Would the atmosphere be poisoned for all life on earth, as in Nevil Shute's *On the Beach*? How likely is the nuclear winter that Carl Sagan and other experts predict—should the sun be blocked by billions of tonnes of dust thrown into the atmosphere? Can you add three or four questions to this list? Try it now for practise.

It's easier to ask questions, of course, than to answer them, but in asking sometimes answers emerge. In asking, you also mark which territory you'll be able to handle best when you focus the topic more. So the first step is to ask the honest questions—the ones you really care about. Tough questions require tough, gutsy details. They'll help to point you toward a good paper.

■ *Practice 10-1:* Ask four or five tough questions about the topics below. Suspend what you do know about them and ask what you really should know.

Bilingual education

Television nature programs

The value of a bachelor's degree in today's job market

 # SURPRISE VALUE

Good informative reports or essays should *surprise the reader with new information.* If you only tell us what we already know, you're not informing us of anything. For instance, most people know that nuclear bombs generate great heat and do awful things to human flesh. But when they read John Hersey's book *Hiroshima,* they learn that some people caught within half a kilometre of the blast were vaporized so suddenly they didn't even have time to scream or turn away. How do we know? Because they stood between concrete walls and the blast, and exact outlines of their bodies are preserved on the concrete—a painter raising his brush, a mother straightening the blanket on her baby. Their bodies shielded the wall from the intense heat just enough to imprint their silhouettes on it.

That is information. Give your reader the same kind of essential, inside information. "General" or "official" information usually tells readers only what they already know, unless you pick exotic topics—such as spelunking (exploring caves), cooking Indonesian food, or teaching sign language to the deaf.

So do you have to do original research to write informative essays? In a sense, yes. However, you don't have to travel to Japan or work 10 years in a lab. Your eyes, ears, fingers, and brain are researching the world every day. If you can imagine a world without electricity, family, schools, police, hospitals, or law enforcement, you may be able to create a plausible essay on the world after nuclear war. If you can use your experience to imagine what it might be like to see a dying relative put on a respirator and can honestly picture a doctor asking you to sign over the person's organs, you may be able to write about some of the issues in "The Gift of Life" essay.

Many informative papers you do for school *will* require some outside research without being full-scale research papers. Be sure to document these sources (see chapter 13). Following is an example by a student writing on bulimia, or binge eating. To enhance her personal knowledge, she cited two sources with surprise value in details:

> Jessica, a thirty-six-year-old financial analyst from Edmonton, gorges herself, then takes three hundred laxatives. She has done this each day for sixteen years. A teenager with bulimia starved herself, gorged herself, and made herself throw up. She died while retching over a toilet bowl (Cauwels 3). Suzanne Abraham recorded one patient's "bad binge": she ate a bag of potato chips, a jar of honey, a jar of anchovies on bread, one pound of rolled oats, two pounds of pancakes, one pound of macaroni, two instant puddings, four ounces of nuts, two pounds of sugar, one box of Rice Crispies, a pound of margarine, two quarts of milk, a gallon of ice cream, a pound of sausage, a pound of onions, twelve eggs, a pound of licorice, a dozen candy bars, and ended with a bottle of Coke. This totals 1,071 grams of protein, 1,964 grams of fat, and 14,834 grams of carbohydrates (85). These violent abuses of the body profoundly affect bulimics' social life, self-esteem, and psychological functioning. It may cause death from suicide or cardiac arrhythmia.
>
> —Andrea Macaluso

■ *Practice 10-2:* Write a senses and an examples brainteaser about a natural disaster you know about: flood, blizzard, fire, and so on. Be especially alert for details with surprise value—little things that many people might not know.

POOR INFORMATIVE TOPICS

1. *Introductory topics*—such as "How to play the piano"—can lead to disaster. There's so much basic definition and terminology that it's hard to write an interesting paper. You might do better to focus on "How to handle your first piano recital" or "What makes jazz piano sound different." Another problem with introductory topics is that most educated people will be familiar with the basic information. Picking topics such as "Techniques of safe driving" or "Basics of gardening" will bog you down in saying the obvious. Pick an *aspect* of the topic that promises more surprise value: "Why truck drivers are the safest drivers" or "Gardening health hazards."

2. Broad topics—such as "What is a good marriage?"—can also doom your paper. You'll only be able to say the most general and superficial things about this topic because you promise more than you can fulfil in sharp, gutsy detail. Better choices: "How to handle a family argument over money" or "Six questions to ask your fiancé before walking down the aisle."

CHOOSING GOOD TOPICS

Lurking inside all poor topics are potential good topics, and keeping two things in mind will help you to recognize which kind you have. First, is it limited to an aspect you can cover *in depth* in your allotted pages? Can you really tell us something fresh and fill the essay with vivid details? Second, do you have a *specific slant* or a message to convey—a thesis? Remember that the steps in writing an essay are interdependent— the thesis helps to determine structure; the structure helps to create ideas. The four steps of the writing process described in this book—getting ideas, arranging order, drafting, and revising—constantly play back and forth with each other.

ORGANIZING INFORMATIVE WRITING

After narrowing your topic and doing some brainteaser lists, you can invent your own scratch outline for the material. But following are six common structuring and thinking devices people use to convey information. If you start with one early in your prewriting, focusing and structuring your informative writing will be easier. However, you shouldn't always rely on these devices—the most creative topics often break new ground.

1. The process
2. The essentials
3. The causes
4. The effects
5. Comparison/contrast
6. Classification

You'll notice that numbers 5 and 6 come from our brainteasers; the other four can also be brainteasers. All not only dig into the recesses of your mind for ideas but also suggest a focus and structure. Let's look at each in some detail.

1. The process: one way of focusing and organizing information is to present it as a *process*. Imagine yourself telling the reader *how to do* something: "How to skydive," "How to con a professor," "How to teach children manners." Process can also be used to focus on issues simply for *understanding*: "How the Liberals won the last election," "The stages of juvenile delinquency," or "The fall of Communism in Eastern Europe." Your scratch outline would consist of *chronological steps*. Try several outlines until you're satisfied. If, for instance, you find yourself with three stages that have very little information and one bloated with examples and ideas, you probably need to divide that step and combine the smaller ones.

If I were writing on skydiving, for instance, I don't think the following outline would work well:

Saying goodbye to family

Arriving at the airport

Preparing my equipment

The flight up

Diving

Cleaning up

The first, second, and last items don't deserve full steps in the process. They can be brief transitions. Preparing equipment seems reasonable as a main heading, but the dive seems the most important and ought to be divided into several stages itself: leaping, free falling, opening the chute, and landing. Organizing chronologically does not imply that you must give equal time to each element. Focus on the key moments and divide the steps accordingly. Slowing time down at a key moment can heighten the informative effect.

The Ontario government, for instance, published an effective brochure that describes an accident at 90 kph. It describes the *one second* after a car hits a solid object. In the first tenth of the second, the bumper and grille collapse. In the second tenth, the hood crumples and hits the windshield. The car frame stops, but the rest of the car still travels at the same speed. The driver braces his or her legs against the crash, and they snap at the knee. In the third tenth, the steering wheel shatters. In the fourth, the front half metre of the car collapses while the rest still moves at 50 kph. The driver is still travelling at 90. In the fifth tenth, the driver is impaled on the steering column, and blood fills his or her lungs. In the sixth tenth, the impact rips his or her feet out of tightly laced shoes, the brake pedal snaps off, and the driver's head strikes the windshield. In the seventh tenth of the second, hinges pop and seats break free, hitting the driver—who is now dead.

After deciding on your scratch outline, braintease again and add details and ideas to each heading. This is true for each of the outline patterns below.

■ *Practice 10-3:* Describe a process in slowed-down fashion, just like the one above. Try a kiss, falling down stairs, or your own topic.

2. The essentials: this approach informs a reader of *essential* characteristics of your topic. For example: "The essentials of a good photograph," "Problems children have when parents divorce," "What's really bad about television," or "What is unique about Leonard Cohen's poetry." Your scratch outline would consist of each of the key elements you explain.

For instance, for children involved in divorces, you might have:

Loss of a father/mother figure

Dealing with parental sorrow

Feelings of guilt about causing the divorce

Loss of home if property is sold and divided

New "uncle-daddies"/"aunt-mommies" in the home

Loss of friends if the family moves

Under each of these you can list the examples, facts, questions, or "bug" items from your brainteasers. If some items have little information, you might omit them. If one item seems to draw most of your attention, you might focus on it. For instance, one common thread in the above list is that of *loss*. You might decide at this point to focus on "The things children lose during a divorce."

■ *Practice 10-4:* Make a list of the essentials of a good relationship with a boss or the essentials of a good shopping mall.

Is There One "Right Pattern" for Your Essay?

The topic on good photographs or the one on divorce would also work as process essays describing the stages of taking a good photo or the stages children go through during a divorce. The organization of the paper changes, but it might be equally effective. On the other hand, the topic on television might not work so well as a process paper—unless you wanted to tell the story of one incident ("A couch potato's guide" or "Controlling your TV addiction"). The point here is to have *a plan* that does not mix approaches. Mixing might confuse a reader—and *you*.

3. The causes: organize your paper by informing the reader of the causes of a particular situation. Here are the same topics from a causal perspective:

What motivates (causes) a person to skydive?

What were the causes of the Conservative defeat and the Liberal victory in the election of 1993?

What causes TV addiction?

Why do children feel guilty during a divorce?

How are juvenile delinquents created?

List as many causes (reasons or motivations) as you can for the situation. Each may become an outline heading and eventually a paragraph in the paper.

■ *Practice 10-5:* Make a list of possible causes for one of the above topics.

4. The effects: instead of looking backward to the sources of the situation, look forward to its effects. Explaining our topics from this perspective, we have:

Long-term effects of skydiving on your body

How the Liberal majority, the Conservative defeat, and the rise of the Reform Party and the Bloc Québécois have changed Canadian politics

The psychological effects of too much TV

When children of divorced parents marry

The effects juvenile delinquents have on their peers

List as many consequences as possible. Then under each, list details from your brainteasers.

■ *Practice 10-6:* Create an effects approach for each of the following topics. Then list four or five possible effects one of them leads to.

Drunk driving

French immersion education

A change in your neighbourhood

Computer education

5. Comparison/contrast: let's try to organize our topics using this structure:

Skydiving is safer than hang gliding

The Reform Party and the Bloc Québécois: two visions of Canada

The CBC versus American television: which would you rather watch?

Is it worse for a parent to die or to divorce?

Teaching manners to kids in Canada and Japan

Juvenile delinquency today and in 1960

List your points of comparison/contrast as headings and support each point with details.

■ *Practice 10-7:* Develop a list of comparisons or contrasts for one of the topics above.

6. Classification: here are some of the topics structured by classification:

Three types of governments emerging from former Communist regimes in Eastern Europe

Four kinds of excuses to use on your professors

Five skydiving styles

Three common reactions for children of divorced parents

After deciding on your main points, fill in each category with details describing it. In your draft, each heading will become a paragraph.

■ *Practice 10-8:* Pick one of the following topics and try to see it in five of the six structures for thinking/organizing. Create a one-sentence statement for each.

Evolution (or any other scientific concept)

Romeo and Juliet (or any other literary work)

Schizophrenia (or any other psychological term)

■ *Practice 10-9:* Create a half-page brainteaser to explore the most promising of your five statements.

■ *Practice 10-10:* Find your own approach to the same topic—one that does *not* fit any of the six traditional patterns. Describe it in a few sentences.

Highlights of Chapter 10

1. In informative writing, adjust your approach according to your audience.
2. Pack in plenty of details with surprise value. Ask questions and use other brainteasers to stimulate ideas.

3. Narrow your topic to one you can handle in your allotted space. Avoid broad, introductory topics; pick ones with a sharp focus.

4. Consider several options when organizing an informative essay. Create your own pattern; describe the process; explain the essentials, the causes, or the effects; compare or contrast; or classify. All these patterns should suggest more ideas and details.

5. Don't mix organizational patterns in short essays.

Writing Suggestions and Class Discussions

1. List five topics on which you think you can write a non-researched, informative essay. Highlight the ones you think will offer the most surprise value for a general audience.

2. Write an "ask questions" brainteaser list (with answers) and one other brainteaser list for two of the best topics in 1.

3. Narrow the best topic further and write three scratch outlines (just main headings). Use three different organizational patterns.

4. Decide which of your three organizational plans conveys your message best and fill it in with details from your brainteaser lists.

5. Write the paper and revise it.

6. Suppose you are writing an informative letter about your first semester. How would your tone and information included differ depending on the following audiences?

   The college or university president

   Your boss (who reimburses your tuition)

   Your best friend (who is not going to school)

   Make a list of information for each letter.

7. Rewrite the following weak topics into sharper, more interesting ones still related to the originals; give two alternatives for each.

   How to bowl

   What is classical music?

   How to balance a chequebook

   Violence after a Stanley Cup game

   Smoking is bad for your health

8. Ask five tough questions about each of the following topics, questions that will lead to surprise-value information.

   Teenage marriages

   The future of gasoline consumption in Canada

   Community colleges versus universities

   Television satellite dishes

9. Write a process or how-to essay, packing as much information as you can into one or two pages. Concentrate on vivid details and smooth organization. Topics:

    How to drink with style

    How to meet men or women at school

    How to deal with a sexist (or racist) boss

    How to give an "A" oral report

    Open topic

10. Suppose you land the job you want. Write a letter to clients or employees explaining a process to them. Choose something you're learning in a course: "How to extract wisdom teeth," "How to help autistic children respond," or "How to conduct a marketing survey for our new product—the solar popcorn maker."

11. Class Exercise in Process Writing: Create a diagram or doodle with about the same complexity as this one:

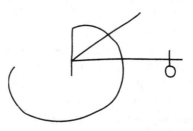

    Write a process description of it so someone else can draw it without seeing the doodle. Proportion is important, but actual size isn't. You will have 10 minutes. Members of the class will try to draw it only from the read-aloud instructions—no changes allowed from your written text.

12. Write an essentials essay on one of the following, packing as much information as possible into one or two pages.

    A good love letter

    A top action film

    The most common clichés of sitcoms

    The joys of being a mature student

    Open topic

13. Write a causes or effects essay on one of the following, packing in as much information as possible in one or two pages.

    Loss of wildlife habitat

Democratization of Russia

High salaries for athletes

A recent career change you made

Open topic

14. Write a one- or two-page informative essay comparing or contrasting two of your current textbooks. Evaluate them based on the standards established in this chapter for conveying information: adapting to audience, using surprise value, and covering readers' tough questions. Quote examples to support your views.

15. Write a classification essay on one of the following, packing as much information as possible in one or two pages.

Male attitudes toward women

Female attitudes toward men

Levels of racism in Canada

Open topic

16. Inform a person you're attracted to of your essential personality features. This should not be a sell, but an honest appraisal. A brainteaser list should give you at least three or four key aspects about yourself that a future spouse should be aware of. Pack in vivid, supporting detail.

17. Write an informative essay on the essentials of a career you're considering. Interview a person in the field, asking honest questions. Some all-purpose starter questions are:

What do you like best about your job?

What piece of advice would you give to someone wanting to enter this career?

What qualities are most important to be a successful...?

What are you most proud of in your career?

What part of your job would you gladly give to someone?

What most frustrates or disappoints you about it?

18. Create four scratch outlines for one of the following topics:

Pet cats

Indoor shopping malls

Credit cards

Aboriginal Canadians

19. Divide the class into six groups. Each should apply one of the six organizational patterns to the same topic. Each group should write a focus sentence, an outline, and some details for each heading.

20. Use the following checklist for peer evaluation of informative essays.

✔ **PEER-REVIEW CHECKLIST: INFORMATION**

Author: _____

The organizational pattern I used for this essay is (describe it if it's your own pattern):

I'd like help with this paper in this area:

Reviewer: _____

	STRONG	AVERAGE	WEAK
IDEAS: surprise value?			
DETAILS: vivid enough?			
enough detail?			
ORGANIZATION: easy to follow?			
TONE: unbiased, informative?			
AUDIENCE: style suits audience?			
RESEARCH: documentation okay?			

Do you agree with the author's assessment of the organizational pattern?

Explain where/how it might be strengthened.

Respond to the author's request for advice.

Evaluate the essay's surprise value. What was new? What wasn't?

What questions about the topic should the essay have answered?

What is the strongest part of the essay?

Give two additional suggestions for revision.
1.

2.

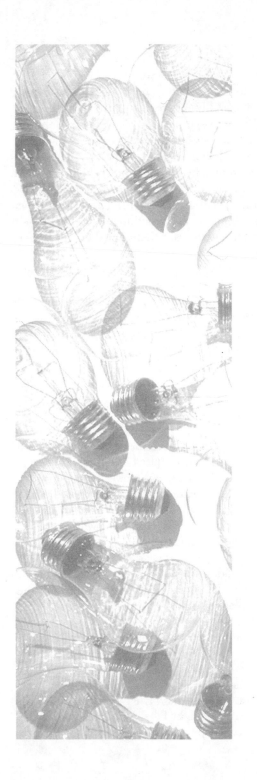

Chapter 11

Persuasive Writing:

Seeking Agreement from an Audience

To me, the most important thing in a piece of art is the thought. Technique is totally secondary.

Robert Bateman

*P*ersuasive writing has a bad reputation. At its worst, we picture a hoodlum twisting someone's arm to "persuade" him to tell where the diamonds are. We think of battleships floating and bombers flying just off the coast of a tiny country to "persuade" its government to change its policies. Automobile advertisements in magazines "persuade" men that owning a particular fast car will make them feel sophisticated, while another company's sexy convertible will make women feel daring and rebellious. How about empty political-campaign speeches or a father screaming at his late, tipsy teenager at 2 a.m.? Persuasion is commonly pictured as forcing, tricking, seducing, or lecturing people to buy or do something not really in their best interests. Too often these tactics work. But that's not the kind of persuasion we're interested in here.

Honest, ethical persuasion means bringing readers—through their own reason and emotions—to believe or act as the writer does. In this sense, readers willingly and *consciously* discover that it is in their best interests to agree. This type of persuasion, required of you in many assignments and in the majority of persuasive writing done in business, professional, and technical careers, is an *honest appeal to reason and feeling.*

AUDIENCE AND TONE

Advertising, political speeches, and barroom debates often imply the audience is so dumb or bullheaded that it must be pounded into submission. Reasonable persuasion assumes your audience is uncommitted (unless you know for *sure* you are dealing with supporters or those holding opposite views). It also assumes your audience is educated and will weigh the strength of your arguments reasonably. This audience will want facts and logic, will be critical of shortcomings in your position, and will not fall for the gimmicks of advertising.

This means that you, as a persuader, must achieve a good persuasive tone. You don't have to be sombre or dull; in fact, humour not only enlivens persuasion but also demonstrates that you are broad-minded. Overall, strive for perspective and common sense. Sentences such as "All people who support abortion are murderers!" and "Anti-abortionists want to enslave women!" share the same hysterical tone. Wild, undisciplined language usually results from wild, undisciplined thinking, and smart readers will be sceptical about such statements. Assume your readers are intelligent, present many facts and reasons for your position, and trust readers will see the logic. If you try to bully them into agreement by shouting, they won't be convinced—they'll only want to get away from you.

Before we can agree with an argument, we must trust the arguer. Is the persuader knowledgeable? Reasonable? Your credibility is damaged by using profanity or threats, by bullying or ranting, by twisting facts or calling rumours "facts," or by relying on slogans, clichés, stereotypes, or other oversimplifications. The writer who calmly *helps* a reader to sort through the complexities of a situation, who honestly *shares the difficulties* of right and wrong in the issue, and who *respects the truth* will open doors with a quiet knock. The persuader who approaches with a battering ram or who tries to sneak in a back window is the one against whom readers build barricades.

So before you begin trying to persuade readers, put yourself in an honest, helpful frame of mind; open yourself to alternate viewpoints in the early stages especially, so that the point you set out to prove is as reasonable and fair as it can be. Keep this statement in mind: "The aim of argument should not be victory but progress."

As long as you consider your audience's reactions, are willing to modify your ideas to strengthen them, and use many brainteasers to open the topic, you'll make honest progress. If you seek victory over a reader, ignore or hide facts that shake your plan, or lose control of your emotions, your case will start to crumble.

■ *Practice 11-1:* Recall two persuasive situations you've been in: one that led to hot tempers, one that led to "progress." Think about the attitudes of the people involved in each.

 ## PERSUASIVE TOPICS

When choosing a topic for persuasion, you have two choices: *to take a stand* on a controversial issue or *to make a proposal* to solve a problem. If you choose to take a stand, you'll have the advantage of some pre-existing arguments, but you'll need to find additional arguments and examples of your own. Freshness of idea will be difficult with some topics, such as pornography, nuclear power, and drug laws, because most supporting arguments on *both* sides are well known. If you make a proposal of your own—a new solution to a problem—you'll have to invent all your own arguments. But you'll have the advantage of freshness. Proposals sound more stimulating:

Students with "A" grades in courses will receive free tuition, while those with "D" or lower will pay double tuition.

No politician should serve more than one term in office.

Put a 25¢-per-litre tax on gasoline and use the receipts for solar research.

But proposals require more careful thinking: can you think of a serious objection to, as well as a positive benefit of, each of these proposals?

In career writing, of course, you'll be making proposals 98% of the time. Most employers pay people for new concepts and plans, not for rehashing old issues. Persuasion will be needed to convince your supervisor and colleagues; even more persuasion will be needed to sell clients, government agencies, customers, and other institutions. The higher you rise in your career, the more persuasive proposals you'll write; in fact, writing proposals for new ideas is one way to rise rapidly. How would your employer react to receiving proposals like the following from you under your own initiative?

1. We can draw more customers to the store by providing a shuttle bus service from three locations.

2. Bookkeeping at the company can be simplified if we adopt the following plan.

3. The summer recreation program can be improved if we stagger the children's nap times and alternate quiet tasks and outdoor activities.

■ *Practice 11-2:* Write a trial proposal for your employer, school, or family. List a few details of the plan.

 RAISING PROBLEMS

As in the examples above, your thesis should be stated in a single sentence, and in most persuasive writing, it appears at the end of the introductory paragraph. This is not an unalterable law, but it is a pattern that makes reading easier. It's a minimap for reader *and* writer. Short persuasive essays may defer the thesis until the conclusion, especially in cases when the writer finds both sides appealing. This approach is used less often simply because it's trickier to bring off successfully.

What does the rest of the introduction do? It makes the reader care about the problem. The introduction can also establish your reasonable tone. For example, one might start an essay on the topic "Grades and tuition" this way:

Teachers complain many students are unmotivated. Whether they graduate with an A or C average, they still get the same diploma at the end. Many graduates wonder if working hard for a high cumulative GPA is really worth the effort when they might end up getting a job based mostly on their personality. Many students just slide through with little effort, while the taxpayers foot much of the bill. Perhaps we can motivate students with something closer to home: cash.

At this point, the writer has established a problem, has considered it from several angles (teachers, graduation requirements, several types of students, and taxpayers), and has probably prompted the reader to say something like this: "Yes, motivation is poor; what should be done about this?" In other words, by showing the problem, by showing how extensive it is, the writer has made the reader hungry for an answer. Then the thesis is presented as the last sentence of the paragraph, followed by the essay in support of it.

A proposal for the shuttle bus might begin this way:

> A customer who wants our product circles the store three times. Our tiny parking lot is full; street parking is full. Will that customer ever return? Unlikely. No one in the area will sell us space for parking, the city has refused to run a bus route nearby, and we have already made our employees park six blocks away. If we can shuttle them, why not our customers?

One way of starting to think about persuasive writing tasks is to raise all the problems you can about a topic—perhaps by writing a brainteaser bug list. Much of this list may turn up in your introduction.

■ *Practice 11-3:* Take an issue you find important and write three or four sentences explaining why it's a tough problem. Be fair to all sides. Then, if you think there's a way to solve this problem, write a trial thesis sentence.

 ## SUPPORTING EVIDENCE

A reasonable person expects reasonable evidence before believing something. In the previous examples, you'd want to be convinced that cash motivation would work for grades: that it would be fair, that the economics of the plan would fly, and that it would be good for students and teachers. Can you imagine three or four questions you'd want answered before investing in shuttle buses if you were the store's manager? *Always anticipate your audience's barriers to belief.*

When you are trying to argue persuasively, you should pack in as much supporting evidence as possible. Think of yourself as a lawyer convincing a jury. There are three types of evidence:

Facts

Appeals to values

Logic

These are new brainteasers for persuasive writing. Make a list of all the relevant facts you know (or need to know so you can research them later), all the appeals to values you can use, and all the logical arguments you can employ.

FACTS

Statistics are one type of fact you can use to support a thesis. A proverb says, "There are two kinds of lies: regular lies and statistics." It means that statistics can be twisted to bolster weak arguments. Maeir's law even says, "If the facts do not conform to the theory, they must be disposed of." Disreputable advertisers or politicians may hold this attitude, but in honest, ethical persuasion, you must be especially careful to handle statistics fairly and accurately. If you say, for instance, "In a recent study, 94% of the people surveyed believed the ban on television advertising for cigarettes is unfair," our reaction to this statistic changes if we learn the survey was conducted by a tobacco company in the town where its factory is located. An ethical arguer must reveal such information or not use the statistic.

The source of your fact strengthens or weakens its impact. Generally, your facts will be more credible if they come from *recent* research conducted by an *expert* and published in a *reputable* journal or book. Material from the *National Enquirer,* facts assembled by astrologers, and work done 30 years ago in fast-changing fields such as psychology or physics are generally not considered reliable.

Another problem with statistics is making the reader *see* them clearly. Today we are bombarded with numbers: millions of dollars, thousands of highway deaths, hundreds of recalled products. Despite our modern sophistication, big numbers seem unreal to most of us, and the writer must help us to *see* in a concrete way what they mean.

Below are three facts. Which is the most visual?

1. Nearly 200 million tonnes of dirt and rocks were dug out to create the Panama Canal.
2. A typical hurricane releases 50 times the energy of the first atomic bomb.
3. The Canadian side of Niagara Falls is 54 metres high, 675 metres wide, and has a flow of 155 million litres per minute.

The second example is the easiest to visualize because we can imagine 50 atomic bombs (even if we cannot fully comprehend the impact); it's more difficult to visualize almost 200 million tonnes of dirt and rocks and 155 million litres of water per minute.

■ *Practice 11-4:* Take a minute to visualize in words those other two facts for a reader.

Which of the following facts about Toronto's CN Tower is the most impressive? Why? Visualize each.

It is the world's tallest free-standing structure.

It is 553 metres high.

Its glassed-in elevator rises 342 metres to the world's highest revolving restaurant.

Plan on doing occasional research for persuasive writing. The facts I've just given took me five minutes to locate in *The Canadian Encyclopedia.* Statistics give authority to your persuasive voice.

Some statistics can come from your own observations. In a letter to the vice-president for Facilities Management at a large university, a student proposed that the parking facilities be expanded. At one point, to produce her own statistics suggesting faculty-student parking spaces were not fairly distributed, she made a trip around the campus counting spaces:

> It may also be possible to turn parts of faculty lots into student parking, since faculty lots are seldom full. There are 18,000 students currently enrolled and 4,000 faculty members. Half of the 10,000 commuter students and, I estimate, one quarter of the 2,000 who live close to the campus drive to class. There are eight student lots on the North Campus, three of which hold approximately 300 cars, five of which hold 200 cars, for a total of 1,900 spaces. Yet there are five faculty lots with a total of 1,000 spaces. On the South Campus, there are four student and two faculty lots, each accommodating 200 cars. I calculate the ratio of faculty to parking spaces is three to one and of students to student parking spaces is eight to one. After viewing the parking lots throughout the semester, I believe you can afford to transfer at least several hundred spaces to students.
>
> —Tina C. Maenza

There's a second kind of fact, one handy for all of us: *examples.* Use examples from (1) what you've seen; (2) what your friends and family have seen; (3) historical or current events; and (4) hypothetical cases.

If you're writing about the law that forbids those under a certain age to drink alcohol, for instance, you probably know a dozen cases that could support either side— from firsthand experience, from what others have told you, and from the news. Everyone can dig up a couple of examples of drunken teenagers causing fatal accidents (or of drunken middle-aged people killing sober teenagers), of teenagers bribing an adult to buy illegal liquor, or of responsible teenagers arranging for a designated driver who will not touch alcohol during the evening.

Historical and news stories carry more weight with a reader—he or she can think, "Oh yes, I remember that." They are verifiable. *Personal examples* may make the reader wonder if you've coloured the facts; however, your own examples give you the chance to write vividly. You can describe the accident scene, quote dialogue from the party, build narrative conflict, and write with a freshness you can't with historical cases—and you should. *Examples you heard from your friends* are less satisfactory because, as lawyers say, they are "hearsay" testimony. They are one step further removed from the reader and hence less reliable. We all know truth has a way of getting watered down (or spiced up!) as it gets passed along.

Hypothetical examples are necessary to fill in gaps when facts are not available or to project future events. Hypothetical examples are simply made-up cases of events *likely to happen.* In the abortion debate, for instance, several hypothetical cases are usually raised: "Suppose a woman gets pregnant through rape" or "Suppose a pregnant woman discovers the fetus is badly deformed." Both scenarios are likely to happen sometime in our society. We might be able to track down facts about actual cases, but if we can't, a hypothetical example can appeal to the reader's common sense. The reader will test *your* common sense in explaining the hypothetical case. You would be on shaky ground in portraying a woman who became pregnant through rape as a person who should forget how she became pregnant, look forward to the experience of childbirth the way an intentionally pregnant woman would, and within months develop normal maternal tenderness. There are noble women who can do this—but they are rare.

Facts and examples are important support for most arguments; pack plenty into your essay, and use them fairly and vividly. Rely most on first-hand experience and reliable sources; secondhand and hypothetical examples should be used as last resorts.

APPEALS TO THE READER'S VALUES

People are persuaded not only by facts but also by realizing that your proposal supports *values they believe in.* Facts without a context of values seem meaningless much of the time. Take, for example, statistics about the James Bay hydro-electric project in northern Quebec, taken from *The Canadian Encyclopedia* (1103–04):

> The $15 billion project entailed massive diversions of water.... A tiered spillway, three times the height of Niagara Falls, has been blasted from the bedrock, and La Grande-2, which was completed in 1982 and has the world's largest underground powerhouse, generated 5,328 MW of electric power.... Five reservoirs...total 11,900 square kilometres—half the size of Lake Ontario—and eight dams and 198 dikes...have been built.

These impressive statistics indicate the size and generating capacity of this monumental project. But what they don't tell you is that huge areas of wilderness were flooded, forests were burned, the Eastmain River lost most of its flow, and the entire population of one village had to be moved. The James Bay project also forced the Quebec government to negotiate with the Cree Indians, who settled their land claims for $225 million. And the controversies continue, for the next phase of the project has already begun. Thus, the significance of statistics is altered when we change the context and begin to look at some of the issues that accompany the "plain" facts.

Some values that writers consider in persuasive writing are *economics, fairness, health, safety, love, environmental impact, freedom,* and *beauty.* Would *you,* for instance, bulldoze a beautiful neighbourhood park for an industrial plant if it meant secure jobs for your family? Would most people? Germany, where most wilderness has been devastated, values nature preserves more than Brazil does; Brazil is burning down its vast tropical rainforest for industry in the hope of improving its people's standard of living—what it sees as a higher value. One of the more interesting aspects of persuasive writing is dealing with the changing, conflicting values of people and groups.

■ *Practice 11-5:* Make a list of *your* most important eight to ten values, trying to include several not already listed here. Star the two or three you think are the most important.

In practical terms, the persuasive writer might start thinking about defending a proposal by going down a checklist of values, asking if each can suggest new arguments to support the proposal. It's another brainteaser. Suppose you're proposing that the government legalize marijuana. Following are some values to question. The list is written so you can use it as a brainteaser for many topics.

1. What economic benefits will my position have? For whom? How great will they be?
2. Will it increase people's security or satisfy their basic needs?
3. Is it fair to all parties involved? Think through—one at a time—how various other people might see it.
4. Will it enhance or limit anyone's freedom?
5. How will my plan affect families?
6. Will it appeal to the reader's concern for beauty?
7. Will it affect the environment?
8. Will it build self-esteem or status for anyone? Whom? Why?
9. How might this proposal help people to actualize their potential?
10. List other values of importance to you. How can you appeal to them in your proposal?

■ *Practice 11-6:* Go through this list to see what support it triggers for your proposal to legalize marijuana. Some questions will lead nowhere; just move on. Try the same list (and perhaps your own list of values) with the following proposals, looking for support.

1. The United Nations ought to be given command of a permanent, powerful military force.

2. Evolution ought to be the only theory of origin taught in public schools.

3. Churches should pay property taxes.

LOGIC

Logic alone rarely persuades people, but it draws together facts and appeals to values. In its simplest form, logic takes one fact (the minor premise) and one value (the major premise) and shows that if both are true, then a reasonable conclusion drawn from them must also be true.

Let's take an example. Suppose I want to persuade people abortion is morally wrong and ought to be illegal. To do this, I present a value—killing a human being is generally held to be morally wrong and is illegal. Then I present a fact—a fetus is a human being. If these two are true, then the conclusion is inevitable: killing a fetus is wrong and should be illegal. Someone who disagrees with me, however, might argue that one or both of these premises are *not* true. With the abortion issue, people usually question whether a fetus is really a human being. Do you see how the logic of my claim disintegrates if that "fact" is proved false? The opposition might also question my other premise by pointing out that killing humans *is* morally or legally acceptable in a number of circumstances. Can you name some?

Logic, then, is rarely perfect. One or both of the premises can be questioned. And there are about a dozen common flaws writers fall into when using logic. We call these flaws "logical fallacies" because they make any argument that uses them invalid. "Invalid" doesn't mean an argument is false, only that we don't *have* to believe it based on what the writer has presented. It means a tight connection between the evidence and the thesis has not been made. They are forms of dishonest persuasion. Following are some of the more common logical fallacies.

1. Endorsement
Wayne Gretzky likes a certain video camera. The commercial claims you'll like it too. Joe Carter drinks milk. Are you persuaded to buy it? Obviously, we suspect that the recommendations are strongly influenced by what these athletes are paid to make them. But endorsement's fallacy isn't really in lying but in logic. There is no necessary connection between the tastes of one person and another. Had a nutritionist recommended milk for its health benefits, we might have a stronger case. An athlete endorsing a video camera is far less effective than an athlete (hockey player or figure skater)

endorsing skates. In such cases, there should also be an explanation of *why* the product is good and the viewpoint correct. This applies to "experts" you may quote in your papers as well. It's not enough to say that it's true because some famous person believed it. For the reader's understanding, you also need to explain how the theory works or what the facts are.

2. Hasty Generalization

"I hate Professor Smith. My friends in the class hate him. Therefore, Professor Smith must be an unpopular teacher." Sorry. You need more evidence. Several students from a class of 25 are too few to support such a claim. Perhaps your group is on Professor Smith's bad side because of poor performance or attitude.

A hasty generalization means you base a conclusion or claim on too few examples or on oversimplified evidence. You can overcome this problem in your essays by deluging your reader with cases and examples. If you're worried you have so many facts or so much evidence that you may be boring a reader, list the "excess" in a note at the end of the paper!

3. Bandwagon

This fallacy is similar to the endorsement, except that instead of picking a prominent person who supports your claim, you say your position must be right because many people support it. There's a quick cure for this fallacy: just remind yourself how many millions of people thought Hitler and Mussolini were saviours. What makes an argument right is that it *is right*, not that millions of people *believe* it's right. Your job is to show how it's right, not how it's popular.

4. Tradition

"It's always been done this way" or "My parents taught me to believe…." This fallacy is a cop-out from thinking. You're hiding behind someone else's thinking when you must take the reader through the arguments themselves. There's a quick reminder you can use if you're tempted to rely on this fallacy: suppose the first human beings one million years ago had latched onto this principle? "We've always eaten our meat raw and slept in trees. No fire, no caves!"

Traditional beliefs prevent people from rushing to each wild, untested idea that floats along, but the fact that a belief was once valid does not mean it still is. Tradition fights most good ideas as well as bad ones.

5. Dicto simpliciter ("Unqualified generalization")

In our enthusiasm for a claim, we sometimes exaggerate: "Television game shows are the worst thing for our children's minds today." Really? Worse than pornography? Worse than fighting parents? Worse than abusive teachers? Such a statement shows the person has simply not thought *through* the idea. *Qualifying the statement makes it more acceptable.* "Television game shows are bad for children's minds." It is no longer at the head of a list of *everything* bad. You could also say, "*Some* TV game shows *may* harm a child's mind as badly as pornography." The reader cannot toss this statement away at first reading—she must first see how you support such a view. Avoid using words such as "all," "always," "never," "nobody," or "everyone." Use considered words or phrases such as "most people," "usually," or "under normal circumstances."

6. Post hoc ergo propter hoc ("After this, therefore because of this")

You commit this fallacy if you claim one thing caused another to happen when the only tangible relationship between the two is that one preceded the other. You may be able to prove the one did indeed cause the other, but a simple time relationship alone does not. "My parents got divorced after I was born. Therefore, I broke up their marriage." Or, "Every time I get a day off, it rains." Or, "The family has deteriorated in the last 20 years—since feminism became strong. That proves how harmful feminism has been." None of these holds water as a complete argument. In the first case, you'd need to prove that your parents' marriage was solid before you came along and that you were the key cause of their arguments. In the second, you'd have to establish that meteorological powers infuse your body on a day off. With the antifeminist statement, think of all the competing explanations for why the family has deteriorated: the decline in church-going; the increases in violence, sexual activity outside marriage, drug use, and materialism; the decay of public morals; and the rise of a highly mobile society. All three cases need to show a *connection* between cause and effect.

7. Ad misericordium ("From misery")

This means pleading a cause based on your feelings (usually misery) rather than on its merits. "You've got to give me a C in this course or I won't graduate"; "You can't withdraw me for absences; I'll lose my funding." Sorry. The grade in a course says you have performed at a certain level, and your misery at not doing well should not persuade a professor your merit is greater than it is. Your funding is given assuming you'll attend class; you earn it by attending and performing at an acceptable level. "A promotion will make me so happy!" By itself, not good enough. Did you earn a promotion? Do you show potential?

8. Ad hominem ("Against the man")

Instead of attacking a position, value, or fact to advance your case, you attack the person who made the proposal. "Don't support a proposal to bring a blue-box recycling program to our community because the alderman who suggested it has just been embroiled in a scandal involving his secretary." The merits of the proposal have nothing to do with his moral lapse. The proposal and its sponsor are separate issues, and the plan should be discussed on its own merits. How about the following cases; are they *ad hominem* or valid criticisms?

We shouldn't have elected Chretien because we've had too many prime ministers from Quebec.

We shouldn't do business with the Captain Computer Company; its head salesman smokes pot.

■ *Practice 11-7:* Think of two arguments—political, parental, peer, or commercial—that infuriate you. Now, using the eight fallacies as a guide, expose the logical flaws in these arguments.

 ## STRUCTURING THE PERSUASIVE ESSAY

If you have the time and creativity to invent your own persuasive structure, do it. But for over 2,000 years, from Roman orators to contemporary editorialists, one model structure has worked over and over again. It helps you not only to organize your ideas but also to generate new ideas, and it makes sure you cover key aspects of any persuasive presentation. The four-part structure is: *introduction, main supporting ideas, refutation,* and *conclusion.*

The introduction should begin by intriguing the reader with a concrete problem that is difficult to solve, and it should end with your solution to this problem, your thesis. You establish a reasonable, knowledgeable tone here by showing the reader your familiarity with several issues involved. The introduction should also outline in detail what you are proposing. *Explain* how your plan will work, define key terms, who will do what, how it will be funded, what the timetable or stages are. Before you defend it, show the reader exactly what you propose. A complex plan may require several paragraphs of explanation. Don't skimp here!

The body of evidence should be arranged tightly, one paragraph or two perhaps for each main supporting idea. The paragraphs should be filled out with examples, facts, appeals to value, and logical statements that support the idea. In papers of three to five typed pages, you should have room to develop three or four supporting ideas. In papers of one or two pages, two ideas may be all you can present in depth.

To outline, list the main arguments and fill in support from brainteasers under each. Try several scratch outlines until your headings are crisp and distinct. Roman orators believed support should start and end strongly, with weaker arguments embedded in the middle. Their rule of thumb: the second strongest argument comes first, the strongest comes last, and the others come in the middle. If you have a flimsy argument, put it in your wastebasket.

The refutation comes next in the paper. After raising your main supporting ideas, take time to consider one major objection someone might have against your views or proposal. Some writers may say, "Why should I attack my own case?" Why indeed? Well, in a written persuasive paper (as contrasted with a debate), you have total control over the presentation of ideas; there is no one else who can raise questions about your ideas—*except the reader!* Hiding weaknesses in your position won't work with a good reader. So be honest. Also, if you don't consider objections, chances are pretty good you'll get carried away and end up with something superficial or full of holes. By considering objections, you can modify and improve your ideas, making them more convincing. It's in your best interest as an arguer to do so. As John Locke once observed, "To judge other men's notions before we have looked into them is not to show their darkness, but to put out our own eyes."

In the refutation, one strategy is to present an objection to your idea, then to show how the objection is flawed. You must state oppositional ideas with full honesty to satisfy the opposition. Present them as valid questions that need answers, never as pesty troublemakers. Then pinpoint *fallacies* in the objection, correct ideas presented as *"facts,"* or question *values* implicit in it. In other words, the brainteasers used to create support can also be used to create refutations to an objection.

Suppose you've written an essay defending television, saying that it contributes much to Canadian culture and is a great educational tool. In your refutation, you must consider objections people might have to your view. One objection would be that watching television has caused a decline in children's ability to read. It contradicts your claim of television's educational value. To be an honest arguer, you might point out that children do seem to watch television more than they read books; perhaps you might acknowledge that reading scores on standard tests have declined steadily in the past 15 years. How do you refute this objection now? Begin by testing if it falls into a logical fallacy. The *post hoc ergo propter hoc* fallacy, for instance, seems to apply. Just because a decline in reading scores followed an increase in television watching does not prove one caused the other. In refuting, you should also suggest possible causes of the decline other than television. Perhaps schools aren't teaching reading in the best way; perhaps problems of discipline disrupt the teaching of reading; perhaps a lack of family togetherness (reading aloud after supper, discussing the newspaper) has contributed to the problem. Perhaps today society as a whole values reading less.

You might question not just the logic but also the facts. Perhaps the reading tests are outdated. Do the lowest test scorers watch the most television? Do the best readers also watch television? You can get examples from your classmates or perhaps do some quick research. You can also *question the values* behind the objection. You might argue it's too easy to blame a machine for our problems as a society when we ought to blame ourselves for not working hard enough to learn, support, and teach reading.

A second way of handling the refutation is to *concede* some truth to the objection. "Television has probably contributed somewhat to a decline in reading ability. However," you would then usually say, "despite this drawback, there are too many good reasons to let it stand in the way." This is often the only solution in moral issues when no compromise is possible. If you're in favour of allowing abortions, for instance, you might concede that aborting a fetus really is the taking of a human or potentially human life. You might even acknowledge that this would be wrong in a perfect world, but that the misery an unwanted or deformed child endures is worse yet.

Another type of concession offers a compromise. People who are against abortions, for instance, might reluctantly agree that a woman in danger of dying in childbirth should be granted an abortion. But they would probably add that the principle of the sanctity of human life is still not compromised—that the taking of a life is to save a life.

The refutation element of a persuasive essay is perhaps the most important; it establishes your integrity as a writer, forces you to consider your thesis more deeply, and gives you the chance to make your argument even stronger. You may place refutation in a separate section of the essay or handle it as objections might be raised against your supporting points.

■ *Practice 11-8:* Raise two objections to one of the following proposals and then see if you can refute the objections by checking for logical fallacies, incorrect facts, or questionable values.

1. The United Nations ought to have a permanent, powerful military force.

2. Evolution ought to be the only theory of origin taught in public school.

3. Churches should pay property taxes.

The conclusion in persuasive writing can be a simple reaffirmation of your thesis, but it's usually better to look forward. You might paint a picture of the world in which your plan is enacted or of how less effective plans than yours would affect people's lives. Or you might end with a dramatic statistic or an example.

Highlights of Chapter 11

1. To find a persuasive topic, use the brainteasers for bug lists, fantasy, or questions. To develop and support your argument, use the special brainteasers for value lists, persuasion, and fact lists (include all the statistics and real or hypothetical examples you can think of, as well as relevant research you do). To develop the refutation, you need to see from alternate viewpoints and then check for logical fallacies, incorrect facts, and questionable values to break down the objections.

2. The traditional order for persuasive writing is introduction, support, refutation, and conclusion.

3. While drafting your persuasive paper, write a concrete, problem-solving introduction, adopt a reasonable, honest tone (be a host, not a preacher), speak to your audience, and visualize statistics and examples.

4. In revising your persuasive paper, ask if the thesis is clear, if there is sufficient support for it, if you fall into any logical fallacies, if your audience would object to anything, and if you are fair and reasonable. Test your word use to qualify generalizations and eliminate extreme language.

Writing Suggestions and Class Discussions

1. a. Make a list of five topics you could develop into persuasive essays. Try for a mix of personal, career, and social issues. Choose topics that matter to you.

   b. Develop one of these topics into a proposal, explaining your plan.

   c. Use several brainteaser lists to develop supporting ideas and details. Begin developing a refutation.

   d. Order the essay in a scratch outline.

   e. Draft and revise the essay.

2. Read the letters-to-the-editor sections of several newspapers and pick out an example of a letter whose tone appealed to you and one whose tone put you off. Explain why one works and the other doesn't. Bring the letters to class.

3. Write an introductory paragraph for a paper on teenage sex. Your job is to show the reader how difficult the problem is to solve yet how important it is to solve it. At the end of the paragraph, establish a tentative thesis that could lead to a paper.

4. List a page of statistics, examples, and hypothetical examples that could be used to support one of these theses:

   a. Canadian football is much more exciting than the American game.

   b. Most white people have little idea what subtle discrimination most visible minorities suffer in an average day.

   c. The rules of normal life are suspended once you enlist in the armed forces.

   d. Raising a child isn't as sweet as many people believe.

   e. High school is a time of continual humiliation for many students.

   f. Old age can be the best time of a person's life.

5. a. Make a list of the 10 values you hold highest. This will be a brainteaser resource for persuasive papers.

   b. Use this list to support or refute the following proposals:

   The Canadian government should allow more refugees to immigrate to Canada from places such as Haiti and Rwanda.

Gay or lesbian teachers should not be hired in elementary schools.

The CBC ought to be supported by a special tax of $50 on all television sets sold.

6. What values would you use to support the following two statements?

    "I am a citizen of the world."—Socrates, Greek philosopher

    "I have no responsibility to save the world."—Richard Feynman, Nobel Prize winner in physics

7. Write examples to illustrate five fallacies. They can be real or made up. Label each example with the fallacy it demonstrates.

8. Pick out a magazine or newspaper advertisement; write a paragraph explaining a fallacy in logic in the ad.

9. Write a response to an essay you've read recently. Respectfully disagree with the author. In your introductory paragraph, accurately and fairly present the author's views, then work on refuting logic, facts, and/or values.

10. Write a one-paragraph letter to persuade your mother you really are working hard at school. Help her to visualize the amount of work you're doing by making the statistics (number of pages read, papers done, hours studying, and so on) more visual.

11. Write a one-page letter to yourself, persuading yourself to reform some habit you know is wrong. Be sure to consider a refutation.

12. Write a one-page persuasive essay on some aspect of school policy. You'll be expected to send a copy to the student newspaper.

13. Write a letter persuading a company to change its television advertisement, which you find offensive. Address it to the Public Relations Department and provide a stamped envelope so your professor can mail it.

14. Write a letter to the proper city official, persuading him or her to change some policy or activity you don't like.

15. Write a proposal to your employer to solve a company problem. After revising it, send it to your supervisor.

16. Write a job-application letter to yourself. Apply for a job you want now or one you'll want after graduation. Honestly sell yourself by referring to your main accomplishments, skills, experience, and personal qualities. If there is an obvious refutation (your lack of experience, for instance), answer it.

17. Group Activity: Open Hearing. The class will be divided into four groups. Each will develop a proposal to solve a local or school problem, doing research and brainteasing for supporting facts, values, and logical arguments. Each group will present its plan to the rest of the class in

an open hearing for feedback: refutations, suggestions for additional research, new ideas. Then each student will write a persuasive paper on the topic. Use the following checklist to review the proposal (or any persuasive essay you are asked to comment on).

✔ **PEER-REVIEW CHECKLIST: PERSUASION**

Author: _____

(Underline your proposal.)
My intended audience is (explain background if necessary):

One concern or problem I have with the paper is:

Reviewer: _____

	STRONG	AVERAGE	WEAK
INTRODUCTION: attention grabbing?			
proposal clear?			
plan detailed?			
TONE: respectful, open minded?			
IDEAS: proposal fresh?			
target audience?			
number/power of arguments?			
DETAILS: enough supporting facts?			
facts visual enough?			
appeal to values?			
logic maintained?			
REFUTATION: objection raised and answered?			
DOCUMENTATION: sources credited?			

Respond to the author's concern or problem.

What is the strongest part of the paper?

Suggest two things the author might work on in revision.
1.

2.

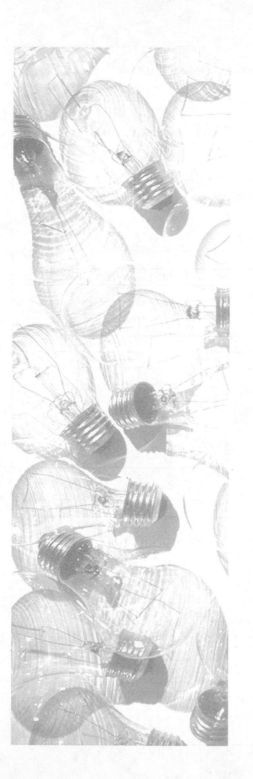

Chapter 12

The Literary
Essay and Review

Men take possession of
art as a means of
covering their nakedness
a little.

Pablo Picasso

*S*ometime during your postsecondary studies, you'll probably be asked to write papers about literature—poems, plays, fiction, or essays. Why? Partly to practise critical thinking and writing. But also because literature often fully expresses our unborn or rejected ideas. Writing about literature not only teaches us how the best writers write but also helps us to develop thoughts we have not been able to ripen alone. Literature's compact intensity often reveals patterns, emotions, and ideas more clearly than does real life—which is watered down with trivia.

Exactly what is a literary essay? What does it do? First, it's *persuasive*, for it tries to convince a reader with evidence that your analysis is valid. It's *informative* as well, because it usually strives for an objective tone and reveals something about the work, not just your feelings. It may require *research*. At heart, the literary essay *explains* or *analyses* a literary work. It is *not a summary*. Analysis seeks the *why* under the surface of a literary work. It discovers not-so-obvious organization, style, or ideas. And it creates a *thesis* to be proved about the work. Examples:

> *Moby Dick* is a book about hunting the God who runs this world, not about hunting whales.

> In Margaret Atwood's collection of poetry *The Journals of Susanna Moodie*, the landscape is more internal than external—it explores the dark places within us.

> In Shakespeare's last play, *The Tempest*, the playwright uses the character of Prospero to comment on his craft.

Notice that each thesis requires supporting evidence from the literary work and that each says something *about* the work that its author does not state; it does not simply retell the story. Here are the same three theses stated as vague summaries—theses that will lead you to "D" papers or worse:

> *Moby Dick* is about a man obsessed with killing a white whale.

> *The Journals of Susanna Moodie* is about a woman's experience in rural Ontario in the nineteenth century.

> *The Tempest*'s main character is a magician who finds revenge by torturing those who set him adrift in a boat.

Each of the previous theses focuses on one work, but analysis may also compare or classify several works. Examples:

> Modern detective stories still use Poe's tricks.

> Marlowe's Dr. Faustus and Goethe's Faust portray two very different men who sell their souls to the devil.

> We can see Irving Layton's changing sense of the role of the poet when we compare one early and one late poem.

■ *Practice 12-1:* Explain what a writer would have to do to prove each of the six theses above.

THINKING ABOUT LITERARY ESSAYS

Read the literary work *slowly* (fast reading is for newspapers). Allow the story or poem to lead you into its world. Suspend judgment at first. Say to yourself, "Maybe what's going on here is..." rather than committing yourself to one idea. Read it again, marking passages that strike you as important or meaningful. They may not always be easy to understand; in fact, sections that seem irrelevant or puzzling may be the most fruitful if you hope to explain the not-so-obvious.

At this point, an *idea* for a thesis may occur to you. The marked passages will be handy *details* for evidence. But if no thesis pops up automatically, common ways of thinking about literature can be applied as brainteasers. Following are four major approaches to getting ideas about literature.

USE YOUR GUT REACTIONS

Reading is a *collaboration* between writer and reader. Writers are helpless without readers' imaginations. They rely on readers to catch suggestions, to feel sad or afraid. Your response is part of the literature.

Start by listing your thoughts on a literary work. Simply freewrite your impressions and observations. Reread significant passages to restart the flow when you stall. If an idea sizzles, continue in paragraph form until the spell cools; then search for new ideas.

There is a drawback to using this approach. If you enjoyed pet garter snakes as a child, for instance, you may allow this personal experience to colour your reading of a poem such as Emily Dickinson's "A Narrow Fellow in the Grass." Her comment that snakes make her feel "zero at the bone" does not allow a cuddly interpretation. *You* may write such a poem, but Dickinson didn't. Remember, you must be able to *support* your gut reactions with evidence from the work.

EXPLORE THE AUTHOR'S INTENTIONS

This approach involves researching what authors have said about their work or biographical events that relate to their work. Poet T.S. Eliot attached more than 50 notes to "The Wasteland"—most readers need these comments and explanations to understand the poem. Another example is poet and novelist Thomas Hardy, who often wrote about chance and fate. Two biographical incidents may explain why. Doctors pronounced Hardy stillborn, but he was revived by a sceptical nurse. Weeks later, he was found with a poisonous snake sleeping beside him. These stories, vividly told to a young Hardy, may have influenced the accidents and twists of fate that afflict his characters.

There are dangers in biographical analysis. A book doesn't necessarily reflect an author's life. Writers often disguise their personal lives, create purely from fantasy, or build mythical public images of themselves. Novelist Frederick Philip Grove wrote an autobiography in which he said that he was the son of a Swedish nobleman who'd lost all his money, forcing Grove to emigrate to Canada. People interpreted his work in the light of this "fact." Later it was discovered that he'd made the whole thing up— that he was, in fact, the son of a middle-class German worker and had spent time in jail for fraud. Robert Browning raised another problem. He was asked late in life to interpret one of his first poems, "Sordello," because no one had ever understood it. Browning stared. "When I wrote 'Sordello,'" he said, "only God and I knew what it meant. Now only God knows." He could no longer explain his own poem! The point is that authors aren't omniscient about their writing. Their intentions—if we can really discover them—may strike us quite differently. It's perfectly reasonable to disagree with an author's interpretation of his or her work—*if* you can prove the work supports your view. Thus, while an author's life or philosophy may be relevant to the work, you must show evidence from the work itself. Most professors will be uneasy with a totally biographical interpretation of a literary work, but some connections may help you to develop your ideas.

USE CRITICAL PERSPECTIVES ON LITERATURE

Like biographical interpretations, these ways of thinking step outside the strict boundaries of the text. Following are some common critical perspectives.

1. Political Perspective

You can interpret literary works as expressions of common social problems. Hugh MacLennan's novel *Two Solitudes*, for example, explores tensions between French- and English-Canadian cultures between the First and Second World Wars. It considers, among many issues, the conscription debate of 1917, during which many French Canadians refused to fight because they felt no loyalty to Britain. Margaret Atwood's *The Handmaid's Tale* shows the dangers of religious fundamentalism and what happens when an apathetic public allows its freedom to be taken away. A paper on MacLennan's book from this perspective could discuss the relationship between current debates about the future of Quebec in Confederation and his depiction of the clash between the "two solitudes." A paper on Atwood's book might explore the Canadian notion of the necessary split between church and state.

2. Feminist Perspective

You can evaluate the portrayal of women in literary works. Shakespeare is often credited with creating smart, witty, independent, strong women (Portia in *The Merchant of Venice*); just as often, however, he is criticized for creating paper dolls who fall apart (Ophelia in *Hamlet*) or shrews who are "tamed" into meek obedience by loud-mouthed and oafish husbands (Kate in *The Taming of the Shrew*). Or, as some critics wonder, has Kate learned to play along with male egos in public so she can be free in private? Your paper can evaluate or define how women and gender roles are handled in the work.

3. Ethnic Perspective

John Richardson's *Wacousta*, one of the first Canadian novels, deals with the siege of Fort Detroit (then part of British North America) in 1763. Although Richardson expresses respect for the Indian leader, Pontiac, his depiction of Aboriginal people is often degrading and ethnocentric. He talks about "the lurking band in the forest," associating the Natives with darkness, savagery, and cunning. He does allow Pontiac to describe the wrongs dealt to the Indians by the British, but Pontiac's complaints are overshadowed by Richardson's depiction of the Indians' massacre of whites. An essay from this perspective could explore Richardson's nineteenth-century blindness to the rights of Aboriginal people or his characterization of them as "other" in a white culture for a white audience.

Shakespeare's portrayal of the Jew Shylock in *The Merchant of Venice* has been considered anti-Semitic. Your paper could gather references in the play, research the way Jews were seen and treated in Shakespeare's day, and draw comparisons to current literature.

Critical perspectives give you new ways to think about a literary work. You can analyse it from a Christian, Jewish, Hindu, or Moslem perspective. Or from a psychological or sociological perspective. All are brainteasers that open up ideas and angles to write from.

The danger in using critical perspectives is that you may distort the literary work to make it fit your idea. Freud's oedipal theory (a son's latent sexual attraction toward his mother) applied to Hamlet can be taken to extremes. As with biographical interpretations, you must return to the text for supporting evidence.

EXPLAIN THE WORDS

Most twentieth-century literary critics have stressed the work itself—the words and form (they are sometimes called "formalists"). They say an author's atheism or comments made to friends and the work's connection to politics are secondary; because words create meaning, the analysis should focus on them. This school has convinced most other critics that *any* analysis should include some *explication of the text*. This means a close reading of the text. Your paper may be a line-by-line interpretation of a poem or a selection from a short story or, more often, an explication of several short sections to show how the literary work supports your thesis.

At the brainteaser stage, work through key passages, explaining lines and tying ideas together. Here's an example from the first paragraph of Sinclair Ross's short story "The Lamp at Noon":

> A little before noon she lit the lamp. Demented wind fled keening past the house: a wail through the eaves that died every minute or two. Three days now without respite it had held. The dust was thickening to an impenetrable fog.

Brainteaser:

The oddity of the opening line and the central symbol of the story established early: the lamp at noon. Who is "she," and why is she lighting this lamp? Noon is the brightest time of day. Why light the lamp? Images of darkness and light. Are they symbolic? "Keening" is a wailing lamentation for the dead. This word combined with the other "wail" and the reference to the wind dying foreshadows the death at the end, but the entire story is a sustained wail of pain—both the man and woman are dead inside. The wind is also "demented," indicating a kind of insane personification, as if the characters will be manipulated by an unreasonable force. Contrast the simplicity of monosyllables—"Three days now...it had held"—with the complexity of the previous sentence. We are disoriented: where are we, and why is the dust so thick and getting worse? Nothing is seen clearly here: both characters are lost, and there is no light.

A few observations on this process. First, the rough brainteaser opens up potential ideas, but must be focused when you develop a trial thesis. Second, notice how long the explication is compared to the original. That's normal—works of literature often compress much into a small space. Third, a rough explication moves backward and outward for connections; you can't simply plod through line by line. Tie ideas together.

 # FIVE BRAINTEASERS FOR EXPLICATION

1. THEME

Don't settle for the first idea you see. Make a list of possible themes. Few literary works have one underlined purpose. And the first ideas that occur to you, as with any brainteaser list, will often be superficial. Also, don't think of theme as the ultimate point of a literary work. Literature is not a sermon in rhyme or dialogue but an experience of life. There's more to it than a moral. In its proper form, a theme must be (1) a complete statement, not just a word, and (2) stated in terms outside the literary work—in universal terms.

Weak: The theme of *Romeo and Juliet* is love. (What *about* love?)

Weak: The theme is that Romeo loves Juliet so much while their families are fighting. (This is not universal.)

Better: The theme of *Romeo and Juliet* is that romantic love cannot exist in this corrupt world.

2. CONFLICT

List the forces in tension in the work. In the quote from Ross, "human life versus the natural world" is the most obvious, but you could also list "vision versus blindness." In a short story or play, conflict occurs between characters, in a character's mind, or between a character and society or nature. List all the conflicts and fill them out with examples or evidence. Then draw a conclusion about the conflict and you have your thesis. Examples:

In *Fifth Business*, Robertson Davies shows the conflict between materialism and spiritual values through the character Boy Staunton.

In *The Stone Angel*, Margaret Laurence details how Hagar Shipley is torn between her desire for propriety and social status and her desire to "rejoice."

Your paper must then illustrate and prove its thesis with detailed evidence.

3. CHARACTER

Drama, fiction, and some essays and poems can be approached by thinking about character. Start with gut reactions, but also apply these questions:

What *consistent* qualities does a character have?

What *motivates* the character?

What *complexities* does the character show?

Does the character *change*? If so, how?

To discover ideas, comment on each question and note details from the work for support. In *The Great Gatsby*, for example, Jay Gatsby is *consistently* polite, gentle, a big spender, mysterious, and somehow detached from real life. He's *motivated* most obviously by his desires for wealth and Daisy, the rich girl he loved, but who married someone else. Underneath, there's also his motive of wanting to live in the past. He's *complex* because he has contradictions and inner conflicts: he has gangster pals and a pover-ty-stricken past, yet he can be naïve and gallant and really doesn't care about money except to attract Daisy. Does he *change*? Scholars have debat-ed this point since the book was published. This brainteaser can supply ideas and details for any paper on fiction or drama.

4. IMAGERY

Most literature can be analysed through its images and symbols—pictures and other sensory details. Scan the work, listing images, searching for pat-terns and repetitions. In *Romeo and Juliet,* for instance, Shakespeare uses religious images (saints, prayer books, a shrine) to refer to Juliet to suggest both love's holiness and Romeo's melodramatic excess in act 1. In *The Great Gatsby,* Fitzgerald repeatedly mentions the green light on Daisy's dock across the bay. Perhaps Gatsby wants a "go" from Daisy to pursue his romance, but this hazy, uncertain light may represent Daisy, who likes the youth and fun Gatsby brings to her settled life, but who is too selfish to risk herself. Like the light, she's a tease. There's usually something significant behind a repeated image. Write down locations and your first interpretations.

5. FORM/STYLE

Each genre or type of literature has its own principles of style and form. *Poetry* can be analysed by looking at rhyme, rhythm, sound devices, figures of speech, and format (sonnet, ballad, and so on). But you can't just *describe* sound patterns; show how they relate to the overall meaning of the poem by having a *thesis* about them. Example:

> In John Donne's "Holy Sonnet 14" ("Batter my heart, three-personed God"), strongly stressed syllables, alliteration, and hard consonants combine to create the impression of violence throughout the poem.

Fiction can be analysed by discussing narrative point of view (who the speaker is and how much he or she knows of characters' thoughts) or by explaining how the time sequence is constructed. As with poetry, show how the form or style contributes to the story's overall effect. Example:

> The narrator in Margaret Atwood's *Surfacing* at first appears believable, but we later discover she has been lying about her past.

Drama's unique element is staging—the props, actors' gestures, lighting, set, and visual effects. Show how staging contributes to the themes or con-flicts. Example:

> The main sets in *Romeo and Juliet*—the street, bedroom, and tomb—set up the three main conflicts in the play.

All literature can be analysed for word choice and "tone" or "mood"—what we might call the writer's *attitude* toward the subject. Example:

Poet bpNichol uses puns and plays with language in his *Martyrology* to show the slipperiness of meaning and the pleasure of words, sounds, and associations.

■ *Practice 12-2:* Read the following poem by Robert Browning.

Meeting at Night

The grey sea and the long black land;
And the yellow half-moon large and low;
And the startled little waves that leap
In fiery ringlets from their sleep,
As I gain the cove with pushing prow,
And quench its speed i' the slushy sand.

Then a mile of warm sea-scented beach;
Three fields to cross till a farm appears;
A tap at the pane, the quick sharp scratch
And blue spurt of a lighted match,
And a voice less loud, through its joys and fears,
Than the two hearts beating each to each!

First reading: What's going on? Is a character or the poet telling the poem? Any vocabulary you need to look up? First reactions?

Brainteasers: List the conflicts. Who is meeting, and why is it so secret? List the images—what pattern emerges? Is there meaning in it? Regarding form, how do the two stanzas mirror each other? Listen to the sounds by reading the poem aloud, especially the end of the first stanza and the middle of the second. Does this poem have a theme?

After answering some of these questions, formulate a thesis you can defend with evidence from the poem.

 # ORGANIZING LITERARY ESSAYS

Many approaches can lead to a paper, but you must focus on an *aspect* of the work; only short poems or very brief stories can be adequately analysed as a whole in a short paper. In developing a thesis, examine your notes for an idea *worth* proving—one with some complexity. In literature, this often means recognizing *multiple truths*. Good versus evil rarely occurs cleanly in life or good literature. More often we face a choice between two partial goods or two partial evils. The most memorable characters interest us because good and evil mix in them. An honest thesis embraces ambiguity. A categorical thesis suggests that either the work or the interpretation is superficial.

Weak: Ophelia goes mad because her father dies and Hamlet rejects her.

Better: Ophelia's madness is a symptom of her complete lack of power as a woman in a man's world, where father, brother, and lover have all abandoned her.

Weak: Ahab in *Moby Dick* is a lunatic, pure and simple.

Better: Ahab may be crazy, but it's a magnificent, sane madness.

After focusing your thesis, assemble evidence from the literary work—quotes, incidents, details of character—and from whatever interesting, relevant bits you've combed from other reading, brainteasers, or research. Place like material together in piles or use the number system (see chapter 4) until you have solid outline headings.

 ## THE DRAFT

A good way to start a literary essay is to explain why your thesis is important or puzzling. Doing so should lead to your support. While drafting, constantly clarify and support your ideas with quotes from the literature. Explicate to *show* how it supports your thesis. Don't fall into summary, and don't plod through your outline. Strive to see more deeply into each quotation used.

Below is a fine example of a student's assembling evidence to build a point. Sinclair Ross's "The Lamp at Noon," referred to in an earlier example, takes place in the 1930s on a farm destroyed by drought. The main characters, Ellen and Paul, are in conflict over whether to stay on the farm. While Paul is attached to the land and refuses to give up his dream of making a success of the farm, Ellen sees that it is a lost cause. The five-year-long drought has destroyed any chance of success, and she longs to return to the town life she is used to. The story takes place during a particularly severe dust storm. Left to herself and her anguish, Ellen wanders into the storm, taking her baby with her. The story ends when Paul finds his wife and son; his wife has gone mad, and the baby is dead, smothered by either the dust or the protecting arms of his mother. The following brief essay examines the symbolism inherent in the story's title.

Sinclair Ross's story "The Lamp at Noon" begins with the sentence "A little before noon she lit the lamp," introducing a symbol that highlights two main themes. First, the lamp represents the harshness of the prairie landscape, a world in which the lamp must be lit at noon; second, it represents the hopes of the main characters.

As the story opens, we learn that a storm has been raging for three days, creating a dust so thick that Ellen, the wife, must light the lamp at noon in order to see. Ross stresses that "The dust was thickening to an impenetrable fog," a fog that stands in for the confusion of both Ellen and her husband, Paul. This couple, after all, is at cross purposes. Ellen longs to leave the farm, for she considers it to be a trap. As she says to her husband, "We aren't living here—not really living." Paul, on the other hand, feels challenged by the harsh conditions under which he lives. He believes that some time in the future all his hard work will pay off, that he will earn enough to give his wife a comfortable life and his son an education.

While Ellen sees the lamp lit at noon as a sign of hopelessness, Paul is blinded by his own desires. Angry at his wife's version of the truth, he retreats to his stable, where he tends to the animals with a care and compassion he does not show his wife. For him, dealing with the storm is "easier with the lantern lit and his hands occupied." Here the lantern represents his hopes, the light that he believes the future will bring. While Ellen concentrates on the darkness of the storm, Paul thinks about its end and the light that will follow it.

In the end, however, he wakes up to the desolation around him. Looking out on the land after the storm ends, he sees "the utter waste confronting him." Ross writes:

> Suddenly like the fields he was naked. Everything that had sheathed him a little from the realities of existence: vision and purpose, faith in the land, in the future, in himself—it was all rent now, stripped away. "Desert," he heard her voice begin to sob. "Desert, you fool—the lamp at noon!"

As Paul begins to see the futility of his struggle, he also begins to see the symbolic truth of the lamp lit at noon. His new way of looking at the potential for light is affirmed when he returns to the house to talk to Ellen, only to find her and their child absent and "the lamp blown out." The lamp, Ellen's only protection against the darkness of the dust storm, is now out, a fitting symbol that she has finally succumbed to her despair and to the madness that the "demented wind" has fostered in her. Her final words indicate her madness and confirm the symbolism of light, which runs through the tale. As Paul holds their dead child in his arms, she turns to her husband and says, "You were right Paul.... You said tonight we'd see the storm go down. So still now, and a red sky—it means tomorrow will be fine." Her embracing of his futile hopes is the final irony. For both Paul and Ellen, the lamp really has "blown out."

Accurately copy quotations. If three lines or fewer, incorporate them into your paragraphs. Should you quote poetry in this way, you must use a slash to indicate the line ending, as in this example from Marvell's "To His Coy Mistress": "Had we but world enough, and time, / This coyness, lady, were no crime." If a quote is more than three lines, set it off, as in this selection from Tennyson's "Ulysses":

> The lights begin to twinkle from the rocks;
> The long day wanes; the slow moon climbs; the deep
> Moans round with many voices. Come my friends,
> 'Tis not too late to seek a newer world.

The lines are *indented* 10 spaces for both poetry and prose, and *no quotation marks* are used. Some people double space all indented quotes, while others stick to the older practice of single spacing. (See chapter 14 for the punctuation of taglines for quotations.) Try not to pour on quotation after quotation. Quote the best, paraphrase the rest. (For the documentation of quotations, see chapter 13.)

 ## REVISING LITERARY ESSAYS

Revise ideas first. Does your thesis still fit what you wrote? Some parts may have to go, or your thesis may need to be rewritten. Have you wrenched the literary work's main idea out of context to make your point? Make sure you introduce quotations so your reader knows who is speaking and why. Cut where you dwell on the obvious. Beef up interesting ideas treated too briefly.

Revise details next. Too little support? Too many quotes? Are your explanations sharp and vivid?

Then revise mechanics and style. Literary essays use the present tense to describe a work, so you would say, for instance, "Sinclair Ross says..." even though he "said" it years ago.

 ## THE REVIEW

Related to the literary essay is the review—of books, restaurants, plays, concerts, art shows, speeches, films, or any other event or work that can be judged by *standards of performance*. Like literary essays, reviews persuade readers through supporting details. If it was a bad dinner followed by a worse speech, describe the limp green beans and mushy potatoes as well as the speaker's bad jokes. Like a literary essay, a review can interpret the purpose or theme of its subject.

Reviews differ from literary essays, however, in several regards. First, descriptive *summary* is expected. Up to half of a review may inform readers accurately about the topic. You should assume that readers of literary essays are familiar with the work being discussed, but a review must help readers to sample the unknown. Second, a review emphasizes *evaluation*. Your purpose is to make a judgment of value and then support it with evidence. As with any persuasion, make your standards of judgment clear. Specify what you mean by "good service" at a restaurant. Some people like a waiter to check on their needs every few minutes; others consider that pesky. In an art review, does "old-fashioned" art mean the red-barn school of painting or anything that does not use lasers or computers?

Chances are good you'll write reviews in your career and in school. In your career, you may be asked to review a new product your boss is considering buying or another employee's job performance. You'll need to set up standards of performance and interpret how well they have been reached, and you'll need specific, descriptive details to support your point. For a product, some standards might be:

Efficiency

Ease of use

Price

Necessity

Safety

Can you add others? Under safety, for instance, you might point out that the new computer tends to give some employees a tan after a week's use. For a job evaluation, common standards of performance are:

Amount of work done

Quality of work done

Reliability

Ability to work with others

Initiative

What else would you add? You might outline your review with these headings, then comment on each with details.

You'll likely review books or theories for courses. Your psychology professor may ask you to contrast how behaviourist and humanist psychologists would deal with a teenage alcoholic and to evaluate which approach will succeed best. What should be the standards of success?

While people don't usually write reviews of dates or parenting styles, in your private life you can use the techniques of a review to help you decide what car to buy or which university to attend. Prioritizing standards and developing a sharp eye for supporting detail will help you to evaluate with more depth and clarity.

■ *Practice 12-3:* Make a list of *your* top five standards of performance for one of the following: artworks, restaurants, movies, books, films, or theatrical events. Now apply these standards to a specific example in your category.

Highlights of Chapter 12

1. A literary essay explains or analyses a literary work. It is not a summary. You aren't ready to begin until you have a thesis to prove about the literary work.

2. These four brainteasers can help you to reach a thesis:

   a. Freewrite or list your gut reactions, but later be sure you really are writing about the work's ideas and not about your own creative fantasy.

   b. Discover the author's intention through biographical research. Doing so may open up new ideas on the work—if it supports what you think the author intended.

   c. Use a common perspective. Each of the following is a separate brainteaser, somewhat like an alternate viewpoint: politics, history, feminism, ethnicity, religion, psychology, and myth. As in a. and b., make sure the work itself can support the ideas these perspectives inspire.

   d. Explicate the text itself. Most literary analysis today explains the work by examining passages in detail. You might limit yourself to one of these aspects: theme, conflict, character, imagery, or form.

3. In a literary essay, you must continually prove your thesis with evidence, so before you begin organizing and drafting, assemble a list of quotations and significant incidents from the work that support your idea. As you draft, explain these passages in detail.

4. The review, like the literary essay, supports a judgment about someone else's work with evidence, but its scope includes performance. In addition to analysing the work, it summarizes and evaluates.

Writing Suggestions and Class Discussions

1. Write a review of a restaurant, film, art show, or other subject using standards of performance. Make your standards clear and support your opinion with specific details.

2. Write a review of your essays written so far for this course. Establish standards of performance and evaluate your work, quoting from the papers to support your points.

3. Write a job evaluation of someone who works with you. Fairly and specifically evaluate his or her work, with supporting details. Conclude with a recommendation.

4. A peer group will research and analyse a literary work. One person each will (a) research the author's life and connect it to the work; (b) apply a critical perspective to the work, doing necessary research; (c) explicate theme; (d) explicate conflict or character; (e) explicate images and symbols; and (f) explicate style or form. The group will discuss and combine ideas and then report to the class.

5. Choose a literary work. Do preliminary brainteasers and turn in three thesis statements you might defend. After reviewing them with a peer group or your professor, organize, draft, and revise the paper.

6. Compare and contrast works by two authors on the same topic.

7. Study how one poet or fiction writer deals with a narrow topic (Yeats on escape, Lawrence on love, Hopkins on nature). Support your thesis with the explication of several works and with any other relevant evidence you can find.

8. Four poems follow this section. Although from different ages and using different forms, all deal with the idea of time. Below are several ways you can use these poems to improve your ability to analyse literature.

   a. Pick one poem and come to class with ideas about it to discuss. Formulate a tentative thesis.

   b. Look for similarities and differences among the poems. Consider theme, imagery, and form. Have specific evidence from each poem to support your ideas.

   c. Research the life of one of the poets and see if you can draw some connections to the poem. Does the poem support your biographical interpretation?

   d. Read the student essay on Atwood's poem and answer the questions following it.

 # POEMS FOR EXPLICATION AND DISCUSSION

Sonnet 73

That time of year thou mayst in me behold
When yellow leaves, or none, or few, do hang
Upon those boughs which shake against the cold,
Bare ruined choirs, where late the sweet birds sang.
In me thou see'st the twilight of such day
As after sunset fadeth in the west;
Which by and by black night doth take away,
Death's second self, that seals up all in rest.
In me thou see'st the glowing of such fire,
That on the ashes of his youth doth lie,
As on the death-bed whereon it must expire,
Consumed with that which it was nourished by.
This thou perceiv'st, which makes thy love more strong,
To love that well which thou must leave ere long.

—*William Shakespeare*

Vocabulary: *thou*: you; *mayst*: may; *boughs*: branches; *fadeth*: fades; *doth*: does; *perceiv'st*: understand; *ere*: before.

To the Virgins, to Make Much of Time

Gather ye rosebuds while ye may,
Old time is still a-flying;
And this same flower that smiles today
Tomorrow will be dying.

The glorious lamp of heaven, the sun,
The higher he's a-getting
The sooner will his race be won,
And nearer he's to setting.

That age is best which is the first,
When youth and blood are warmer;
But being spent, the worse, and worst
Times still succeed the former.

Then be not coy, but use your time,
And, while ye may, go marry;
For, having once but lost your prime,
You may forever tarry.

—*Robert Herrick*

Vocabulary: *ye*: your; *succeed*: follow; *coy*: shy or flirtatious; *tarry*: linger behind.

For Francoise Adnet

It is that time of day, time
To chop the beans, to peel
Potatoes for the evening meal.

The fullness of time
Grows, at this hour,
Like the shadows on the crockery.

Mademoiselle's mauve gloves,
Alone, tell of the afternoon, the dried
Flowers, the delicate hands among the stalks.

For once things are what they are,
Until my little girl
Comes in from outdoors, the melting snow

Cool in her nostrils,
Sky, blue without clouds,
Behind her eyes.

But even these dissolve.
Fingering an orange
She lets her bare legs dangle.

Time is space, it glows
Like the white tablecloth,
The breadboard where I slice the onions.

The kitchen floats in my tears—
And the sun
In its brazier of urban trees.

—D.G. Jones

(From A *Throw of Particles,* © 1983 by D.G. Jones. Used by permission of
Stoddart Publishing Ltd., Toronto.)

A Night in the Royal Ontario Museum

Who locked me

into this crazed man-made
stone brain
where the weathered
totempole jabs a blunt
finger at the byzantine
mosaic dome

Under that ornate
golden cranium I wander
among fragments of gods, tarnished
coins, embalmed gestures
chronologically arranged,
looking for the EXIT sign

but in spite of the diagrams
at every corner, labelled
in red: YOU ARE HERE
the labyrinth holds me,

turning me around
the cafeteria, the washrooms,
a spiral through marble
Greece and Rome, the bronze
horses of China

then past the carved masks, wood and fur
to where 5 plaster Indians
in a glass case
squat near a dusty fire

and further, confronting me
with a skeleton child, preserved
in the desert air, curled
beside a clay pot and a few beads.

I say I am far
enough, stop here please
no more

but the perverse museum, corridor
by corridor, an idiot
voice jogged by a pushed
button, repeats its memories

and I am dragged to the mind's
deadend, the roar of the bone-
yard, I am lost
among the mastodons
and beyond: a fossil
shell, then

samples of rocks
and minerals, even the thundering
tusks dwindling to pin-
points in the stellar
fluorescent-lighted
wastes of geology

—*Margaret Atwood*

(From *The Animals in That Country,* © 1968 by Margaret Atwood. Used by permission of Oxford University Press, Toronto.)

THE NOTION OF TIME IN MARGARET ATWOOD'S "A NIGHT IN THE ROYAL ONTARIO MUSEUM"

Margaret Atwood's "A Night in the Royal Ontario Museum" describes a nightmarish journey back through time and history. In the poem, a nameless speaker wanders through the labyrinth of corridors and exhibits, lost in the symbols and artifacts of civilization. We do not know how the speaker found her way into the museum or why she is compelled to remain there; all we know is that she is an unwilling participant who is forced to confront the preserved pieces of history.

The poem begins with a question: "who locked me / into this crazed man-made / stone brain" (1–3). The comparison of the museum to a "brain" makes sense: it is a repository of the creations of the human mind—the dead objects of vanished cultures.

And the speaker, like all human beings, finds herself born into a culture at a particular time and in a particular space. We make our way, observing the signs and symbols of the past and trying to make sense of the present by understanding history. The wandering speaker is disoriented by the strange jumble of objects that she is forced to observe—the concentrated power of these objects creates a "crazed" cultural overload that she cannot absorb:

> Under that ornate
> golden cranium I wander
> among fragments of gods, tarnished
> coins, embalmed gestures
> chronologically arranged,
> looking for the EXIT sign (8–13)

She is only able to observe pieces of this puzzle, small "fragments" and preserved "gestures." Ironically, gestures, animated movements of the body used to express ideas and emotions, are here frozen, "embalmed" and represented through the fragments of time in the glass cases.

The speaker is lost in this world; she cannot find her position in space or understand her relationship to the objects that she is observing:

> but in spite of the diagrams
> at every corner, labelled
> in red: YOU ARE HERE
> the labyrinth holds me (14–17)

Like all human beings, she is locked into her own time and cannot find a way out. Atwood uses the metaphor of the museum to comment on our compulsion to view the past and try to understand what it means. We have all seen the diagrams of large museums and the little red dots that tell us where we are. Atwood uses this common experience to show the confusion of the speaker who, almost against her will, is propelled by the museum through the "labyrinth" of history.

In the middle of the poem, the speaker, emotionally overwhelmed, can no longer endure this rush of historical data: "I say I am far / enough, stop here please / no more" (31–33). She has gone "far / enough," confronted too many lost cultures, whose traces are contained in the glass cases and displays. We are never told overtly why she is crying out, why she cannot take it anymore. We must assume that the experience has traumatized her because there is no life in the museum: just room after room of artificial displays and preserved remains.

Despite her plea, "the perverse museum" (34) has a mind of its own. The wandering observer is "dragged" (38) deeper into time, and she is finally forced to confront her primitive beginnings: "I am lost / among the mastodons / and beyond" (40–42). She completely loses her bearings as she is "dragged to the mind's / deadend" (38–39). The crazed museum and the disintegration of her sanity come together as she experiences something even more primitive than "mastodons": "the stellar / fluorescent-lighted / wastes of geology" (47–49)—the ancient origin of the planet, preserved under the fluorescent lights of the modern world.

Atwood's poem is a study in contrasts: the living and the dead, the present and the past. She uses the metaphor of the museum to comment on our curious relationship to time and our tendency to place whole cultures "under glass." We attempt to control the past by packaging it; we try to make sense of the chaos of history by preserving it in forms that we can understand. Atwood does not give us an answer. Her speaker is not soothed by the museum's control of history, but is lost in the labyrinth of time, unable to get her bearings, know where she is, or even find her way out.

Works Cited

Atwood, Margaret. "A Night in the Royal Ontario Museum." The Animals in That Country. Toronto: Oxford UP, 1968. 20–21.

Discussion

1. What is the thesis of this paper? Do you agree with this interpretation of the poem? Support your view.

2. Consider how the author uses quotations to support the main points. Why these quotations and not others? Do you think the author has chosen the best examples?

3. Notice that the writer makes a distinction between the poem's nameless speaker and Atwood, the poet. Why is it useful to separate the two?

4. What aspects of the poem does this paper not discuss?

5. Do you agree with the author that the central theme of the poem has to do with our relationship to the past? Have you ever had this kind of experience at a museum—a sense of being overwhelmed by history?

6. Find a quote that the author explicates thoroughly and another that you feel needs more explanation.

✔ **PEER-REVIEW CHECKLIST: LITERARY ESSAY**

Author: _____

I would especially like the reviewer to comment on:

Reviewer: _____

State the author's thesis as you see it (you and the author should discuss the accuracy of this statement).

	STRONG	AVERAGE	WEAK
IDEA: insight into literary work?			
sticks to thesis?			
DETAILS: supporting evidence?			
interpretation of quotes?			
ORGANIZATION: smooth and logical?			
FORMAT: documentation of quotations?			
punctuation of quotations?			

What was the strongest section of the paper?

Respond to the author's request.

Use three or four adjectives to describe this essay.

What else about the literary work ought the writer to cover to prove the thesis or dig out its complexity? What questions do you have after reading the paper?

✔ **PEER-REVIEW CHECKLIST: REVIEW**

Author: _____

A question or problem I have for the reviewer is:

Reviewer: _____

	STRONG	AVERAGE	WEAK
IDEAS: depth/creativity of analysis?			
clear standards of performance?			
DETAILS: support for evaluation?			
vivid description?			
ORGANIZATION: clear and logical?			
TONE: reasonable?			

Respond to the author's question or concern.

What is the best part of the review?

Is there anything the author ought to cut or cover in more depth? Why?

Offer a possible refutation to the author's evaluation (hint: see the evaluation from the viewpoint of the person being evaluated).

Offer two other suggestions for the review.
1.

2.

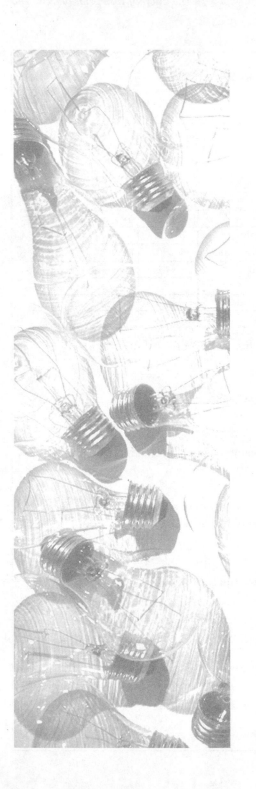

Chapter 13

Research

*An investigator should
have a robust faith—and
yet not believe.*

Claude Bernard

*I*t's 2 a.m. Books are piled on the desk and floor. A thousand scraps of paper snow you in. Blank, fanned-out note cards await entries. You've been waiting for someone to return the most important book you need to the library. Earlier tonight, the microfilm reading machine snapped your spool. You've quoted so much that your paper will be one long footnote. You forgot to copy the publication dates and publishers for three sources; now you pray to the god of libraries that they'll still be there tomorrow so you can get the information. In 12 hours, your finished copy is due.

OR

It's 2 a.m. Five weeks ago, the day your research paper was assigned, you typed a schedule:

WEEK ONE:	Do general reading (reference section)
	Narrow topic
WEEK TWO:	Assemble bibliography
	Get books (request interlibrary loans)
	Get magazines
WEEK THREE:	Read sources and take notes on cards (carefully note bibliographic info)
WEEK FOUR:	Weigh all evidence
	Decide on thesis
	Make outline
	Do rough draft
WEEK FIVE:	Revise paper
	Type bibliography
	Make final copy (extra copy for security)

Beside each item, as relentless as marching soldiers, checks appeared as the weeks passed. *You* took the books first, your interlibrary loan book arrived last week, and there was time to repair a broken microfilm. Note cards stacked aside, you're about to proofread the paper. The only thing wrong, really, just nagging the back of your mind, is that the paper turned out kind of flat. It seems too tame, bland.

The first example describes the research chaos many people suffer; the second outlines an idealized process, but also what may happen to those who follow it mechanically. Both, of course, are exaggerated. And excess—whether of organization or of disorganization—has given research writing a bad reputation. Some people view research as dry, mechanical drudgery; others build it up as the "ultimate creativity" done in rapture by inspired geniuses touching the secrets of creation. In fact, it contains the same opportunities for both drudgery and creativity as other writing, and it demands the same skills. Most undergraduate research assignments aim to prepare you for more extensive research later—in graduate school or in your career. They make you prove you can learn a subject alone and accurately analyse or evaluate it. Your job, as with all other writing, is to explore an idea deeply and honestly and bring it to life with specific details.

RESEARCH REPORTS AND ESSAYS

A *research report* summarizes what others have said on the topic, setting your opinions and experiences aside. However, it's not enough simply to glue together a pile of quotes; you must highlight key ideas and give vivid details to show you know the subject thoroughly. In college and university, research reports include article or book summaries or analyses of factual topics: "How have immigration policies changed in Canada over the last 20 years?" "Write a brief biography of scholar Northrop Frye." "Describe two small-business accounting systems." In a career, your boss might ask you to research the costs of starting a company recycling program or the services competing companies offer customers. A research report gathers the most accurate, detailed information available.

In a *research essay,* you must *interpret* the research as well as report it. You wouldn't, for instance, simply write Northrop Frye's biography; perhaps you'd relate his life story to his ideas about literature. For the accounting topic, you might be asked to advise a certain business to adopt one system. This type of research combines informative and persuasive writing; you draw conclusions, evaluate or apply the facts you've dug up.

You may use research for personal as well as academic and career reasons. For example, you might want to do research about a company you have a job interview with. It would certainly be to your advantage to know the latest information about the company's products and performance.

A research paper follows the same writing process as any other writing: *thinking, organizing, writing, revising.* But instead of relying entirely on yourself for details and ideas, you also use other sources during the thinking stage. These sources become your brainteasers. But it's still *your* paper, and your voice should control it. A reader wants to hear the writer's voice speaking, not a robotic databank quoting long passages from experts. Your challenge in honest research writing is to avoid the temptation to pile up quotes. Sources should support *your* idea.

Research writing counts in academic, career, and personal life. The academic term paper helps students to explore course ideas on their own. In organizing and presenting material, you learn far better than you do through exams or quizzes. You won't be writing papers per se in most jobs, but you'll probably have to do research. You may research the cost of recycling cardboard packaging for the furniture store where you work, assemble facts and quotes from others to respond to a weak job-performance evaluation from your supervisor, or gather information on new insurance procedures to make a seminar presentation.

This chapter will introduce basic research methods and give you enough information to write short research papers.

THINKING ABOUT RESEARCH PAPERS

Choose a topic you care about. If the paper becomes an exercise done just to get a grade, *you've* missed an opportunity. As always, narrow the topic. If your topic for a history course is World War I and you're interested in cars and engines, research transportation technology during this era. If you love sports, study new sports emerging from World War I or games soldiers played during it. If your boyfriend is in the armed forces, you might research how the wives and girlfriends of soldiers handle loneliness or grief. Or you might research the way women were treated during World War II, both within the military and as wives of soldiers. *All* topics hold thousands of possible topics inside them—some will excite you; some will put you to sleep. And remember this: in most cases, your reader cares half as much about the topic as you do. So how much enthusiasm you can evoke in a reader depends largely on how much *you* have. Pick a topic you really care about. If you fear you're narrowing the topic beyond the professor's limitations, simply ask.

You already know that narrowing the topic and creating a thesis are not as simple as the outline at the beginning of this chapter suggests. Thinking is messy and redundant. Before, during, and after your research, you must refine and rewrite your topic and thesis.

■ *Practice 13-1:* Find one or two research angles that interest you in three of these topics:

Child psychology

Astronomy

Western Canadian writers

Marketing

Before you begin your research, consider not only your interest in the topic but also *how* to research it. One modified brainteaser to use is *a list of key questions you want answered.* Finding the answers will be your research. For instance, suppose you decide to research the Internet computer network. The following preliminary questions might occur to you.

What is the Internet—how can we define its features?

Who invented it, and what was the original intention?

What services are available, and what kind of information can be found?

How many people are using it today—and for what reasons?

How do they access the Internet?

Can anyone use it?

Who pays for the Internet?

Asking key questions keeps you focused on the important issues as you dive into research. But be alive to new questions, and scratch ones that grow stale or seem obvious.

Also do some brainteasers to draw out what you already know. On the Internet topic, an examples brainteaser could record your current knowledge of computer-network applications. Find someone who is on the Internet or has an electronic mail (e-mail) account and experience cyberspace for yourself. Doing your own brainteasers and experiencing your topic directly help to ensure that *you* will be in the paper. Brainteasers for breaking stereotypes, listing examples, or finding analogies will keep the research from smothering you. *Plan ahead,* and *be an active thinker.* Figure out what's important. Most of the time, research doesn't discover unexpected answers; it verifies or denies hypotheses and questions the researcher has in mind from the start.

■ *Practice 13-2:* For one of the topics in the previous practice, create a list of four key research questions, and do a half-page brainteaser to see what you already know.

 # SOURCES

Let's start our discussion on sources with learning how to find facts or opinions. Then we'll look at how to take notes that *help* you to write the draft.

LIBRARY RESOURCES

The library contains four main sources of information. The most important is the *librarians.* They can guide you through confusing pamphlet files and computerized databases. A librarian can send you to the correct book in the reference section and save you time in the process. Ask for help with periodical indexes or microfilms too. But a word of caution: to keep this primary resource on your side, come prepared with specific questions, not just a general topic such as "war" or "music." The more specific you are, the more specific information you'll get. Do the obvious work *before* asking for help—check out basic references, on-line catalogues, and periodical indexes.

The Reference Section

The reference section includes dictionaries, encyclopedias, almanacs, and other books that summarize large bodies of information. This section of the library is best for providing raw facts and statistics you can interpret. If you want comparative statistics about global economics or other world facts, *The Information Please Almanac* is a good place to start. For research on any topic, you might go to an encyclopedia for a quick overview before writing your list of key research questions. However, don't rely on encyclopedias as main reference sources—they're too superficial for most research essays. Following are some recommended reference books.

General background:

> *Encyclopaedia Britannica*
>
> *Encyclopedia Americana*
>
> *Van Nostrand's Scientific Encyclopedia*
>
> *The Canadian Encyclopedia*
>
> *Occupational Outlook Handbook* (for careers)

Facts and statistics (updated yearly):

> *The Information Please Almanac* (American and world facts)
>
> *The Canadian Global Almanac*
>
> *Canadian Almanac and Directory*

Find a reference book's call number in the on-line or microfiche catalogue and then locate the book in the reference section.

A few minutes of browsing in almanacs can yield some interesting statistics that can often lead to good ideas for topics. On random pages of *The Canadian Global Almanac*, for example, you can find such facts as the largest profits and losses of Canadian companies; the changes in the price of gasoline, heating oil, natural gas, and electricity over a 20-year period; or the population projections for every country in the world.

■ *Practice 13-3:* For the topic you developed in the previous practice, list the reference works you'd use, the specific headings you'd search under, and the specific facts/statistics you'd like to find.

Finding Books

Most college and university libraries are now on-line—you access information about library holdings through terminals that are linked to a central computer. This saves you an enormous amount of time compared to the old system of looking up individual entries in the card or microfiche catalogue. But remember that the catalogue, whether traditional or computerized, only lists books *your* library has, not all books written on the topic.

With most systems, you have a choice of whether to search under subject heading, title, or author. In the case of preliminary research, you'll probably start with the subject headings in order to see a list of books on a particular subject.

Following is a sample screen you might see if you requested the subject "INTERNET" on an on-line catalogue.

```
Request: INTERNET

1: (12 records)      Internet (Computer network)
2: (2 records)       Internet (Computer network): periodicals
3: (1 record)        Internet (Computer network): directories
4: (1 record)        Internet (Computer network): handbooks, manuals
```

You choose number one because you notice there are 12 records, and you assume these general-interest books are a good place to get started. Later you might want to check out periodicals, directories, handbooks, or manuals, and you may return to the catalogue to access these records.

In a second or two, you see the following screen.

```
Subject heading: INTERNET (12 records)

1: The Internet Companion               LaQuey, Tracy          1993
2: Doing Business on the Internet       Cronin, Mary J.        1994
3: Netguide                             Rutten, Peter          1994
4: The Internet for Dummies             Levine, John R.        1993
5: The Internet Navigator               Gilster, Paul A.       1993
6: The Internet Starter Kit             Engst, Adam C.         1993
7: On Internet 94                       Abbott, Tony           1994
8: Internet: Getting Started            Marine, April          1993
9: The Internet Guide                   Dern, Daniel P.        1994
10: Zen and the Art of the Internet     Kehoe, Brendan         1993
11: Exploring the Internet              Malamud, Carl          1992
12: The Whole Internet                  Krol, Ed               1992
```

If you choose number three, the following screen gives you more specific information about *Netguide*.

Author:	Rutten, Peter; Bayers, Albert F.; Maloni, Kelly
Title:	Netguide: your map to the services, information and entertainment on the electronic highway
Publisher:	New York: Random House Electronic Pubs
Date:	c1994
Phys. Feat.:	xix, 356 p. ill.
Notes:	Includes index
ISBN:	0-679-75106-8
Subjects:	Internet; Computer networks; Information networks; Wide area networks
1 item:	

Your College or University Library—Main Collection

TK 5105.5 R8 1994
Available

The call number at the bottom of the screen tells you how the book is filed and where it is located. The "Subjects" heading tells you that the book is listed under these additional headings and may give you another idea of how to search for similar books on this topic. How do you decide if you want to find and read this book?

The *title* looks good. You may or may not recognize that the *author* is famous. Next check the *date*. Is it recent? Older books won't have the latest information. How important the date is depends on your topic. Books on scientific and technological topics often must be published within the last five years to be up to date. Psychology considers books 10 years old to be out of date. In books about literature, "recent" can mean one published 25 years ago. For books about the Internet, the more recent the better.

Compare the *number of pages* the book has to the *size of the topic* suggested by the title. A history of music in 400 pages will be more superficial than a history of the blues in 244 pages. Does the book have an *index?* If you only want certain facts, this is important; if you want to read the whole book, you won't care so much. Does the book have a *bibliography?* If so, it means the author researched previous sources. A bibliography also provides the titles of other books on the topic that the author found worthwhile. A few seconds evaluating sources now can save you from investing an hour in a weak source later. All books are not equal.

For books worth investigating, write down the titles and call numbers. Many people write down *all* the bibliographic information (author, title, city, publisher, and date) on separate cards before scanning the books. Others wait to see if a book contains relevant information. When you find good books in the library stacks, cruise the adjacent books. Related books hang out together.

What do you do if you find a reference to a book in a bibliography and that book is not in your library? If you want the book badly enough and it exists in a library somewhere in the world, you can get a copy by requesting an interlibrary loan. Your librarian knows how to search a number of national and international databases to determine the closest location of a copy of any book or periodical. Two of the more popular services are the OCLC or Online Computer Library Centre (11,000 institutions worldwide are now tied into this system with access to 22 million volumes) and the Hytelnet feature of the Internet, which connects users directly to the on-line catalogues of university libraries (you can use this yourself if you have an Internet account). After finding the book, your librarian will fill out a form and process your request. There may be a slight charge for this service. Remember that interlibrary loans can take anywhere from three to eight weeks, depending on the distance, so try to be patient.

■ *Practice 13-4:* Find two book titles for your topic from the on-line catalogue (or microfiche catalogue) and record complete bibliographic information.

Finding Journal and Newspaper Sources

Why would you want journal articles if you have books? For one thing, most "new" books are already one to five years old the minute they reach the bookstore. This is the time lag in writing, editing, and producing books. Journals and newspapers stay closer to the latest developments. Pollution problems and figures change yearly, computer technology changes monthly, and politics can explode weekly. Also, journals can cover topics too small for books and are often specialized—that's the difference between journals and magazines. Magazines appeal to a popular audience, whereas journals are specialized publications that appear periodically—that's why they're also called periodicals.

There are thousands of such periodicals covering the latest developments in every field. It's useful to walk through the periodicals section of your college or university library to see the range of topics and the extent of the collection. You'll probably be amazed just how specialized (obscure) the periodicals can be.

Periodical indexes are like card catalogues for journals, magazines, and newspapers. They list all articles written on a topic, giving the author, publication, date, page range, and sometimes other information (abstracts, for instance, summarize articles). Because thousands of periodicals exist, there are many indexes, each covering up to 400 journals. You must first choose the appropriate index for your topic. Most are printed yearly, so you must examine the 1987 indexes for firsthand magazine accounts of the stock market crash of that year or the 1988 indexes for reports about the Calgary Olympics. If you're studying a continuing topic, such as blues music or pollution, start with the latest indexes and work backward until you have enough sources.

Most periodical indexes are also available on CD-ROM, a compact disk loaded with information instead of music. Many libraries have a number of these indexes, which are accessed through a menu on a computer terminal. You choose the index you are interested in, and the computer searches the data on the CD-ROM.

When using an index in book form, you must locate the volumes by year and search them one at a time. All indexes are organized by subject—you look up a subject, and the index tells you what articles appeared on that subject in a particular year. The indexes also give related subject headings, as some articles are listed more than once. You can use these related headings to do a cross-referenced search, but the process is slow and cumbersome, as you must flip pages and check entries one at a time.

With CD-ROM indexes, the process is much easier. You simply type in your subject or topic, and within seconds a list of articles appears on the screen. You can scroll through this list and mark the ones you're interested in printing or save the list to a disk.

Another advantage of CD-ROM indexes is that they make cross-referenced searching easy. For example, if you wanted to locate articles on the topic "Internet and education," you could specify both these topics in your search request. Some indexes allow very flexible searching—you can indicate multiple subjects, titles, authors, or keywords in abstracts.

A very useful index on CD-ROM is *Canadian Business and Current Affairs*, which includes the *Canadian Business Index*, *Canadian Foreign Relations Index*, *Canadian Magazine Index*, and *Canadian News Index*. A search request for articles on the topic "Internet" yielded 119 items. Following are three.

---

7 of 119 Complete Record
Internet pioneers worry that hackers are taking over
Globe & Mail Metro Edition March 22, 1994 pg C4
Special Features: Photograph; Graphic
Descriptors: Internet network

46 of 119 Complete Record
Inside Internet: the "net" is crammed with scholarly and scientific data, public records, recipes, weather reports, airline schedules and endless chatter
Maclean's v.107 (3) January 17, 1994 pg 45
Descriptors: Internet network

64 of 119 Complete Record
First nation in cyberspace: twenty million strong and adding a million new users a month, the Internet is suddenly the place to be
Time (Canadian Edition) v.142 (24) December 6, 1993 pg 44–46
Descriptors: Internet network

If you were doing research on this topic, the *Canadian Business and Current Affairs Index* would give you a long list of sources.

Following is a list of some major indexes. The extent of your library's holdings will depend upon the size of your institution and the kinds of programs it offers. But these give a rough indication of the kinds of things periodical indexes cover. Most of them are available in both CD-ROM and book formats.

Applied Science and Technology

Art Index

Business Periodicals Index

Canadian Periodical Index

Canadian Book Review Annual

Canadian Education Index

Environmental Index

The Humanities Index

The New York Times Index

Psychological Abstracts

The Reader's Guide to Periodical Literature

The Social Science Index

Hospital Literature Index

MLA Bibliography (articles on language and literature)

Two of the most commonly used general indexes are *The Reader's Guide* and *The New York Times Index*. *The Reader's Guide* lists all the articles written in over 200 magazines with the largest circulations. Many of these magazines contain articles that are thought provoking and carefully researched, but some are too lightweight for academic research.

Specialized indexes tend to be more detailed and scholarly. In-depth research on Michelangelo's paintings, for example, will more likely turn up in magazines listed in *Art Index* than in magazines listed in *The Reader's Guide*. *Hospital Literature Index* is not the place for general medical information on natural childbirth; however, if you are a nursing student writing a term paper on procedure in natural childbirth, it will provide stronger sources than *The Reader's Guide*. In your first-year English course, *The Reader's Guide* may do quite well, but as you move up in your field, search for sources in the more specialized indexes.

Before shutting an index, write down the information needed to locate the article: page, date, title of magazine; for a newspaper article, also write down the section (unless you enjoy winding microfilm through page after page of a weekend paper).

Each year all the issues of a magazine are either bound together in a book or reduced to a reel of microfilm. You should find both bound and microfilmed periodicals near the reference section.

■ *Practice 13-5:* Which periodical index(es) would you use to find articles on the following topics?

Robertson Davies's latest novel

Acid rain

Problems with the welfare system

Fibre optics

Employment potential in hotel management

NON-LIBRARY RESOURCES

Libraries are great repositories, but there are other resources. The yellow pages telephone directory is a powerful brainteaser. For example, if you're interested in doing research about an environmental issue in your community, try local conservation organizations or the environment or natural resources department of the federal or provincial government. A student researching funeral rituals might call an undertaker for information, an interview, or even a tour of the facilities. Food, death, sports, housing, technology, child care, and a host of other topics all have local experts. Most will give information over the phone to courteous callers.

Following are a few tips for soliciting research in person.

1. Ask for the person's time a week ahead and explain exactly why you want it. Suggest a few sample questions and how much time you'll need. (30 minutes is reasonable.)

2. Do your preliminary reading first. If you show some awareness of the topic, you'll stimulate your source to provide better information.

3. Prepare questions, but be alive to pursuing new ideas.

4. Come with paper and pen. If you want to tape a formal interview, ask permission.

5. Dress professionally—you'll get better information.

6. Start with an easy question to loosen things up, but move to the key research questions quickly so you don't run out of time before asking them.

7. Thank your sources and tell them they'll be cited in your paper. Send a typed thank-you note.

8. Immediately after an interview, fill out your notes and record your reactions before they go cold. Be sure you indicate which are quotes and paraphrases and which are your own comments.

NOTETAKING

There is no "right" way to take notes; they come with the uniqueness and messiness of other brainteaser lists. But following are a few suggestions.

1. Resist the urge to photocopy sources. Notetaking should condense the material and make it *workable*. Record only the pearls of wisdom.

2. Should you take notes on cards? On regular notebook paper? On a computer? Note cards have been advocated for years because of two advantages: first, they stack neatly and fit in purses or pockets, unlike a ragged mess of papers; second, they can be easily rearranged when you organize the paper—*provided* you limit yourself to one fact or idea per card. Otherwise you'll have two ideas on one card wanting to go different places in the essay, and like Solomon, you'll have to debate how to divide the brainchild.

Notebook paper encourages writing. You have room to keep going if you get hot or into the flow. But to organize, you must tear it into one-idea bits and then sort through the confetti. Despite what textbooks have said over the years, some professional writers operate this way, and it may work for you in *short* research papers. But most researchers find that notecards rescue them from chaos.

Unfortunately, you can't haul your desktop computer into the library. If you are lucky enough to have a laptop, you'll be able to make quick notes on the fly. Otherwise, you'll have to settle for handwritten notes and later incorporate them into the first draft on the computer.

3. Paraphrase instead of copying long quotations when notetaking. Condense the original. Only quote key sentences or phrases. Doing so will help your voice to control the draft. Of course, if you unearth an absolutely sparkling paragraph, take it whole. *In notes, always quote accurately and use quotation marks.*

4. Comment on and analyse source material while reading. *You are not a stenographer but a thinker when you take notes.* Raise an objection, add a personal anecdote, or connect sources. Doing so is easy on full-size notebook paper. For note cards, you may use separate cards to react to sources. In either case, be sure to label "My Ideas" or "My Comment" at the top so you never confuse your ideas with research. Staple or clip comment cards to the source cards. The following example on blues music shows actual student notes. Notice the blend of paraphrase, quotation, and commentary.

5. Record the complete *bibliographic information* with your notes—as in the previous notes. Also write page numbers after each paraphrase or quotation. This recording will interrupt you a bit, but prefer it to having no publisher or date after the library closes for the weekend. Some researchers record bibliographic information on separate "bib" cards, which are easy to reshuffle when it's time to write the bibliography. In this system, cards with ideas on them only list the source's title and page number.

Bibliographic Information

-_Blues People_, Le Roi Jones. Wm. Morrow and Co. N.Y. 1963
Yoruba tribesmen from Dahomy thought "the universe is ruled by fate and the destiny of each man worked out according to a predetermined scheme." Music was one of the few ways -they defied fate (p.9).

Page Reference

Comment Card

MY IDEAS HERE.- Did this belief in fate allow them to be made slaves to people who believed in free will? How did it affect their music? Blues may be music of defiance of establishment rules. goes way back.

One Card combines Comments with Source Matter

Black Music in America, John Rublowsky, Basic Books, N.Y. 1971
On Sundays slaves dressed in "hand-me-down" finery from the big house and would do a "take-off" on the high manners of the white folks" by prancing and high-kicking. Then the "masters" would gather and watch, awarding a cake to the fanciest dancer (that's how "cakewalk" got its name), not knowing that they awarded a prize to the one who mocked them the best. (p. 96) MINE.- Is this how they used music to get even with the gods / fate?

■ *Practice 13-6:* To help you study for an upcoming exam, take notes on any important idea from one of your textbooks. Fill out one note card by summarizing a key idea and quoting a key phrase. Comment on how the idea relates to other major concepts in the chapter. Include complete bibliographic documentation and the page number.

ORGANIZING RESEARCH PAPERS

Organize research papers as you would informative or persuasive writing. Whether you have note cards or paper torn into strips, organize them into related piles and create headings. Another option is to read through the cards and then put them aside. Then, focusing on your main ideas, write a scratch outline of the main points you want to cover. Last, assign note cards to these headings. With long papers, it's especially important to narrow your topic and formulate a thesis before attempting an outline. A thesis helps you to visualize and shape your blizzard of notes. Make a trial thesis statement and then read through your notes, marking ones that relate. Or read through your notes and make a list of trial thesis sentences from them. Remember, your thesis should be a *statement*, not a question. One sentence is preferred.

Many professors require students to submit their research papers in stages for approval, particularly topic or thesis choices and outlines. Try to think of this not as an extra chore but as an aid in writing: it forces you to think and organize early, stimulating your subconscious to incubate, and it provides feedback before a grade is at stake. Get used to preliminary reports. Much business and professional research requires an "abstract"—a statement of thesis and a paragraph summary of the main points. This is usually submitted for approval before the paper is written and may accompany the final paper.

WRITING THE RESEARCH PAPER: CITATIONS AND QUOTATIONS

Drafting a research paper involves the process discussed in chapter 5. You want a sharp introduction that grabs the reader with an anecdote, your key research questions, or a strong fact and leads to a clear statement of thesis. Often the introduction will preview the areas you'll cover and explain why you won't cover other areas. Work quickly on the first draft so you don't get hung up on correcting little problems. Your main goals are to clarify your sketchy ideas and to make them visual with sharp details.

HANDLING SOURCE MATERIAL

Research drafting differs from writing other essays because of outside sources. You must incorporate them smoothly into your text and document them as you draft. The bibliography can be left until last so it doesn't disrupt the flow of creation.

1. Quotations, paraphrases, and facts from other sources must flow with your paper. They are valuable only if they directly relate to *your* thesis. So you must clearly show that relationship to the reader by *smoothly introducing* all source material and by *commenting*, not just stringing quotes together like beads on a necklace. Start with simple taglines: "As one social researcher says..." or "According to the editors of *Time Magazine*..." or "After 30 years as a judge, Deborah Paine believes...." A tagline not only prepares us for a new voice but also tells us *what authority* your source has. The tagline should show us why we should trust what follows.

There are two main methods of incorporating quotations into the text. One is the smooth integration of quoted material. In this style, the quotation is simply integrated into the grammar of your sentence—it is spliced smoothly with the flow of your introductory words, as in the following example:

> Keats describes "Negative Capability" as the experience of living with "uncertainties, Mysteries, doubts, without any irritable reaching after fact & reason" (qtd. in Perkins 1209).

You may also introduce quotations more formally by setting them up with a tagline followed by a colon. Here is another example:

> In a letter dated December 21–27, 1817, Keats describes his famous theory of "Negative Capability": "I mean *Negative Capability*, that is when man is capable of being in uncertainties, Mysteries, doubts, without any irritable reaching after fact & reason" (qtd. in Perkins 1209).

Remember that a colon is only used after a complete sentence and gives your reader the signal that something is going to follow directly. It is almost like a pointing arrow.

If you want to omit words from the middle of your quotation, use an ellipsis, a set of spaced dots. If you are leaving out words, use three dots; if you are leaving out a complete sentence, use four dots (the last dot is the period of the sentence you've omitted from your quotation). You don't need to use an ellipsis if you are omitting something from the beginning or end of your quotation, as long as you end with a complete sentence, which is usually the case.

When choosing quotations, always keep in mind that their purpose is to provide information to support the thesis. These connections may grow from the comment cards you attached to source cards when you were doing your research reading, or they may be spontaneous ideas.

Following is an example from the opening paragraph of a student essay. The writer begins by citing statistics about McDonald's and its labour force in order to establish a context for an argument in favour of restaurant employees having a union.

According to <u>Report on Business Magazine</u>, "McDonald's and its franchises employ more than 65,000, largely teenage workers at 700 or so outlets across the country, and a stunning 7% of all people in Canada and the United States—1 in 15—got their first job at a McDonald's restaurant" (Kidd 48). You have seen them many times—those smiling, uniformed kids who hope you have a nice day, while they rush to and fro, madly attempting to fetch your burgers and fries before the customer standing behind you gets too grumpy. This is the story of one such employee, a 17-year-old woman from Orangeville, Ontario, and her failed attempt to organize the not-always-happy workers at McDonald's by establishing a union.

2. Condense quotations from your notes even more by paraphrasing all but the most important passages. You cover ground more quickly with paraphrases, and strings of quotes frustrate a reader, who assumes correctly that the real message is in *your* voice. If two or three writers agree on one point, quote or paraphrase the best one, and simply mention that two others agree; don't drag a reader through redundant quotes. Following is a student example of a nice paraphrase mixed with bits of quotation from a clinical description of an animal test. All of the information comes from the same page of a single source, so there's no need for more than one parenthetical citation (see below):

The Draize Test involves testing cosmetics for eye damage that might occur to humans. Researchers smear mascara, for example, over the eyeballs of rabbits. Unlike humans, rabbits have no tear glands to wash it off. The animals are "immobilized" in a stockade device. In some cases, their eyes are held open with clips. As a result, they cannot blink to get even a moment's relief and ultimately suffer "eye ulcers, bleeding, and blindness" (O'Connor 94). And for what purpose? The tests do not even resemble how humans use the product.

Should you need a long quotation (5 lines or 50 words minimum), set off the entire passage with a 10-space indentation. No quotation marks are needed. With block-style quotations, remember to place the parenthetical reference outside the final punctuation mark, unlike the regular in-text reference, which is set within the punctuation marks of the sentence.

3. Research papers use citations in the text to document sources. Until about 10 years ago, documentation required a system of notes (either placed at the bottom of each page as footnotes or assembled on one final page as endnotes). But notes were cumbersome for both readers and writers, required Latin expressions such as "loc. cit." or "ibid.," and needlessly repeated the information contained in the bibliography. So the format has been

changed, and most instructors will expect you to use one of two systems: the MLA (Modern Language Association) system for essays in the humanities, and the APA (American Psychological Association) system for essays in the social sciences and most other disciplines.

Both of these systems of documentation are based on the premise that the reader should be able to find the source of the quoted material. It's a courteous way of acknowledging that the information doesn't belong to the writer but has been borrowed from another source and incorporated into the essay. The documentation sends a signal to the reader that the information is available, should he or she wish to look it up.

Both APA and MLA are two-part systems. The first part is a reference in parentheses placed directly after a quoted, paraphrased, or summarized passage. It lists author, page number, and (in APA style) date. The second part is a list of bibliographic details in the Works Cited (MLA) or References (APA) page at the end of the document. If the reader is interested in looking up the book or article indicated by the parenthetical reference in the text, he or she can turn to the back and find all the needed information in the alphabetically arranged list.

The parenthetical references in the text show the reader which ideas or words "belong" to the writer and what has been "borrowed" to support the thesis. Documentation, then, has something to do with intellectual property—it indicates what originated with the writer and which facts or ideas have been imported to support or provide background to the argument.

MLA STYLE OF PARENTHETICAL REFERENCES

The MLA system is simple. All quoted, paraphrased, or summarized material must be followed by a parenthetical citation, which usually includes the author's name and the page number (don't put a comma between them). Try to place this information as close as possible to the material it refers to, preferably at the end of a sentence:

> "The second element in the Ghost's message that squeezes Hamlet's life into narrowing limits is the interruption of the habits, such as they are, of Hamlet's life" (Frye 87).

The main idea behind this system is to try to avoid redundancy whenever possible. If Frye is your principal source and you refer to his ideas or words again soon after, your second and subsequent references only require a page number as long as it's clear you're still referring to Frye:

> The ghost speaks again to Hamlet, and it is "not a reassuring recommendation" (87).

Likewise, if you mention the author's name in the introduction to the idea or quotation, there's no need to repeat it in the parenthetical citation:

Frye goes on to suggest that "Hamlet's feelings are still fixated on his mother, and he has to keep working up his hatred of Claudius" (87–88).

If you have two books by Frye in your bibliography, then obviously a reference to Frye's name alone in parentheses will not indicate to your reader which of the two books you are referring to. In this case, you must indicate the title of the book as well (or an abbreviated version of it):

"The second element in the Ghost's message that squeezes Hamlet's life into narrowing limits is the interruption of the habits, such as they are, of Hamlet's life" (Frye, *Shakespeare* 87).

Following are a few other examples you might run into in the course of your research. For a more exhaustive list, refer to the fourth edition of the *MLA Handbook for Writers of Research Papers*, the standard guide to MLA style published by The Modern Language Association of America.

Work by Two or More Authors

If a work is by two or three authors, give their names in the parenthetical citation: (Smith, Jones, and Brown 35–59). If a work has four or more authors, use the first author's name followed by the abbreviation "et al.": (Reed et al. 99).

Article in an Edited Collection

Your reference should indicate the name of the author of the article, not the editor of the book. If Josephine Seward has written an article in a collection edited by Stewart Snodgrass, you refer to Seward in the parenthetical reference: (Seward 87).

Work of Literature

If you are quoting from or paraphrasing a prose work (novel or short story), indicate the page number and chapter immediately after the quotation or paraphrase: (175; ch. 8). For Shakespeare and other classic verse plays and poems, omit the page number, but refer to the act, scene, and line numbers or other divisions: (*Hamlet* 1.1.22–23).

Indirect Source

If the author of the book you're using quotes from a source that you want to include in your paper, you should indicate the names of both by using the abbreviation "qtd.," which stands for "quoted": (qtd. in Cameron 450).

Multivolume Work

If you are quoting from a multivolume work, indicate which volume you are referring to by placing the volume number after the author's name, followed by a colon and the page number: (Boswell 2: 450). If you've already indicated the author's name, give only the volume and page numbers: (2: 450). If you have only one volume listed in your Works Cited, there's no need to indicate the volume number in the parenthetical citation.

Corporate Author

Use the name of the corporate author in the parenthetical citation if there's no individual author: (Government of Alberta 23). If possible, indicate the author in the introduction, rather than having a long citation in parentheses.

APA STYLE OF PARENTHETICAL REFERENCES

The principle of APA style is the same as MLA; you must indicate the sources of all quoted, paraphrased, or summarized material. But the details are a little different. In APA style, the date is part of the parenthetical material because it is important in the social and natural sciences to establish quickly the currency of the information and findings. The only other difference is that you are encouraged to paraphrase if quotations are fewer than 40 words. If you use the author's name to introduce the quoted or paraphrased material, you must place the date in parentheses immediately after the name and refer to the page number after the quotation or paraphrase:

> According to Dolan (1986), cocaine is an expensive drug that can cost users from $500 to $5,000 per week (p. 87).

Some instructors may ask you to leave out the page number if you are paraphrasing or summarizing. It is optional in this case, but the inclusion allows the reader to find the reference easily. Ask your instructor which method he or she prefers.

If the author's name and year of publication don't appear in the introductory material, you must include all three elements in the parenthetical reference that follows the quotation or paraphrase:

> Doctors are still not certain how cocaine works. "A leading theory is that cocaine, like many other stimulant drugs, produces an action on certain body chemicals when it enters the bloodstream. These chemicals are called neurotransmitters. The cocaine prompts them to activate the nerve cells and send tiny electrical impulses coursing through the nervous system" (Dolan, 1986, p. 86).

Note that commas separate these elements and that page is indicated by "p." for a single page and "pp." for multiple pages.

As in the MLA system, the main idea is to avoid unnecessary repetition. For example, if you only have one book by Dolan in your References list, there's no need to include the date or author's name in subsequent references if it's clear you are still quoting Dolan—simply include the page number immediately following the quoted or paraphrased material.

If you refer to two articles by the same author and they appeared in different years, the year of publication should distinguish one from the other. If you refer to two articles written by one author in the same year, you must put them in alphabetical order on your References page with a letter beside the year (1995a). In the parenthetical references, use this designation to make it clear to your reader which one you are referring to:

> Falk (1995a) suggests that too much television causes the brain to turn to mush (p. 3).

Following are a few more examples of APA parenthetical documentation. For a more exhaustive list, refer to the *Publication Manual of the American Psychological Association*.

Work by Two or More Authors

If you are referring to a work by two authors, simply include their names in the introduction to the quoted or summarized passage:

> Arnold and Hall (1887) suggest that there is a direct correlation between the size of the pinkie finger and creativity (p. 89).

If you don't mention the authors' names in the text, use an ampersand (&) to link the two names in the parenthetical reference:

> Important early studies suggest that there is a direct correlation between the size of the pinkie finger and creativity (Arnold & Hall, 1887, p. 89).

If a work has more than three but fewer than six authors, refer to the last names of all the authors in the first reference, but only refer to the first author followed by "et al." in subsequent references. If you have six or more authors, use the first author and "et al." for all parenthetical citations:

> Jones, Krishna, Rosenberg, and Cooley (1990) argue that the original intention of the legislation was to provide greater access to information that had been protected by government agencies. The legislation was a good idea in theory, but the practical result is far from ideal. This discrepancy between the intent of the legislation

and its implementation (Jones et al.) has not freed information, but simply created a tangled bureaucracy that gives the illusion of free access.

Note that the second parenthetical reference occurs in the middle of the sentence. In APA format, you are encouraged to place the in-text citation as close as possible to the paraphrase, even if it's in the middle of a sentence. In this case, the idea of the discrepancy between the legislation's intent and implementation comes from Jones et al., whereas the conclusion that follows belongs to the author of the paper.

Reference to Two or More Sources

If you are referring to two or more sources, alphabetize the list and separate each item with a semicolon:

> To date, research on the qualitative changes effected in writing by the word processor has been either contradictory or inconclusive (Auten, 1989; Collier, 1983; Curtis, 1988; Hawisher, 1987; Hill, Wallace, & Hass, 1991; Nydahl, 1991; Vockel & Schwartz, 1988).

Corporate Author

If there is no individual author, indicate the corporate author's name in the first reference followed by an abbreviation in brackets. For subsequent references, use the abbreviation only:

> In the report (Canadian Radio-Television and Telecommunications Commission [CRTC], 1994), many of the applicants were turned down.

■ *Practice 13-8:* For your textbook note card, write a brief paragraph that introduces the source smoothly and uses a proper citation.

 ## AVOIDING PLAGIARISM

Under current copyright law, everything anyone writes, including student essays, is copyrighted—that is, protected by law from being used by anyone else without written permission. The law was designed to protect authors and publishers from other people profiting from their efforts. However, this would create havoc if millions of students needed publishers' permission to quote sources in papers or if all professors doing research needed permission for scholarly papers. So publishers have agreed that proper documentation will substitute for written permission to use copyrighted material for scholarship. You document, then, not only to show your material came from reputable sources and to allow your professor to check the accuracy of your research but also as part of an agreement to "pay" an author and publisher for using their work.

The reader should never doubt which ideas are yours and which are from sources. Introductory taglines tell readers where source material begins, and citations in parentheses tell them where it ends. Anything else you claim as your idea. "Naked" quotes or paraphrases without citations create doubts, and they may result in a teacher accusing you of plagiarism—academic stealing. What must have citations? Quotations, ideas from sources rewritten in your own words, and statistics or facts.

Rewriting doesn't make an *idea* yours; it only makes the *words* yours. A citation credits the idea to someone else; quotation marks credit the *words* to someone else. Ultimately, most of what we know comes from other sources—books, teachers, parents, the media, and so on. The core of knowledge that most educated people have is called "common knowledge" and does *not* have to be cited: it is considered common property. This can include famous quotations, ideas, and facts—anything you didn't take from a source but knew as part of your background of knowledge. Examples:

Capitalism stresses individual rights and freedoms, while socialism stresses group rights and freedoms.

Most major religions say death is a release from the pain of life, not a dreaded event.

Shakespeare lived in England 400 years ago and wrote the plays *Hamlet* and *The Tempest*.

DDT spraying 25 years ago still pollutes water today and kills fish and birds.

Michelangelo painted the ceiling of the Sistine Chapel.

The speed of light is 300,000 kilometres per second.

Water consists of two hydrogen atoms bonded to one oxygen atom.

You may not know all these facts, but they'd be considered common knowledge by most educated people. They don't require citations or bibliography entries. If you go to a higher degree of specific knowledge, it may cease being common knowledge. If, for instance, you described the specific chemical reaction DDT causes in bald eagle eggs, it would cease to be common knowledge for the general educated public. Among *experts* it may be common knowledge, but until you establish yourself as an expert, you must document this more specific information. Anything you learn from reading specifically for a paper *must* be documented. If you read something three or four times in different sources, you'll suspect that it is common knowledge. Ask your professor if you're not sure. Someone once said, "Whatever isn't nailed down must be mine." This anonymous person is a likely candidate for a charge of plagiarism. Anything not your own should be documented.

REVISING RESEARCH WRITING

Revising research papers proceeds as does any other revision. Start with the big things—the thesis and the details—then move to paragraphs, sentences, and words, and finally proof for mechanics. Keep in mind the following points as you revise.

1. Edit long-winded quotations or paraphrases. Pick the most vivid or relevant; eliminate the rest.

2. Make sure each source has a smooth introductory tagline, a citation with a page reference at the end, and your own commentary tying it to the thesis.

3. Research papers usually require a stronger conclusion than other papers. Restate your thesis.

BIBLIOGRAPHY

The last step in drafting a research paper is compiling a bibliography. In addition to citations in the body of your paper, you must provide complete information on book, magazine, or interview sources you used. At first glance, bibliography format may seem like a jumble, but it has an inner logic. You must give enough specific information to identify each source and allow a reader to find it.

MLA and APA formats are, as you'd expect, different in subtle ways. For one thing, bibliographies have different names. In MLA, it is called either Works Cited, if you are only referring to the sources cited in the parenthetical documentation, or Works Consulted, if you are listing all the works you consulted in the course of your research. In APA, the bibliography is simply called References.

Note to students: Yes, these two systems ought to be united into one simple, logical form of documentation for all areas of study so that researchers can concentrate on ideas and evidence, not on format. Eventually, the APA and the MLA will cooperate. But for now, you must check with your professors to see which system you should use for which paper.

Some publications omit identifying information. Substitute these abbreviations for missing information:

n.p. (no place of publication listed)

n.d. (no date given)

n.p. (no publisher given)

n. pag. (no page numbers given)

MLA Bibliography Format

The fourth edition of the *MLA Handbook for Writers of Research Papers* (1995) does not recommend any significant format changes from previous editions. It does, however, include a greatly expanded section on citing CD-ROMs and on-line databases (see examples below). Not only is it the definitive guide to the MLA documentation style, but it also offers detailed information on the process of writing and research.

The MLA format has the following characteristics:

- The entire list is alphabetized by the authors' last names so that citations are easy to locate.
- The second and subsequent lines of each citation are indented five spaces to keep the author's name visible.
- The entries are double spaced.
- Punctuation and the order of items in each entry are consistent.
- The list is entitled "Works Cited" or "Works Consulted" on a separate page at the end of the paper.

There are three main parts to each entry: author(s), title, and publication information. Begin with the author's name: last name first, followed by the first name and initials (as you find it on the title page of the book or article) and a period. Leave two spaces and then give the title of the work. Underline it and capitalize the main words, just as you find it on the title page. Include any subtitle by separating it from the main title with a colon followed by a single space. This part also ends with a period followed by two spaces. The third part is the publication information, which includes the place of publication, followed by a colon and a space; the publisher's name, followed by a comma and a space; and the date of publication, followed by a period.

Following are sample formats for the most common sources you'll encounter.

Basic Book Format

Use the *latest* date listed on the copyright page.

Abbey, Edward. <u>The Monkey Wrench Gang</u>. New York: Avon, 1975.

Book with Two or Three Authors

Flick, Jane, and Celia Millward. <u>Handbook for Writers</u>. Toronto: Harcourt, 1993.

Book with More than Three Authors

Use "et al." after the first author's name.

Voss, Richard D., et al. <u>Mastering the Art of Documentation</u>. Toronto:
Scholarly, 1995.

Book with an Author and an Editor

If you refer to the primary text, the citation should begin with the author's
name, followed by the editor, referred to as "ed."

Spenser, Edmund. <u>The Faerie Queene</u>. Ed. Thomas P. Roche, Jr. Markham:
Penguin, 1978.

If you refer to the editor's comments, the citation should be reversed.

Roche, Jr., Thomas P., ed. <u>The Faerie Queene</u>. By Edmund Spenser.
Markham: Penguin, 1978.

Corporate or Group Author

Give the full name of the group author, followed by the title.

American Psychological Association. <u>Publication Manual of the American
Psychological Association</u>. 3rd ed. Washington, DC: APA, 1984.

Two or More Books by the Same Author

When listing two or more books by the same author, the second and subsequent citations should begin with three hyphens and a period, instead of
with the author's name again.

Frye, Northrop. <u>Northrop Frye on Shakespeare</u>. Markham: Fitzhenry, 1986.

– – –. <u>Fearful Symmetry: A Study of William Blake</u>. Princeton: Princeton
UP, 1974.

Book Not in First Edition

After the title, specify the edition number, because page references and
wording may change from edition to edition.

Breland, Osmond, et al. <u>Principles of Biology</u>. 3rd ed. New York: Harper, 1964.

Book in More than One Volume

Refer to the volume you use if you are citing a book in more than one volume.

Daymond, Douglas, and Leslie Monkman. <u>Literature in Canada</u>. Vol. 2.
Toronto: Gage, 1978. 2 vols.

If you use both volumes, cite the entire work.

Daymond, Douglas, and Leslie Monkman. <u>Literature in Canada</u>. 2 vols.
Toronto: Gage, 1978.

Selection from an Anthology or Edited Book

The selection is placed in quotation marks, while the book title is underlined. "Ed." refers to the editor of the collection. Page numbers must also
be cited.

Kennedy, Elizabeth. "The Marketing of Madonna." <u>Selling Culture</u>. Ed.
Philippa Jones. Toronto: Oxford UP, 1995. 145–49.

Article in an Encyclopedia

Unsigned articles need no volume or page number—just the title.

"Canada." <u>Encyclopaedia Britannica: Micropaedia</u>. 1993 ed.

Signed articles require the author's name.

Freeman, Minnie Aodla. "Inuit." <u>The Canadian Encyclopedia</u>. 1988 ed.

Lecture

Cite the information in the following order: speaker, title of lecture, spon-
soring group, location, and date. If there is no title, label the kind of presentation: lecture, keynote address, and so on.

Gould, Stephen Jay. "Wonderful Life." Mount Royal College Arts Lectures,
Calgary, AB. 26 Apr. 1990.

Monthly Magazine

Cite the details in the following order: author, title of article (in quotation
marks), title of magazine (underlined), date, and page numbers.

Jervis, Nancy. "Waste Not, Want Not." <u>Natural History</u> May 1990:
70–74.

Weekly Magazine

In this case, include the precise date.

Kael, Pauline. "The Current Cinema." <u>New Yorker</u> 29 Nov. 1982:
162–65.

Article in a Journal with Continuous Pagination

In such journals, usually published quarterly, the page numbering continues in each issue for an entire year (e.g., the page numbers in the summer issue continue where those in the spring issue left off). The volume number is followed by the date in parentheses and the page numbers.

Collier, Richard M. "The Word Processor and Revision Strategies." College
  Composition and Communication 34 (1983): 149–55.

Article in a Journal with Separate Pagination

In this case, add a period between the volume number and the issue number.

Bridwell-Bowles, Lillian. "Designing Research on Computer-Assisted
  Writing." Computers and Composition 7.1 (1989): 81–95.

Article in a Newspaper

If the city of publication isn't in the title, include it in brackets. The plus sign (+) indicates that the article continues on another page that isn't consecutive.

Cernetig, Miro. "Probe Ordered into Hockey Riot." Globe and Mail
  [Toronto] 16 June 1994: A1+.

Personally Conducted Interview

Indicate what type of interview: personal or telephone.

Raines, Tim. Personal interview. Montreal. 18 May 1990.

Pamphlet

List the author, title, publisher, and date, if available. Try to follow book format as closely as possible. If there is no author, enter the title and publishing information.

Swinburne, Elizabeth, and Albert Roberts. Gardening Tips in a Short
  Season. Inuvik: Polar Bear Garden Supplies, 1990.

Television Program

List the program title, producer, narrator or main actors, network, station name, location, and date.

CBC Alberta News. Narr. Brenda Finley. Prod. Laurie Long. CBC. CBRT-
  TV, Calgary. 14 June 1995.

Video or Film

Be sure to include the medium after the title.

Antony and Cleopatra. Videocassette. Writ. William Shakespeare. Prod.
Jonathan Miller. With Colin Blakely and Jane Lapotaire. BBC
Enterprises, 1980. 177 min.

CD-ROMs and Other Portable Databases

Most portable databases are issued on CD-ROM only, although some can
be found on diskette. There is a wealth of information currently issued on
CD-ROM, such as the full text of books, newspapers, periodicals,
abstracts, encyclopedias, and catalogues. The entries for such databases
are much like those for traditional print media, with the following special
considerations:

1. You must cite the medium: CD-ROM, diskette, etc.
2. For periodically published CD-ROMs, you must cite the vendor (similar to the publisher of a book).
3. You must cite the date of electronic publication. This may be a little
   tricky. For example, if you are citing an article that originally appeared
   in print, you must cite the date it was first published as well as the date
   the CD-ROM database was released. Most CD-ROM databases are
   updated at regular intervals, and sometimes this information is only
   available on the title screen.

1. PERIODICALLY PUBLISHED CD-ROM DATABASE WITH PUBLICATION
INFORMATION FOR A PRINTED SOURCE

These CD-ROMs include material that also appears in print, either previously or simultaneously. For example, the periodical indexes and
abstracts you find on computer terminals in the library are linked to
a remote CD-ROM. Sometimes newspapers are made available on
CD-ROM, such as the *Globe and Mail on CD-ROM* and the *New York
Times Ondisc*. The bibliographic information (author, version, vendor,
etc.) is usually found on the opening screen. Cite the article exactly as
you would using standard MLA format, followed by the title of the database (underlined), publication medium, name of the vendor, and electronic publication date.

Kienetz, Alvin. "Ethnic Identity in Northern Canada." Journal of Ethnic
Studies 14.1 (1986): 129–34. ERIC. CD-ROM. Knight-Ridder.
Mar. 1995.

2. PERIODICALLY PUBLISHED CD-ROM DATABASE WITH NO PRINTED SOURCE SPECIFIED

These databases are updated regularly, but they don't refer to previously printed sources. When citing these sources, include the name of the author (if indicated), title of the material, date, title of the database, medium, vendor, and publication date.

"Aboriginal Affairs (Alberta)." 13 May 1994. <u>FundMel Sources</u>. CD-ROM.

    IGW Canada. 1994.

3. NON-PERIODICAL PUBLICATION ON CD-ROM

These CD-ROMs are much like books: they are published once and may or may not be updated. They include encyclopedias, dictionaries, games, works of literature, and any number of multimedia packages. Include the following in your citation: author (if available), title of work (in quotation marks if you are citing only part of the work), title of product (underlined), edition or version, medium, city of publication, publisher, and year of publication.

<u>The Oxford English Dictionary</u>. 2nd ed. CD-ROM. Oxford: Oxford UP, 1992.

If citing only part of the work:

"Redundancy." <u>The Oxford English Dictionary</u>. 2nd ed. CD-ROM. Oxford:

    Oxford UP, 1992.

On-Line Databases

On-line databases are electronic sources of information accessed through a computer that is connected to either a private service or the Internet. Such references require special consideration, as the material may be updated frequently. The citation of on-line databases must include the publication medium, name of the computer service or network, and date of access. In the case of material with publication information for a printed source, you may have to include both the date the publication originally appeared and the date you accessed the on-line version.

1. MATERIAL ACCESSED THROUGH A COMPUTER SERVICE WITH PUBLICATION INFORMATION FOR A PRINTED SOURCE

In this case, cite the article or information as you would normally and follow it with the title of the database (underlined), publication medium, name of the computer service, and date you accessed the information.

"Angry Tobin Blasts Spain as Turbot Talks Fall Apart." <u>Winnipeg Free</u>
    <u>Press</u> 15 Apr. 1995: A3. <u>Canadian Business and Current Affairs</u>.
    On-line. Dialog. 27 June 1995.

2. MATERIAL ACCESSED THROUGH A COMPUTER SERVICE WITH NO PRINTED SOURCE

In the following example, the database of CanCorp Canadian Financials
was accessed through the Dialog on-line service for information on Corel
Corporation.

"Corel Corporation." <u>CanCorp Canadian Financials</u>. On-line. Dialog. 27
    June 1995.

3. MATERIAL ACCESSED THROUGH A COMPUTER NETWORK SUCH AS THE INTERNET (ELECTRONIC JOURNALS, ELECTRONIC TEXTS, DISCUSSION LISTS, ETC.)

References to material from electronic journals must include the following:
author (if given), title of article (in quotation marks), title of journal (underlined), volume and/or issue number, year or date of publication, number of
pages or paragraphs (use n. pag. if no pagination), medium, network, and
date of access.

Yule, Jeffrey. "Waxing Kriger." <u>Postmodern Culture</u> 5.2 (1995): 26 pars.
    On-line. Internet. 28 June 1995.

You may, if you like, follow this information with a statement that describes
exactly where the information can be found. In this case, the information
was accessed through FTP (File Transfer Protocol) on the Internet.

Yule, Jeffrey. "Waxing Kriger." <u>Postmodern Culture</u> 5.2 (1995): 26 pars. On-line.
    Internet. 28 June 1995. Available FTP: jefferson.village.virginia.edu

SAMPLE STUDENT ESSAY USING MLA DOCUMENTATION

Most instructors won't want a title page for a short paper. Instead, follow
the model below by placing your name, the professor's name, course name
and number, and date at the top of the first page beside the left margin.
Also remember to include your last name with the page number on every
page. The title should be centred, without quotation marks.

Irina Reyzelman

Professor J. Altman

English 1112, Section 33

23 November 1995

The World of Our Dreams

The woods are dark, past sunset. People or animals lurk behind the trees. I am naked. I begin to run, but know they are running after me. I am lost. The creatures are bloody, half human, half animal. I fall. I try to scream, but nothing comes out. One of the creatures approaches, reaches out, and.... I wake screaming. It was only a dream.

In dreams you can air-swim, stop buses with bare hands, wear regal finery or nothing at all. You may receive gifts or learn lessons or experience intense love, courage, loss, or fear. Some people change their jobs, plane reservations, even lovers, based on dreams. Since ancient times, humans have been curious about the essential stuff of dreams: why and how people dream and what meaning the theatre of sleep has with its phantasmagoric denizens.

First comes a preliminary stage of drowsiness, when the practical senses drift out of control and the sable wings of sleep enfold us. According to Sharon Begley, about 90 minutes later, your brain awakens with a start, crackling with mental electricity. The brainstem at the base of your skull fires a random barrage of high-voltage impulses, nonsensical and chaotic, and unleashes waves of chemicals into the forebrain. You are paralysed, a victim of events in your head (41). One researcher reports that before you return to consciousness, you will pass through four or five dreams that increase in length as the night goes on and that total about two hours (Dolnick 48).

What do people dream about? There is an impression that dreams are full of sex and violence because people remember more of these types of dreams and tell others about them. But a study done by Calvin

Hall and Robert VandeCastle on 1,000 dreams collected from hundreds of male and female students showed that almost any subject, event, or person can become a dream theme. They found that "dreams bear the unmistakable stamp of gender." Females' dreams contained more indoor scenes, while males' dreams were set out of doors more often. There was less sexual content in females' dreams, but when it did occur, the person was familiar. Males dreamed more about aggression and sex, usually with a stranger as a partner. Females emphasized emotions, while males' dreams tended to be more "action-oriented" (Begley 42).

The nature of dreams and their frequency change with age. Our earliest dreams are brief and almost without action—a child might dream of herself asleep in a bathtub, for instance. Dreams lengthen in children from five to seven years old, but the dreamer is still a passive participant. By age eight or nine, children's dreams begin to become as complex and lengthy as adult ones. But while the young tend to dream more about morality and guilt, the middle aged dream more about aggression and sexuality, and the elderly dream more of illness and death (Garfield 93).

Throughout history, humans have sought to understand the meaning of dreams. Prophets, shamans, and oracles traditionally receive divine messages through dreams. In the Bible, for example, Joseph's elucidation of Pharaoh's dream averted seven years of famine. Other cultures, according to Scientific American, have interpreted dreams as inspirational, curative, or alternative reality (Winson 86).

Dreams never seem more powerful than when they solve a problem. There's the example of Elias Howe, who was trying to invent a sewing machine and reportedly dreamed he was captured by savages carrying spears with holes in their tips. Upon waking, Howe realized he should put the thread hole for his sewing machine needle at the end, not at the middle (Begley 42). Another episode concerns a dreamer who earned a Nobel Prize. Otto Loewi, a German scientist, was researching how nerves send their signals. Did they transmit electricity or chemicals? The answer came to him in a dream on Easter Sunday, 1920.

Loewi woke and wrote it down, but in the morning, he couldn't read his writing and forgot the dream. But the next night the dream returned. He rose, went to the laboratory, and performed the experiment. He found the chemical now called acetylcholine, known to be the neurotransmitter that triggered Loewi's dream in the first place! (Dolnick 60). Of course, these cases are unique—gifts of the gods—and biochemistry cannot fully explain the creativity of dreams.

Sigmund Freud believed there are two essentially different methods of interpreting dreams. The first studies the dream's content as a whole and seeks an analogy to the dreamer's waking life. This method is called "symbolic dream interpretation." The second method is the "cipher method," since it treats the dream as a secret code in which every image can be translated by an established, universal key. The symbolic method, however, only works for a fraction of dreams, and the cipher method depends on the reliability of the dream-book key (Freud 9). For instance, one school says pointed things symbolize the penis, round, whole things represent the vagina, and rhythmic movements signify coitus. Not everyone agrees! Carl Jung felt dreams express ancestral fears and experiences. Some believe we dream our desires—the theatre of the night. I think the world of our dreams remains a riddle.

Reyzelman 4

Works Cited

Begley, Sharon. "The Stuff That Dreams Are Made Of." <u>Newsweek</u> 14 Aug.

    1989: 40–44.

Dolnick, Edward. "What Dreams Are Really Made Of." <u>Atlantic Monthly</u>

    July 1990: 41–45.

Freud, Sigmund. <u>The Interpretation of Dreams</u>. New York: Modern, 1978.

Garfield, Patricia. <u>Creative Dreaming</u>. New York: Ballantine, 1990.

Winson, Jonathan. "The Meaning of Dreams." <u>Scientific American</u> Nov.

    1990: 86–88.

APA BIBLIOGRAPHY FORMAT

The APA system has recently been revised (see *Publication Manual of the American Psychological Association*, fourth edition, 1994). Most of the changes do not affect undergraduate writers. They have to do with the elimination of bias and the application of ethical principles in scientific writing. As well, there are new guidelines for referencing electronic material (on-line and Internet documents). The following chapter reflects the format recommended in the Fourth Edition. It may be useful to summarize the major changes.

- APA now recommends a minimum one-inch margin on all sides, as this is the default on most word processors.
- Right margins are not justified, and words are not broken at the end of a line (it's recommended that you disable the hyphenation feature of your word processor).
- On formal manuscripts, the running header now goes before the title of the article.
- The first line of each reference citation is now indented as a paragraph is (generally, five spaces). All subsequent lines of each entry maintain the normal margin.
- APA now recommends the use of continuous underlining for titles and volumes of journals or magazines, including the commas before and after the volume numbers. The period is now underlined at the end of a book citation.
- You must now indicate the volume number for magazines and newsletters as well as journals. As before, don't put "Vol." in front of the volume number, and be sure to include the issue number in parentheses following the volume number if each issue of the publication is paginated separately.
- Electronic and on-line references must include an availability statement that generally indicates the protocol, directory, and file name. This replaces other publication information (see example below).

Here is a list of general rules that distinguish APA from MLA:

1. Only initials are used for first names (middle initials are also included).
2. "Works Cited" is called "References."
3. Only the first letter of all titles of articles and books is capitalized, except proper nouns and words after colons. Capitalize all major words in the titles of journals.
4. The date appears in parentheses immediately after the author's name. The year always appears first in any date used.

5. Quotation marks are not used around the titles of articles from magazines or newspapers.
6. "p." or "pp." is used before page numbers (there are some exceptions); "p." is for a single page, "pp." for consecutive multiple pages.
7. The first line of each entry is indented five spaces (one tab).
8. In the References, space only once after the periods that separate each part of a citation.

Following are some sample entries done in APA format.

Basic Book Format

Abbey, E. (1975). <u>The monkey wrench gang.</u> New York: Avon.

Book with Two or Three Authors

Flick, J., & Millward, C. (1993). <u>Handbook for writers.</u> Toronto: Harcourt.

Book with More than Three Authors
List all authors in standard APA format.

Voss, R. D., Chow, M., Hunt, A. N., & Klaeber, L. (1995). <u>Mastering the art of documentation.</u> Toronto: Scholarly.

Book with an Author and an Editor

Spenser, E. (1978). <u>The faerie queene</u> (T. P. Roche, Jr., Ed.). Markham: Penguin.

Corporate or Group Author
Give the full name of the group author, followed by the title. Use "author" to show that the author and publisher are the same.

American Psychological Association. (1994). <u>Publication manual of the American psychological association</u> (4th ed.). Washington, DC: Author.

Selection from an Anthology or Edited Book
There are no quotation marks around the title of the selection, and the word "In" tells the reader where it is found.

Kennedy, E. (1995). The marketing of Madonna. In P. Jones (Ed.), <u>Selling culture</u> (pp. 145–149). Toronto: Oxford.

Book Not in First Edition

Wyrick, J. (1993). <u>Steps to writing well</u> (5th ed.). Fort Worth: Harcourt.

Book in More than One Volume

Indicate the volume(s) consulted.

Daymond, D., & Monkman, L. (1978). <u>Literature in Canada</u> (Vols. 1–2). Toronto: Gage.

Article in an Encyclopedia

Remember to use "In" to introduce the title of the reference book.

Canada. (1993). In <u>The new encyclopaedia Britannica</u> (Vol. 3, pp. 234–239). Chicago: Encyclopaedia Britannica.

Signed articles require the author's name.

Freeman, M. A. (1988). Inuit. In <u>The Canadian encyclopedia</u> (Vol 2, p. 1084). Edmonton: Hurtig.

Lecture

Gould, S. J. (1990, April 26). <u>Wonderful life.</u> Mount Royal College Arts Lectures, Calgary, AB.

Monthly Magazine

Note that the titles of magazine or journal *articles* are not in quotation marks, while the titles of magazines are underlined. Be sure to use capitals for all periodical titles. Page references don't use the "p." or "pp." abbreviation. Include the volume number (if available).

Cannon, M. (1995, February). No boys allowed. <u>Saturday Night, *110,*</u> 18–24.

Weekly Magazine

In this case, include the precise date.

Laver, R. (1995, January 2). Mood of a nation. <u>Maclean's, *108,*</u> 10–12.

Article in a Journal with Continuous Pagination

Note that the volume number is underlined and that there is no abbreviation for page(s).

> Collier, R. M. (1983). The word processor and revision strategies. College Composition and Communication, 34, 149–155.

Article in a Journal with Separate Pagination

> Bridwell-Bowles, L. (1989). Designing research on computer-assisted writing. Computers and Composition, 7(1), 81–95.

Article in a Newspaper

> Cernetig, M. (1994, June 16). Probe ordered into hockey riot. The Globe and Mail, pp. A1, A4.

Personally Conducted Interview

In APA format, personal interviews are not included in your references. You must, however, give parenthetical documentation when citing an interview in your text: (personal communication, July 11, 1994).

Pamphlet

> Swinburne, E., & Roberts, A. (1990). Gardening tips in a short season. Inuvik: Polar Bear Garden Supplies.

Television Broadcast

Follow the standard APA format: name(s), date, title, etc.

> Long, L. (Producer), Finley, B. (Narrator). (1995, July 13). The CBC Alberta news. Calgary: CBRT-TV.

Video or Film

> Miller, J. (Producer). (1980). Antony and Cleopatra [videotape]. Toronto: BBC.

On-Line Sources

The citation for an on-line source should include an availability statement, which must indicate the protocol, directory and filename. The reference should enable the reader to find the source by following the path. Following is an example of how to document an on-line journal (available on the Internet) that is accessible to the public. The reference indicates how to get the article through FTP (File Transfer Protocol), but could just as easily include instructions for how to access it through e-mail or the World Wide Web.

Yule, J. (1995, January). Waxing Kriger [26 paragraphs]. Postmodern Culture [On-line serial], 5(2). Available FTP: Hostname: jefferson.village.virginia.edu Directory: pub/pubs/pmc/issue.195 File: yule.195

Abstracts on CD-ROM

Most conventional databases, such as abstracts and indexes, are now available on CD-ROM. The author, date, title, and publication elements are the same as the conventional APA style. Following the title and publication information, indicate the vendor, name of database, and retrieval number. There is no period at the end of the citation.

Kienetz, A. (1986). Ethnic identity in northern Canada [CD-ROM]. Journal of Ethnic Studies, 14(1), 129–134. Abstract from: Knight-Ridder File: ERIC Item: EJ 335338

SAMPLE STUDENT ESSAY USING APA DOCUMENTATION

It's best to check with your instructor to determine the information he or she wants on the title page. There is a standard format, but it refers more to papers submitted for publication than to less formal undergraduate essays. Papers written in strict APA format usually include an abstract—a summary of the content and findings—but this is often not required. The margin on the right shouldn't be justified. When in doubt, ask your professor.

The following information should be on a separate title page (see below).

1. The page header is placed at the top right of each page. Include the first two or three words from the title, and place it five spaces to the left of the page number.
2. Put the running head (abbreviated title) flush left at the top of the page (below the page header), all in uppercase letters. It should look like this: Running head: YOUR TITLE
3. The title and by-line should be centred on the page and double-spaced. Include the title, author, institution and course.

Running head: STEROID ABUSE

Steroid Abuse in Bodybuilders
Jill Cameron-Thachuk
University of Calgary
English 2201

(Please note: APA Style requires a separate title page. The text starts on a new page.)

Steroid abuse has long been a problem among professional and amateur athletes. With the findings and publicity about the adverse effects of anabolic steroids, one would think that the number of users would decrease. Instead, steroid use is becoming more prevalent. The following essay will examine the mental and physical effects of steroids by looking closely at how they are used in the sport of bodybuilding.

The abuse of anabolic steroids has its foundations in the desire to create a "wonder drug" that would enhance physical strength and muscle development. The hormone testosterone and its derivatives are found naturally in the human body and are responsible for the physical changes that occur at puberty in males, especially the change in musculature (Donohoe & Johnson, 1989, p. 39). If naturally occurring testosterone has the effect of creating muscle mass, then it is little wonder that bodybuilders use anabolic steroids, which are concentrated synthetic versions of these powerful hormones (Walder & Hainline, 1989, p. 55).

In the early fifties, Russian athletes were the first reported users of anabolic steroids. Canadian and American coaches, seeing the effects this chemical had on the Russians, were eager to try it out. Steroid use quickly spread from weight lifting and bodybuilding to other sports, including swimming, baseball, football, running, and gymnastics (Walder & Hainline, p. 56).

Since then, bodybuilders have adopted anabolic steroids as their drug of choice. Tricker (1989) found that 54% of male bodybuilders and 10% of female bodybuilders in his sample all reported the regular use of some anabolic steroids. When they were asked the reasons for using these drugs, they identified the desire to win as the main motive (pp. 313–325). In fact, it is almost impossible for the average bodybuilder to stay on top in competition without the use of steroids.

How do athletes get away with this if the drugs are banned and testing is done regularly? The answer is simple: it is easy to fix the evidence. Samples of urine are taken from the athletes, but the actual process goes unsupervised. Athletes who are non-users will donate a sample of their urine for friends who are users. Another way the athlete can escape drug testing is to take drugs that dilute the urine, making the steroid undetectable (Walder & Hainline, p. 67). In the sport of bodybuilding, drug testing has been particularly sloppy, for the professional organizations may have a stake in maintaining the bulked-up look that is the unmistakable sign of steroid use.

Athletes often pay dearly for such performance enhancement. Dolan (1992) describes a number of health problems and side-effects of anabolic steroid use. Water retention often leads to what is called "steroid bloat." To counter this problem, athletes ingest diuretics to rid the body of excess fluids. This can lead to dehydration, excessive urination, electrolyte depletion, and even heart failure (p. 38). According to Dolan, the "types of damage caused by steroids are usually not reversible—meaning that the damage will not disappear when usage is stopped—when steroids have been taken heavily for prolonged periods" (p. 39).

The psychological effects of steroid use can be just as devastating. Lubell (1989) describes the increased potential for steroids to induce violent antisocial behaviour: "Some research shows the danger of steroids in inducing severe, adverse psychiatric effects. Certain lawyers use this abuse to plead insanity for their clients" (p. 176). Dolan describes wild mood swings as a common side-effect, in addition to disturbed sleep, aggressive behaviour, and even a kind of addictive dependence on getting the drug regularly in order to feel good (pp. 44–45).

Despite all of the evidence of physical and psychological damage, bodybuilders are willing to take the risk because they are convinced that the results are worth it. There is no doubt that steroids increase body mass. Kuipers, Wijnen, Hartgens, and Willems (1991) tested male bodybuilders who received weekly injections of steroids for eight weeks, against a control group who received placebo injections. Both groups increased their body mass, although the increase in the group who received the anabolic steroids was obviously superior (pp. 413–418). This simply corroborates what bodybuilders have known all along—they can have bigger muscles more quickly by using steroids regularly.

Athletes are trained to win, sometimes even at the cost of their lives. Many turn a blind eye to the facts about steroids, risking everything for a stronger, more muscular body. Perhaps the problem of drug abuse in sports has its origins in a culture that makes athletes media celebrities and promotes winning as the highest good. The old notions of doing your best, working hard for results, and playing fair have been challenged by the power of these drugs to create supermen and superwomen without the usual struggle. We must continue to improve the ways of testing for steroids so that sports can become (again) a real test of human potential and not a measure of chemical manipulation.

Steroid Abuse   4

References

Dolan, E. F. (1992). Drugs in sports (2nd rev. ed.). Toronto: Watts.

Donohoe, T., & Johnson, N. (1989). Foul play. New York: Blackwell.

Kuipers, H., Wijnen, J., Hartgens, F., & Willems, S. (1991). Influences on body composition, blood pressure, lipid profile and liver functions in body builders. International Journal of Sports Medicine, 12(4), 413–418.

Lubell, A. (1989). Does steroid abuse cause—or excuse—violence? Journal of Physical and Sports Medicine, 17(2), 176.

Tricker, R. (1989). The incidence of anabolic steroid use among competitive bodybuilders. Journal of Drug Addiction, 19(4), 313–325.

Walder, G. I., & Hainline, B. (1989). Drugs and the athlete. In A. J. Ryan (Ed.), Contemporary exercise and sports medicine (pp. 55–75). Philadelphia: Davis.

Writing Suggestions and Class Discussions

1. Ten years from now—in your chosen career—what two research projects are likely to come your way?

2. What research does your employer need done now?

3. List three topics you'd like to research in school.

4. What topic would you like to research for personal use (consumer, health, or hobby topics, for instance)?

5. Take one topic or research project from writing suggestions 1–4 and do a brainteaser list of key research questions. What do you want to know?

6. Narrow two of these topics until they interest you:

    Changing family patterns

    Advertising

    Medieval castles

    Religious principles

7. Make a list of key research questions and do a brainteaser list on one narrowed topic from 6.

8. Suppose you had to write a research report on one of the following. Without actually doing the research, make up a list of places to go for information—in the library and elsewhere. Be specific about the headings you'd search under in catalogues or indexes.

    Violent patients in hospitals

    Abstract art

    Solar-heated houses

    Students' rights in your school

9. Pick any famous historical event that happened since 1920: the stock market crash of 1929, the bombing of Pearl Harbor, or the first moon landing, for example. Use *The New York Times Index* to locate an article written on the topic; use *The Reader's Guide to Periodical Literature* to locate a second article. Or use a computerized index to find two articles. Find and read the articles, summarizing both and quoting one strong sentence from each. Turn in your notes with complete bibliographic information attached.

10. Do the same as in 9, but use a book and a reference book as sources. You only need to read enough to fill out one note card for each.

11. Look up your local newspaper for the day you were born. What were the main headlines on that day? For fun, name a headline that secretly "announced" your birth ("Budget Deficit Again" or "Madman Holds Bank at Bay," for example). Explain why it fits you.

12. Do the same for a weekly magazine such as *Maclean's* or *Time*.

13. Using an almanac, find an interesting fact about each of the following topics. Be sure to include complete bibliographic information and page numbers. Comment on the significance of each fact.

>   Crime
>
>   Marriage
>
>   Sports
>
>   Ecology

14. Find a non-reference section book source for one of the topics in 13 and quote a short section you find interesting. Then paraphrase and condense the material, keeping only a key phrase or two in quotes. Comment on the material and include bibliographic information.

15. Combine 13 and 14 into a short (one- or two-page) research paper.

16. Here's a list of current topics for research:

>   Doctor-assisted suicide for the terminally ill
>
>   Overcrowded national parks
>
>   Reducing the federal deficit
>
>   Laws protecting homosexuals from discrimination
>
>   Illegal immigrants
>
>   Confidentiality in AIDS testing
>
>   Single fathers
>
>   Characteristics of Generation X
>
>   Salaries of athletes
>
>   Canadian national identity

Peer groups will develop research questions for one topic and establish a list of sources to contact or read.

17. Bibliography Exercise: Find 10 sources on a topic on which you might write a research paper. Try for a mix of books, reference works, magazines, and newspapers. Assemble your list in proper bibliographic form.

18. Find three reviews of a book you enjoyed reading. Try using *The Canadian Book Review Annual* or some other index. Write a one-page paper summarizing the reception the book had, citing each source and giving a proper bibliography. Also, comment on the reviews.

19. Write a research paper (consider expanding any of the above assignments).

>   Choose a topic and narrow it.
>
>   Make a list of key research questions.
>
>   Assemble a list of sources to answer these questions.
>
>   Take notes and comment on the sources.
>
>   Write the draft.
>
>   Revise the draft.

20. Write a thorough research paper on a career you're considering entering. Combine library and non-library resources, including one formal interview with a person who holds the kind of job you want. Your list of key research questions should target all the hard information you want to know about the career—the gutsy, naked truth about its ecstasies and agonies. Finally, evaluate your research and decide if this career fits your interests and abilities.

✔ **PEER-REVIEW CHECKLIST: RESEARCH**

Author: _____

One aspect of this draft I'd like the reviewer to comment on is:

Reviewer: _____

	STRONG	AVERAGE	WEAK
INTRODUCTION: purpose clear?			
IDEAS: fresh, insightful?			
DETAILS: plenty of them vivid enough?			
ORGANIZATION: logical, easy to follow?			
CITATIONS: proper format? research smoothly worked in?			
BIBLIOGRAPHY: proper format?			

Respond to the author's request.

What is the strongest part of the paper?

Give two suggestions for improvement.
1.

2.

Chapter 14

Handbook of
English

Sanity is perhaps the
ability to punctuate.

W.H. Auden

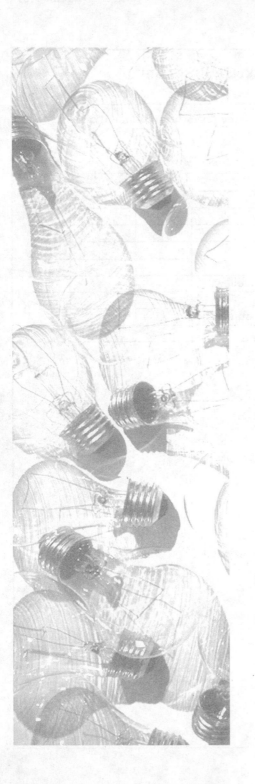

*T*his handbook is a simplified guide to correct writing. It covers the most common, serious errors in punctuation, sentence structure, and usage. If you attend graduate school or write for publication, you should add a more complete handbook to your reference library. But for undergraduate writing, this should be adequate 95% of the time.

You should refer to this handbook *after* you've written your paper. Don't let commas and capitalization distract you from stringing good ideas together or from searching for vivid, exact words to express your ideas. But *do* use the handbook before your final draft is typed. A great idea described with sentence fragments is like the Mona Lisa smoking a cigar—who can appreciate its beauty? In the resume that lists your academic achievements, should you stumble over those three stooges—"their," "there," and "they're"—a potential employer might decide you can't tell the difference between a debit and a credit either.

CORRECTNESS AND THE ENGLISH LANGUAGE

If you've ever diagrammed sentences or been asked to define a nonrestrictive adjectival clause, you know Egyptian hieroglyphics can be easier to master than grammar. However, don't blame your English teachers. The complicated rules simply record the various ways we use our language. If people hadn't been creative hundreds of years ago, we wouldn't have irregular verbs. If people in the past hadn't sometimes left out connecting words in sentences or experimented with new sentence structures, that tiny terror—the comma— might not even exist today. English teachers only report people's standard practice.

Imagine for a moment what it was like before we had a system of grammar. William Caxton, the man who compiled the first English dictionary back in 1490, did so because he was fed up with all the varieties of English being used. There were no formal rules for language then, and people became so inventive that Caxton said he couldn't understand a book written in the English of 200 years earlier. The language had changed tremendously even since his birth. Once, not far from his London home, Caxton grew hungry and knocked on a farmhouse door. He asked the woman who lived there if he could buy some eggs ("eggys") from her. The farmwife answered that she didn't speak French. Caxton snapped back that he wasn't speaking French but "goode englishe." They needed a mediator to translate his "eggys" to her "eyren." After many such confusing incidents, Caxton decided the country needed a dictionary to make the meaning and spelling of words the same throughout the land. Over the next 200 years, people decided they should no longer capitalize or punctuate according to individual feeling, but only for definite reasons. "Rules" of grammar were born.

Rules not only help us to understand each other today but also slow down the evolution of English so we can understand our past and so future people can understand us. Study the following versions of the same biblical passage from different years. They are all correct English for their day.

1. About 1000: Ure Faedir, þu þe eart on heofonum, si þin nama gehalgod. Tocume þin rice. Geweor þe þin willa on eorþan swa-swa on heofonum.
2. About 1390: Oure fadir that art in heuenes, halewid be thi name. This kyngdom come to. Be thi wille don in earthe as in heune.
3. 1611: Our father which art in heauen, Halowed be thy name. Thy kingdome come. Thy will be done, in earth as it is in heauen.
4. 1952: Our father who art in heaven, Hallowed be thy name. Thy kingdom come, Thy will be done. On earth as it is in heaven.

Notice how much more our language changed in the early years. This was largely the result of not having fixed rules. When the Normans invaded England in 1066, thousands of French words, spellings, and sentence structures simply mixed haphazardly with what the native English already spoke and wrote. Different regions went their own way, making governmental, cultural, educational, and even religious communication a nightmare. Caxton's dictionary and, in 1611, King James's Bible further standardized English vocabulary, grammar, and usage. Notice also that while change has slowed, it hasn't stopped, as new words, especially those reflecting technological or scientific change, become part of the language every year.

SPEAKING, WRITING, AND GRAMMAR

In informal conversation, we rarely worry about whether our sentences are grammatically correct. So why is it so crucial when we write?

As we have just seen, the rules of grammar describe the correct way to put words together. They evolved so that we could better understand each other when we speak or write: grammar standardizes language to enhance communication.

Our speech is held together by grammar, otherwise we wouldn't understand each other: we'd talk in a stream of meaningless gibberish. But the rules often get bent in the rush of talk. We often use incomplete and fragmented constructions, and we don't worry about it (unless we're talking with an English professor) because the conventions of conversation are relaxed. If we were making a formal presentation to a class or a client, then we would probably be much more careful about the form of our spoken language. It all depends on the expectations of our audience.

When we speak, our words fly by and are quickly lost, replaced by other people's words or silence. But when we write, our language is permanently fixed on the page for future inspection.

In written communication, we connect individual words into units that express complete ideas: that is what sentences are. Punctuation allows the reader to see where these units begin and end. Paragraphs are groups of related sentences that explore or develop a topic. Indentation is used to indicate when paragraphs begin and end.

The conventions of grammar and punctuation have evolved to make written communication understandable and clear. It is obviously more formal than speech. For example, when writing we don't run sentences and paragraphs together as we might do when speaking. In conversation, we may be asked to clarify a point, but when we write, the reader often doesn't have access to the writer, so the writer can't be approached to explain what he or she meant.

When sentences are grammatically correct and punctuation is properly placed, writing possesses a kind of unity that should enhance understanding. But not all grammatically correct writing is good or effective writing. It is certainly possible to compose an essay of unintelligent yet grammatically correct discourse. But when the rules of grammar are followed, even empty writing has a more sophisticated shape.

Again, the importance of grammar relates to the expectations of your audience. If you're writing a letter to your friend back home, it may not matter if you throw in the occasional sentence fragment or run-on. But if you're applying for a job, it may mean the difference between rejection and an interview. Correct grammar says something about our education and position in society. Whether we like it or not, we are measured by our proficiency in written language, and therefore it is important to understand a few basic principles.

 ## A BRIEF REVIEW OF TERMS

English grammar can be very confusing, mostly because there is so much terminology and so many obscure rules. For most writers, the exercise of identifying each part of speech will not necessarily translate into prose that is grammatically flawless. Most English handbooks make the obvious seem complicated. They take things that most writers do intuitively and break them down into obscure little parts, each with its neat label and set of instructions. This section presents a few important terms, not because it is essential to memorize them, but because we need a common vocabulary with which to begin our discussion of grammar and punctuation. Following, then, are a few simplified definitions.

Nouns

A noun is the name of a person, place, idea, thing, or quality. It can be concrete, abstract, proper, singular, plural, or possessive. It is the most easily recognizable element of a sentence.

Pronouns

A pronoun takes the place of a noun. The word it replaces is called its *antecedent*—something that goes before—and it should always be clear to the reader what the pronoun is replacing. You are familiar with the obvious personal pronouns.

Singular: I, you, he/she, him, her, it

Plural: you, we, them, they, us

Possessive singular: my, mine, your, yours, his, hers, its

Possessive plural: our, ours, your, yours, their, theirs

But you may not recognize the following words as pronouns: who, whose, which, that, those, myself, themselves, all, anyone, each, anybody, few, many.

Verbs

Verbs express an action or a state of being. The action verbs are easy: She *studies* grammar. In this case, "studies" is the action that she performs. States of being are sometimes a little trickier. In these cases, we use a *linking verb* to show the relationship between the subject (see below) and its complement: She *is* confused. Here "is" describes her existence in this condition.

Helping verbs limit or modify the action of main verbs. The most common include shall, will, would, should, might, may, can, could, be, do. Example: She *may study* grammar.

Adjectives

Adjectives modify or describe nouns and pronouns.

The *sadistic* computer just ate my *perfect* essay.

He is baffled by all the *obscure* jargon.

Adverbs

Adverbs modify or describe verbs, adjectives, or other adverbs.

I read the instructions *carefully*, but it didn't help.

I purchased an *extremely* large salmon.

The clerk acted *very rudely* to the customers.

Prepositions

A preposition is linked to a noun or a pronoun (the object of the preposition) to indicate a relationship in time or space. Here are some common prepositions: to, by, from, as, at, above, below, for, in, during, on, off, of, until, than, through, despite, near, over, with.

The preposition and its object form a prepositional phrase. Here is a sentence with a prepositional phrase: She was happy *until the end*.

Conjunctions

Conjunctions are connecting words. The *coordinating conjunctions* (and, but, for, so, or, nor, yet) connect words, phrases, or clauses. The effect is always balanced—the conjunction coordinates grammatical units of equal value. Example: I want to buy mangoes, papayas, pineapples, *and* grapes for my fruit salad. Here the coordinating conjunction connects the final unit of a list to those that precede it. Coordinating conjunctions often connect two independent clauses to make a compound sentence (see below).

Correlative conjunctions perform a similar connecting function, but they work in pairs: both/and, either/or, neither/nor, not only/but also, whether/or.

Subordinating conjunctions introduce subordinate or dependent clauses and create a dependent relationship with the rest of the sentence. The subordinate clause conveys incomplete information and needs an independent clause in order to convey the whole idea. Here are some subordinating conjunctions: although, before, as, if, since, when, where, while. Example: *Although* English is my first language, I don't know all of the rules.

Subjects and Predicates

Every sentence has a subject. It is the thing or person that acts, is acted upon, or exists in some fashion. Every subject can be found in relation to a verb, which describes an action or a state of being. Here is the simplest kind of subject-verb relationship: *Elizabeth moves gracefully*. Here "Elizabeth" is the subject or agent of action, and the verb "moves" and its modifying adverb "gracefully" describe the condition of the subject. There are many variations on this subject-verb theme, but all involve the notion of agency: in every sentence, there is a thing or a person (subject) that is acting or existing in some condition (predicate). The predicate is the verb and its modifiers. In the example above, "moves gracefully" is the complete predicate.

Sentences, of course, are not usually so simple. Subjects can be more complicated than a single word; when this is the case, the complete subject can include all sorts of associated words: *Elizabeth's long, muscular legs* move gracefully. The variations of subject and predicate create all the intricate patterns of sentence construction. We can have subjects after the verb, parallel pairs of subjects and predicates, and any number of modifiers that add colour and detail to nouns and verbs.

SENTENCE STRUCTURE

INDEPENDENT AND DEPENDENT CLAUSES

The most important material of sentence construction is the clause, which is a group of related words that has a subject and a verb. As we have seen, it is not difficult to identify the subject and the verb in a clause: the subject is the thing that acts or exists, and the verb is the word that indicates an action or a state of being. In every clause, there will be an agent that either does something or exists in some state.

Examine the following clauses.

1. The cat came back.
2. Go to bed.
3. Although the program was over.
4. If I am allowed.
5. When I am well enough.

It's easy to see that these examples fulfil the definition of a clause: the words are related, and there is a subject and a verb. It becomes a little trickier, however, when we consider the two kinds of clauses: independent and dependent.

An *independent clause can stand alone* because it forms a complete idea. It must have a subject and a verb; that is part of our definition of a clause. But most importantly, it must be able to stand by itself (independently) as a finished statement. Every sentence must have at least one independent clause, or it is not a sentence. The independent clause is the foundation or core of sentence building. There must be at least one complete idea at the heart of every sentence, or it will not hold together.

A *dependent clause*, on the other hand, *cannot stand alone*. It is incomplete and needs something else in order to finish its idea. It must be connected to an independent clause; it cannot function grammatically on its own. In any case, it doesn't make sense by itself.

Let's look again at the list of clauses above. Which ones are dependent, and which ones are independent?

1. The cat came back.

This is the simplest kind of sentence. It is made up of one independent clause, contains a subject and a verb, and makes complete sense by itself. An independent clause and a simple sentence are the same thing. Every complex sentence must have at least one of these at its core.

2. Go to bed.

The second example is also an independent clause. In this case, the subject is not actually present, but it is understood: (You) go to bed. The command is a completely independent statement; there is no confusion, doubt, or ambiguity. It fulfils the requirements of an independent clause or simple sentence. There is an understood subject, a verb, and a complete idea.

3. Although the program was over.

Obviously, there is something incomplete about this statement; we recognize this immediately because it begins with a subordinating conjunction. There is a subject (program) and a verb (was over), so the group of words fulfils the definition of a clause. But we are left hanging. Something happened, even though the program ended. What was it?

Although the program was over, we were still unsatisfied.

Although the program was over, I couldn't get the images of death out of my head.

Although the program was over, Karen sat mesmerized in front of the screen.

I was still in the mood to watch television, although the program was over.

In these cases, we have connected the dependent clause, "although the program was over," to an independent clause in order to complete the idea and make a grammatically correct sentence. The dependent clause cannot stand alone because the idea that it puts forward is unfinished.

By adding a dependent clause to an independent clause, we discover a new world of sentence complexity. The dependent clause adds important information to the main clause of the sentence and creates a more finished structure.

The next two clauses pose the same problem. They need to be connected to something else in order to make sense.

4. If I am allowed.

If I am allowed, I will stay up and watch the eclipse.

Next year, if I am allowed, I will get my pilot's licence.

After the semester ends, I will move out of the house, if I am allowed.

5. When I am well enough.

I sometimes think that when I am well enough, I will travel around the world.

When I am well enough, I will eat lots of greasy food.

I will go back to school and learn about clauses when I am well enough.

All of these dependent clauses are easy to connect to main clauses because they begin with subordinating conjunctions. A dependent clause is sometimes called a subordinate clause because it needs an independent clause in order to function grammatically. The subordinating conjunctions express this relationship. Each conjunction creates a different kind of dependent relationship to the sentence's core. For example, *after, before, since, until,* and *when* create a relationship of time, while *although* and *whereas* describe a relationship of contrast.

Some sentences begin with a dependent clause connected by a comma to an independent clause: When I am well enough, I will eat tons of greasy food. Some sentences begin with an independent clause connected to a dependent clause. The comma is optional in this case: I will go back to school and learn about clauses[,] when I am well enough.

These examples show the remarkable flexibility of the English language. Every sentence must have its core statement, the independent clause. But its placement is variable. It may even be surrounded by multiple dependent clauses, as in this example: Although I enjoy cutting the grass, I'd rather sit in the backyard and drink beer, even though the delicious calories make my tummy grow and tighten my belt. Here the main clause is surrounded by two dependent clauses that begin with subordinating conjunctions.

It is even possible to split the main clause and surround it with dependent clauses. Example: I am, although I cannot prove my current state of consciousness, one with the universe, despite the fact that my personality is somewhat fragmented. The main clause is "I am one with the universe." The dependent clauses are "although I cannot prove my current state of consciousness" and "despite the fact that my personality is somewhat fragmented." The art of sentence structure is based on the creative arrangement of clauses, and the possibilities are unlimited, as long as the sentence has at least one main clause at its core.

The choice of which clause to begin with is based on the effect you want to produce: I will go back to school and learn about clauses, when I am well enough. Here the core statement is emphasized because it comes first. You emphatically state your intention right from the start: "I will go back to school and learn about clauses." This declaration is followed by a dependent idea that describes a condition of time: "when I am well enough." If you wanted to emphasize this limitation, you'd place it at the beginning: When I am well enough, I will go back to school and learn about clauses.

The arrangement of dependent and independent ideas changes the effect of a sentence. Our choices, therefore, can subtly influence a reader's response to our writing. The placement of every word is significant. If we begin with the independent clause, we are emphasizing the core idea and following it with a causal, temporal, or contrary condition. Or we may choose to begin with a dependent clause in order to emphasize the limitation.

■ *Practice 14-1:* The following pairs of sentences show how independent and dependent clauses can be combined to achieve different effects. Consider the relationship between the two main ideas in each sentence: the one that is dependent and the one that contains the sentence core. Describe how the order of clauses affects the reader's response.

1. a. He barged into my office, as if he deserved a higher mark on the paper.

   b. Although he barged into my office, I did not give him a higher mark on the paper.

2. a. When you are finished eating that disgusting, chocolate-covered, cream-filled delicacy, please wipe your mouth.

   b. Wipe your mouth after you are finished eating that disgusting, chocolate-covered, cream-filled delicacy.

3. a. Whether you know it or not, the government has its hand in your pocket.

   b. The government, whether you know it or not, is stealing from you at every turn.

   c. The government has picked your pocket, whether you know it or not.

4. a. You will have to appear in court unless you remove the jungle of dandelions in front of your house.

   b. Unless you remove the jungle of dandelions in front of your house, you will have to appear in court.

5. a. Even though terrorists blew up the Uffizi gallery, we are still going to Florence.

   b. We are still going to Florence, even though the Uffizi gallery is in shambles.

6. a. I turned on the television, although I knew that I would be disappointed.

   b. Even before I turned on the television, I knew that I would be disappointed.

7. a. As far as I am concerned, the senators should all be sent out to pasture.

   b. The senators should all be fired, because the senate is not a democratic institution.

8. a. If you are going to chew tobacco, please go outside.

   b. Please go outside if you are planning to spit brown juice.

9. a. Although you can memorize all the nit-picking rules of grammar, you will probably forget how to apply them.

   b. You will probably forget how to apply the nit-picking rules of grammar, even though you have memorized them.

10. a. I would advise you not to touch that cable, unless you are unconcerned about your future condition.

    b. Unless you are unhappy with your present incarnation, I would advise you not to touch that cable.

■ *Practice 14-2:* Look at the following sentences and again consider the way the clauses are arranged. Compose one or two of your own sentences for each example by rearranging the clauses or by making dependent structures independent and vice versa.

1. While Rome burned and Nero fiddled, I lit the barbecue and turned on the stereo.
2. Despite my best intentions, I was simply exhausted, although I had eaten enough and had had plenty of sleep the night before.
3. If it rains another day, my seeds will rot in the ground.
4. Thousands of people, although they lack running water, are living in refugee camps all over the world.
5. Even though the *Sun* has better pictures, I would rather read the *Globe and Mail.*
6. As long as my kids brush their teeth every night, they will continue to have no cavities.
7. Baseball is a more intellectual game than hockey because fans have time to think and philosophize between pitches.
8. You will learn how to make wonderfully complicated sentences when you master the art of combining clauses.
9. Mr. speaker, despite the fact that my learned colleague is a horse's ass, I am forced to grant him a little respect.
10. Since I started paying attention to the sound of my writing, I have come to appreciate the sweet music of a well-constructed sentence.

PHRASES

Unlike an independent clause, a phrase can never stand alone. Phrases differ from clauses because they contain a subject or a predicate, but never both. They are perhaps the most common word groups in the English language: bunches of related words that function as nouns, verbs, adverbs, or adjectives. Following are some examples.

Prepositional Phrases
These include prepositions and their objects (see above) and usually function as adjectives or adverbs in a sentence. Example: The man *with the funny smell* sat next to me on the bus. Here "with the funny smell" is a prepositional phrase that modifies the noun "man."

Verbal Phrases
These ones get a little complicated. A verbal is a verb form that doesn't convey the usual action or state of being; instead, it functions as a noun, adverb, or adjective. There are three kinds of verbals: *gerunds, participles,* and *infinitives.* Gerunds and participles are often the "ing" form of the verb

(although the past participle always ends in "ed"). Gerunds function as nouns in a sentence: *Walking* is great exercise. Here "walking" is a gerund because it functions as a noun. Participles usually act as adjectives: Her *dancing* feet moved across the floor, despite her *bruised* ankles. Both "dancing" and "bruised" are participles that function as adjectives. The infinitive is the "to" form of the verb. It can also function as a noun, adjective, or adverb.

Verbal phrases include the associated words that surround the verbal and contribute to its function as noun, adjective, or adverb.

> *Gerund phrase: Writing with a computer* can be very rewarding. (functions as a noun/subject)

> *Participial phrase:* The student *wearing the baseball cap backward* looks very silly. (functions as an adjective modifying "the student")

> *Infinitive phrase:* Amy can't stand *to wait in line*. (functions as an adverb modifying "can't stand")

Absolute Phrases

These always include a participle and are found as elements that begin or end a sentence. Examples:

> *Having studied phrases and clauses*, I can now construct complicated sentences.

> I woke from my nightmare, *tossing my sheets and sweating profusely*.

■ *Practice 14-3:* Label the phrases and clauses in the following sentences. Make sure each sentence has an independent clause or clauses. Remember that phrases are often contained within clauses—a phrase may serve, for example, as the subject of an independent clause.

1. Working hard from dawn until dusk, the professor marks paper after paper, although she knows that the students will never read her comments.

2. Even though the problems in Quebec are still unresolved, I have faith that the country, with all its divisions, will still hold together.

3. In this country, while we now take air travel for granted, we used to have to take the train to travel any distance.

4. I couldn't wait to hear the new Rolling Stones CD, even though I knew they were past their prime.

5. After supper, watching *The Flintstones* gives me indigestion, but my kids seem to enjoy it.

SENTENCE TYPES

Sentences can be categorized according to four types: *simple, compound, complex, compound-complex*. You should understand how these differ if you want to become aware of the potential for variety in your writing. If you use one type over and over, your writing will become monotonous, choppy, or cumbersome. Most good writers like to use a variety of sentence types to create changes in rhythm and emphasis.

Simple Sentence
A simple sentence is made up of one independent clause and any number of phrases: In the morning, I like to drink one cup of strong coffee.

Compound Sentence
A compound sentence is made up of two or more independent clauses and any number of phrases: At the beginning of the semester, I like writing essays, and I usually get them written on time.

Complex Sentence
A complex sentence is made up of one independent clause, at least one subordinate clause, and any number of phrases: While you were doing the dishes, I pulled all the weeds in the garden with my bare hands.

Compound-Complex Sentence
A compound-complex sentence contains two or more independent clauses, at least one subordinate clause, and any number of phrases: In the beginning, I had high hopes for my car, and I expected to get at least one year out of it, although I didn't feel very good about the blue smoke coming out of the exhaust.

COMMON SENTENCE ERRORS

SENTENCE FRAGMENT

The "normal" English sentence has a subject, a verb, and possibly a modifier (adjectives or adverbs that modify or describe nouns and verbs). Anything less is a sentence fragment or incomplete sentence. Why do English teachers make a big deal about it? Because it shows whether or not you recognize the basic unit of the language. (Psst—the previous sentence is a fragment.)

Most sentence fragments are not like the following: "John the house early" or "Left the house early." Most fragments occur in complex collections of words where one of two things usually happens: the writer, nervous about writing a long sentence, makes a break even though there's no grammatical reason to do so, or the writer confuses a verb form with a main verb.

Look at the following examples of fragments.

Margaret put away her teddy bear, kissed her goldfish goodbye, and tore up the photos of her high school boyfriend when she headed off to college. *Which turned out to have more fish than good-looking guys.*

The first college guy she dated reminded her of her guppy. *Because he puckered every time she looked at him.*

Margaret asked the guy to take her to the aquarium to meet his family, and he agreed. *Making her wish for the boys of high school.*

Each is a typical fragment that should be attached to the previous sentence. The first fragment lacks a subject—it needs to refer back to "college" to make sense. The second does have a subject and a verb, but it begins with a "because," which turns what follows into a *dependent clause*. It *depends* on the first part to have complete meaning. The third fragment has a verb form ("making"), but it is a participle, not a main verb, and lacks a subject.

Beware of these key words: because, since, if, although, as, who, which, words ending in "ing." If any of these words begins a sentence, it should be in an introductory phrase or clause with a comma separating it from the main subject and verb. If not, you've probably written a fragment that should be joined to the sentence preceding it.

There are legitimate uses of sentence fragments: use them to answer your rhetorical questions or in dramatic scenes to create a fragmented impression. Examples:

Why do politicians lie to the public? Because the public wants to be lied to.

Whack! The stick caught the side of his head. Whack! Dizzy. Spinning images of the windows. Whack! Sal went down.

In most formal writing, however, sentence fragments are unacceptable. If you want to use them for rhetorical effect, then make sure your instructor understands your intention, or they may be counted as grammatical errors.

RUN-ON SENTENCE (FUSED SENTENCES) AND COMMA SPLICE

A run-on sentence is two sentences joined together without proper punctuation. What difference does it make? Consider this invitation sent to a professor for an end-of-semester party: Come to the party and forget your exams spouses and other attached persons are welcome. Are the people attending the party supposed to forget their exams as well as their spouses? In this case, the writer should have either substituted a semicolon for the comma or put a period there and capitalized the "s" in "spouses."

Comma splices are the same as run-ons, except that a comma is used to splice two complete sentences together: Although I understand some principles of punctuation, I don't always remember the details, they can be so obscure. "They can be so obscure" is an independent clause, and you can't use a comma to attach an independent clause to another sentence.

Following are three ways to fix run-ons and comma splices (see also the section on punctuation, below).

1. Use a period to separate the two sentences.
2. Use a semicolon to indicate that there is a related sentence on either side.
3. Use a comma and a coordinating conjunction.

The choice of whether to use a period, a semicolon, or a comma and a conjunction will depend on the emphasis the writer wants to achieve. Two complete sentences make the ideas more separate than does a semicolon, which separates the ideas but keeps them together in the same sentence. A comma and a coordinating conjunction indicate a clear relationship between the two parts, depending on the conjunction that is used—"and" shows a parallel relationship, while "but" indicates a contradiction.

Below are other examples of run-ons and comma splices, followed by corrections.

1. From the parking lot, Emily listened to the roar of the jets landing at the airport she wished she were going somewhere.

   a. From the parking lot, Emily listened to the roar of the jets landing at the airport. She wished she were going somewhere.

   b. From the parking lot, Emily listened to the roar of the jets landing at the airport; she wished she were going somewhere.

   c. From the parking lot, Emily listened to the roar of the jets landing at the airport, and she wished she were going somewhere.

2. Tom's biology experiment had an unexpected result, his frog grabbed a scalpel and hopped for freedom.

   a. Tom's biology experiment had an unexpected result. His frog grabbed a scalpel and hopped for freedom.

   b. Tom's biology experiment had an unexpected result; his frog grabbed a scalpel and hopped for freedom.

3. The security guards pursued the frog toward the student cafeteria, however, the amphibian made good its escape.

   a. The security guards pursued the frog toward the student cafeteria; however, the amphibian made good its escape.

   b. The security guards pursued the frog toward the student cafeteria. However, the amphibian made good its escape.

   c. The security guards pursued the frog toward the student cafeteria, but the amphibian made good its escape.

"However" (along with "moreover," "also," "nevertheless," "therefore," "thus," etc.) is a conjunctive adverb, not a coordinating conjunction.

When you use it to separate two independent clauses, you must use a semicolon before and a comma after.

You can begin sentences with conjunctive adverbs, but such introductory elements are usually followed by a comma. Likewise, you can use a conjunctive adverb to separate two halves of an independent clause. Note that it is bracketed on both sides by a comma: The amphibian, however, made good its escape.

MISPLACED MODIFIERS

A modifier is a word or a group of words that describes or adds details to another word or group of words. The italicized sections in these examples are modifiers:

He played *the Baldwin grand piano*.

With tenderness, Rudolph rocked *the beautiful, bald baby*.

A modifier must be placed next to the thing it modifies, or it may accidentally describe something else with comic results:

For sale: One maple table by elderly lady *with chipped legs*. (an actual newspaper ad)

I was on my way to the doctor's *with rear end trouble* when my car's rear axle gave way, causing the accident. (from an actual insurance claim form)

The accident was caused by a little guy in a small car *with a big mouth*.

The placement of one modifying word can change the meaning of a sentence. How do the following sentences differ?

In the poker game, John almost won $500.

In the poker game, John won almost $500.

Consider this gruesome, unintended meaning:

Misplaced: The police arrested a man in the Mt. Hope Cemetery who said he was digging up corpses trying to make some extra money.

Corrected: The police arrested a man digging up corpses in the Mt. Hope Cemetery; he said he was doing it to make some extra money.

The following are actual newspaper headlines. Where do the modifiers really belong?

Calf born to farmer with two heads.

Man shot in head accidentally dies.

Or in this letter from a woman to the social services department:

In answer to your letter, I have given birth to twins in the enclosed envelope. (The thing modified isn't even present here!)

■ *Practice 14-4:* Correct any run-on sentences, comma splices, sentence fragments, or misplaced modifiers in the following.

WHAT YOUR PROFESSOR'S OFFICE TELLS YOU

A <u>Campus News</u> Special Report
Angela Johnson, Social Editor

So you're thinking about visiting your professor in his or her office? Cornering the lion in its den. As a veteran faculty-watcher, let me tip off incoming freshmen about what to expect.

Relax if you see family pictures on the professor's desk, a child's hand-made pencil holder or a finger painting means you're in real luck. You might even be offered a cup of coffee, this professor is a pussycat, no lion. With chubby, sticky cheeks, your professor loves children; how can you go wrong?

But covered with debris and centuries of dust, the professor in the messy office will be a trial. You won't be able to sit though, he'll have the chair stacked with old magazines and memos. Which he can't find time to read because he worries about the meaning of life and where his grade book is. Crammed with unopened letters, his mind is as disorganized as his office.

Professor Neat, is a steel trap. Beware! A polished desk, an empty wastebasket, and a coat hung on a hanger instead of flung over a chair are warning signs, you should enter with care. Because Professor Neat plans to vacuum clean your mind with ruthless efficiency.

 # PUNCTUATION

Punctuation is a quiet signal to an experienced reader. You don't stop to think, "What does an apostrophe or comma mean?" You absorb the punctuation without thinking, as you do with small words such as "if" or "and."

When you mispunctuate, readers can usually figure out what you intended to say, but you make them read twice what should only have to be read once, you put doubts in their minds about the clarity of your ideas, and you may give them an entirely wrong idea. For instance, read the first sentence in this paragraph without the first comma. Doesn't it sound for a second that you're punctuating readers?

Sometimes punctuation errors can be more serious than making someone reread a sentence. Look at these two sentences:

All foreign fruit plants and vegetable seeds are free from duty.

All foreign fruit, plants, and vegetable seeds are free from duty.

The first means that young trees and bushes that will bear fruit and any vegetable seeds may enter the country duty-free. The second means that all fruit as well as plants and seeds are duty-free. Imagine the difference the first comma would make in the interpretation of import duties and accompanying revenues.

COMMA

Beyond a doubt, the comma is punctuation enemy number one. So we're starting with it to prove you can handle it; other punctuation will be a snap.

At the outset, let's forget the two extremes of comma theory. One school says, "Put commas wherever you hear a pause." The other recites rules in high-tech tweedle: "Use a comma to set off a conjunctive adverb when used in the middle of a sentence, except when the conjunctive adverb is next to a verb." Both extremes lead to trouble. Commas frequently do coincide with pauses, but so do other punctuation marks, as well as with places where there should be no punctuation at all. Follow this school and you'll be correct only 70% of the time—we're shooting for 95% or better. The high-tech school causes problems because it takes a whole semester to learn the terminology, and you won't have time to face the real problems of writing—developing interesting, honest ideas with vivid details. Let's try a middle ground that will work well for you in college, university, and most business writing.

1. *Use a comma to separate an introductory clause or phrase from the main subject and verb of the sentence.* The comma signals the end of introductory words and the beginning of the sentence's main subject and verb. As we have seen, the "normal" English sentence starts with its subject (a noun), then tells what the subject does (the verb), and usually ends with a modifier that further explains what these two are up to. Here are two examples of the subject-verb-modifier sequence:

S   V   M

Amy reads science fiction novels.

S   V   M

Jeremy hit a home run yesterday.

Even when sentences are more complicated, the "normal" pattern holds:

S   V   M

In a minute, Cindy will drive us to the late show.

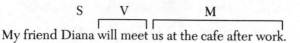

```
         S        V            M
       ┌──────────┐ ┌──────────────────────┐
My friend Diana will meet us at the cafe after work.
```

If you *vary* this pattern by delaying the subject and verb, the comma tells the reader where the main actor and action of the sentence begin. When the modifier comes first (as it does in this sentence) and the reader is desperately looking for the main subject and verb, you must help him or her by marking the end of the introductory words with a comma. Consider the following examples.

```
          INTRO              S  V        M
      ┌─────────────────────┐ ┌──────────────────┐
If I get an "A" in Chemistry, I think I'll explode with joy.
```

Wearing only his track shoes and a smile, John dashed out of the locker room and into class.

Since starting her new job this year, Marcella has been promoted twice.

Thinking time had not been called Benny kept running toward the goal. (Time's name is not Benny—insert a comma after "called.")

Because he came back to school, after four years in the navy, Kevin thought he'd forgotten all his math. (The first comma misleads us—delete it so that a comma comes only at the end of the introduction.)

If it's a short introductory phrase, there's no need for the comma, because a good reader can see the sentence as a unit. Even if it's short, however, words that would confuse a reader if unpunctuated or those that are place markers need to be separated. Look at the following examples.

```
  INTRO   S   V   M
┌──────────┐ ┌──────┐
In a moment we'll join you.
```

When it snows I get so angry.

Next to Janis, Bob is ugly. (Bob looks ugly when compared to Janis. If the comma followed "next," it would mean that Janis thought Bob was ugly.)

Second, the war proves humans still have a lot to learn.

One final point: if the modifier comes *after* the main subject and verb, you usually do *not* use a comma, but this will depend on whether a pause is needed between the main clause and its modifier.

2. A comma separates items listed in a series.

Mario walked into the faculty locker room by accident and found a pile of mouldy papers, a textbook, and a retired Latin professor on the floor. He dropped his sneakers, socks, and towel.

The comma before the conjunction is preferred, but not necessary.

This rule also applies to a series of adjectives modifying the same noun—but *only* if you can substitute an "and" for the comma.

Correct: The Latin professor gave a long, musical, sputtering snore. His nose was a pinkish red and matched his pink, red, and tan socks.

Wrong: The professor gave a most, musical snore.

3. A comma separates two independent clauses joined by a conjunction. This comma tells the reader a complete thought has just ended, and he or she must regroup to begin looking for a new subject and verb.

<pre>
     S   V   M   C   S
Mario nudged the Latin professor with one foot, and the professor

     V   M
muttered a few phrases from Cicero.
</pre>

He could scream for help, or he could leave quietly and say nothing.

If the reader sees an "and" or another conjunction and *no comma,* the signal is different. It tells the reader that whatever is on the other side of the conjunction still refers back to the subject or verb on the first side:

<pre>
     S   V   M   C   M
Mario asked if the professor was hurt or if he could get him a Latin text.
</pre>

("Mario asked" applies to both "if" clauses.)

The professor grunted and said, "Julius Caesar was a Roman geezer." ("Professor" applies to both verbs "grunted" and "said.")

When you come to any conjunction, separately read what is written before and after it. If both could be punctuated as complete sentences, use a comma; if either part is a fragment, don't use a comma.

4. Commas separate nonessential parts from the main sentence. This use of the comma coincides with pauses in a sentence, but you'll do better if you understand the logic behind it. When you have a *parenthetical comment,* which (like this) sounds as though it belongs between parentheses, you need to separate it from the main sentence. It signals to the reader that you are making a side trip into a less important area.

To test whether you need commas, see if the sentence makes sense without the words in question.

```
    S                 M              V              M
    ┌─────────────────┐  ┌──────────┐ ┌────────────────
Mario, his pulse starting to race, began backing toward the locker

──────────┐
room door.
```

The Latin professor, who wore only grey tweed undershorts, shouted, "Illiterati non carborundum."

Mario, however, was racing for the health office.

If the words in question are essential to understanding the sentence, *don't* use commas; they are meant only to set off extra information. Compare the following, both correct as they are.

George Smith, who plagiarized a term paper, was expelled from college.

All students who plagiarize term papers should be expelled from college.

The following sentences are both correct, but they have quite different meanings.

The president of the university says the professor is misinformed.

The president of the college, says the professor, is misinformed.

A group of words at the end of a sentence can also be considered extra information. But if the words are necessary to the main idea in the sentence, *don't* use a comma.

Write all test answers in the blue book, remembering to skip lines. ("Remembering…" is extra information.)

The war is over because we starved the enemy into submission. (The reason the war is over is the key idea, so "because…" is necessary.)

Don't drive home from the party if you've been drinking. ("If…" is necessary.)

5. *Use commas to separate quotations from taglines.* (See the section on quotations on page 266–68.)

6. *Use a comma after the greeting in a personal letter. Business letters are introduced by a colon.*

Dear Wendy,

Dear Prime Minister Chrétien:

7. *Use a comma to separate the direct address of someone.*

Sarah, would you come here?

I wish you'd look at this, doctor.

8. *Use a comma to separate the day from the year in a date.*

September 19, 1962

9. *Use commas to separate what would be separate lines in an address.*

I visited my former lawyer at Cellblock 33, 12 Dawson Street, Saskatchewan Maximum Security Prison, Somewhere, Saskatchewan.

■ *Practice 14-5:* Correct any comma errors in the following.

TO: ALL STUDENTS
DATE: OCTOBER 31 1995
FROM: Dr. R.J. FACTOTUM, Dean of Academic Studies
RE: GRADUATION COMPETENCY EXAM

The college is instituting a competency examination that must be passed to graduate so all students should study the following questions carefully.

BIOLOGY PRACTICUM. Part 1. Create life with your Bunsen burner a test tube and two spoonfuls of the cafeteria's jello. Part 2. After your professor approves your life form you should make it evolve to the level of an earthworm or a TV talk show host whichever comes first.

BIOLOGY WRITTEN TEST. The platypus lays eggs like a bird, swims like a fish, and has hair like a mammal but it has no wings, gills, or eyelashes. If a female platypus were to mate with a polar bear describe the genetic make-up of the offspring and draw an accurate lab sketch.

PHILOSOPHY. Using Socratic and Aristotelian methods of inquiry explain life. What will humans assuming they still exist then believe life means in the year 2050? Be concise, and specific.

ENGLISH. From memory, rewrite <u>Moby Dick</u>, also called <u>The Whale</u> or <u>Hamlet</u>.

MATH. Part 1. Applying the principles of probability studied in Math 151 you must defeat your math professor at blackjack poker or gin rummy. A deck of unmarked unopened cards must be supplied by the student. Part 2. Students must divide any number by zero, and record the result if they live.

Semicolon

Semicolons connect two complete sentences (independent clauses) that are closely related. To test whether a semicolon is correct, read the words on each side of it; each side must stand independently as a complete sentence.

Correct: Computers make even bad writing look neat; pens cause messy blots and illegible scratches.

We can satisfy almost all our energy needs with solar power; the main energy needed is the effort to pass the laws.

Wrong: Our soccer team lost by a 7-4 score; even though we had twice as many shots on goal as our opponents.

Don't use a semicolon when two sentences are joined by a conjunction; a comma is used there.

Wrong: The boss wants sales; and he wants them now.

Do use a semicolon if two sentences are separated by a conjunctive adverb (see above).

Correct: Canadian movies are popular in Europe; however, most Canadians never see them.

Colon

A colon's main use is to emphasize a sharp break between a statement and something that follows: a list, comment, quotation, question, or explanation. Think of a colon as meaning "that is" or "namely." If one of these sounds right, a colon is your best choice.

Three things would make the students' union perfect: a popcorn vendor, sawdust spread on the floor, and a ringmaster.

I love tropical fruit best of all: mangoes, papayas, guavas, and pineapples.

Because the colon is used only when you want to make a dramatic break, don't use it when your list or explanation follows *smoothly* from what comes before.

Wrong: This handbook consists of: rules, rules, and more rules.

■ *Practice 14-6:* Correct any errors in comma, semicolon, or colon use in the following.

April 1, 1995

Dear student,

It has recently come to my attention that some of you registered
for last semester's courses in less than one hour, let me assure you
that this was an error. All students will receive their full registration line time four hours.

Last semester we experienced two problems: all our computers
were on-line and the operators were well trained. We have cor-
rooted these problems, several operators have been properly
misinformed.

If you can handle boredom, and learn how to waste time cro
atively; the administration's goal will be achieved. We hope to
increase registration line time in future semesters to 8–10 hours in
our effort to be number one, therefore, your administration will
ask the curriculum committee to give college credit for registration.

Very truly yours;

B.N. Doublethink
Office of Student Affairs

OTHER PUNCTUATION

Exclamation Point
They're overused! They shout too much!! Save them for big moments!!!

Dash
You are never required to use a dash—commas, a colon, or parentheses can
always substitute for the dash, for it separates a nonessential part of the
sentence from the main idea (see comma rule 4). Dashes have more flair
than commas, and for this reason poets—Emily Dickinson, for instance—
have liked to use them. A dash is typed by striking the hyphen key twice.

> Professor Snerdman—a burly bull of a man with a flaming shock of
> red hair—charges into his lectures just looking for a student foolish
> enough to wave his hand.

Hyphen
A hyphen indicates a word split at the end of a typed line. *Only* divide
words at syllables, which are indicated in dictionaries. Hyphens also connect a group of words that functions as a noun or an adjective: a happy-go-
lucky boss is not a happy boss, go boss, or lucky boss. If you can substitute
an "and" at the location in question, use a comma.

sister-in-law

my thirty-first birthday

two-thirds of Canadians

the hairy, old horse

Parentheses

Parentheses separate nonessential information (definitions, citations for sources, or by-the-way comments) from the main text. No punctuation marks should precede a parenthesis, and all punctuation that would normally come at that point should follow the closing parenthesis. (The exception is a parenthetical statement that is a complete sentence, such as this one.)

> When the enrolment figures were finally released (7,000 full-time, 6,000 part-time, and 1,300 rejected students), the officials at the ministry realized that they hadn't solved the problem of access.

> The enrolment figures indicated 7,000 full-time, 6,000 part-time, and 1,300 rejected students. (The officials at the ministry hadn't solved the problem of access.)

Quotation Marks

1. *Put quotation marks around the titles of short works* (poems, articles, chapters of books), but use italics (underlining when you type) to indicate works long enough to be published on their own (books, long plays, magazines, newspapers).

> In his research paper, Michael documented the following sources: the *Globe and Mail*, Wiebe's "The Naming of Albert Johnson," *Jaws*, a *Saturday Night* article entitled "Was Ben Cheated?" and the entry "Lobsters" in *The Canadian Encyclopedia*.

2. *Use quotation marks to indicate direct citations.* If you're doing research, you must record exactly what the author wrote. If you want to leave out some of what was said, use ellipses (see chapter 13).

> The press secretary reported, "the premier left 3,500 hours of tapes, 10,650 pages of diary...and 45 recorded dinner conversations."

> Joseph Campbell's best advice was, "Follow your bliss."

Similarly, if you're writing dialogue in a narrative, you must use quotation marks around what the speakers say. If you summarize, though, *don't* use quotation marks.

> "What a blast!" Billy yelled as he lit the fuse.

> As he lit the fuse, Billy said he was having a blast.

If you record dialogue in anything you write, follow the guidelines below to clarify what's happening.

a. Never have two or more people speak in the same paragraph. If a second person speaks, start a new paragraph, even if only for one word.

b. Use *taglines* to identify speakers. A simple "he said" is usually better than "he threateningly implied." In dialogue between only two people, you may leave the taglines out once in a while if it's clear who's speaking.

c. Punctuate taglines with commas.

d. People's thoughts are *not* put in quotation marks.

Example of dialogue:

Greg approached the registration counter waving a letter. "This says I can't graduate," he said.

"That's right," the secretary said. "See, you haven't completed your program's new course in witchcraft."

"Witchcraft! I'm going into computers."

"Well," she said, "maybe the college curriculum committee thinks you need a broader perspective."

Great, Greg thought. Maybe I'll learn how to cast a spell on my transcript.

3. *Use quotation marks around a word or phrase being referred to as such.*

The word "computer" comes from "compute."

4. *Use single quotation marks for a quotation within a quotation.* If you quote a speaker or writer who quotes someone else, handle it in this way:

Doctor Seaver says, "We must understand poverty, not simply 'pity the suffering of the poor,' as my colleague stated."

Single quotation marks are made by striking the apostrophe key on keyboards.

5. *Punctuating Quotations:* At the end of quotations, periods and commas go before the quotation mark; semicolons and colons follow it. Question marks and exclamation marks go before the closing quotation mark if they are part of the quotation, after it if they apply to the sentence as a whole.

Merle said, "Trick or treat?"; then he snapped open his suitcase.

How can we elect a man who says, "There is no revenue problem"?

Darren's last question was, "What's for supper?"

Don't combine a comma with other punctuation marks in quotations.

Apostrophe

1. *Use an apostrophe to form a contraction;* the apostrophe is located where the missing letters would normally be.

don't (do not)

who's (who is)

2. *Use an apostrophe to form possessives.* To form the possessive of *all singular nouns* (including those ending in "s") and *plural nouns not ending in "s,"* simply add "'s."

Pete's ball

James's hat

men's cars

people's park

For *plural nouns ending in "s,"* only add an apostrophe.

schools' rules

enemies' weapons

cats' tails

What does the following sentence mean? "I saw cats' eyes staring at me from the woods." It means more than one cat was staring. If it had been "cat's," only one cat was staring.

When grammarians codified the English language, the apostrophe's two uses ran into conflict where they overlapped: at possessive pronouns. The grammarians decided to award the apostrophe to the contractions—who's (who is) and it's (it is)—and to allow pronouns to be possessive even though they don't have apostrophes: whose, its, his, ours, hers, and so on.

It's raining outside.

The sky let loose its heavy rains.

Who's coming to whose party?

CAPITALIZATION

1. *Capitalize the first letter of the first word in every sentence or intentional fragment.*

2. *Capitalize the first letter of all words in a proper noun.* A proper noun is the name of a specific person, place, thing, organization, or event.

Kim Campbell

Prince Edward Island

Halifax County

Lake Ontario

the planet Earth

October

the North

Kodak Corporation

The Shrine Circus

The Montreal Expos

Funk & Wagnalls Standard College Dictionary

Tuesday

Grandma (but "my grandmother")

Don't capitalize the seasons (winter) or general directions (Go northeast a kilometre).

3. *Capitalize the first word and all important words in a title.*

The Moon and Sixpence

A Dance of Thieves

"Rommel the Desert Fox"

■ *Practice 14-7:* Correct any errors in punctuation and capitalization in the following.

Marla G. Snooker
President
Snooker sales corp.
17 Profits Place
Friendlyville, Manitoba
R3L 3K6

May 22, 1995

Dear President Snooker,

I regret that my wife Loretta and I will not be able to attend the companys annual dinner dance at the Elegant Memories diner. Since Loretta returned to college full time I'm living with a human volcano and its tough keeping up with her. She tears through four classes, and three hours in the library. When Loretta and I arrive home she's still full of energy, however, I'm ready for a nap.

All of a sudden she knows about Psychology and history and even talks to me in french. She wants to discuss "Hamlet," and Literary theory with me. It's wonderful she's learning so much but I'm worn out listening. "Do you feel like discussing picassos paintings?" she'll say. "It's two a.m.!" I'll groan. "Oh, don't be so predictable. Put some zip in your life," she'll say.

A fancy dress-up four-hour party will kill me and Loretta has to finish her research paper about illegal whale hunting. There's one thing I need most rest. I hope that you our president will understand.

Sincerely,

Boris Backwater

 # AGREEMENT

"Agreement" means the parts of a sentence are in harmony so that readers aren't confused. Following are three kinds of agreement to strive for.

TENSE

All verbs must agree in tense unless you clearly prepare a reader for a time shift. Generally speaking, if your essay starts in the past tense, it should remain in the past throughout. Stay in the present if you start there.

> *Correct:* Jose *came* to my house and *asked* to use my encyclopedia.
>
> Jose *comes* to my house and *asks* to use my encyclopedia.
>
> Jose *came* to my house often, but now that he *has* his own encyclopedia, he *stays* away.
>
> *Wrong:* Jose *came* to my house and *asks* to use my encyclopedia.

SUBJECT-VERB AGREEMENT

Subjects and their verbs must agree: singular subjects require singular verbs, and plural subjects require plural verbs. It gets a little tricky because the singular verb often has an "s" on the end, while a plural verb has no "s."

> The girl finds the subject difficult. (Singular subject agrees with singular verb.)
>
> The girls find the subject difficult. (Plural subject agrees with plural verb.)

Pay attention to the following special cases.

1. Ignore words that come between the subject and the verb, especially if they take the form of a prepositional phrase that modifies the subject.

The power of the jet engines is overwhelming. ("Power" is the subject, not "engines.")

The trees in the yard are beautiful. ("Trees" is the subject, not "yard.")

2. Treat compound subjects connected with "and" as a plural.

Jack and Jill are still looking for the pail of water.

The only exception occurs when the two things connected by "and" suggest a single person or thing.

Bacon and eggs is my favourite breakfast.

3. The following indefinite pronouns are always singular: each, every, one, anyone, everyone, either, neither, another, anything, everything, none, something, somebody.

Each of the computers was inspected at the factory.

Everything I learned in school is not necessarily worth remembering.

Every one of the members is responsible for the rules.

The following indefinite pronouns are always plural: both, many, few, several.

Many of the ideas are mine.

4. With compound subjects connected with "or," "nor," "either...or," or "neither...nor," have the verb agree with the subject that is closest to it.

Neither the government nor the citizens on the hill are responsible for the riot.

Either late nights or lack of exercise is the cause of premature aging.

5. When using a collective noun as a single unit, use a singular verb.

The faculty is negotiating in good faith. ("The faculty" is a single unit engaged in collective bargaining.)

When the collective noun represents all the individuals or things in the group acting separately, use a plural verb.

The faculty are happy with the new computers that were installed in all offices. (The experience of each faculty member is emphasized.)

6. When using the relative pronouns "who," "that," or "which," make sure that the verb agrees with the pronoun's antecedent—the person or thing that the pronoun refers to.

The woman who represented my case is very talented.

The pictures that were painted by Harris are on display at the gallery.

7. When using linking verbs (verbs that indicate a state of being), make sure that the verb agrees with the subject and not its complement—the thing that the subject is linked to.

My favourite part of going to the movies is the popcorn and candy.

Popcorn and candy are my favourite part of going to the movies.

8. If a subject refers to money, distance, or measurement, use a singular verb.

Two dollars is a lot of money to pay for a cigar.

Five kilometres is all I could jog.

9. Some subjects look like they're plural because they have an "s" on the end, but they're really singular. Make sure they take singular verbs.

Ethics is an important part of philosophy.

Measles has been wiped out because of vaccination programs.

The news is never very uplifting.

■ *Practice 14-8:* Some of the following sentences are correct; others have problems with subject-verb agreement. Mark the correct ones with a C and make the other ones agree.

1. Mumps were a very infectious disease that are now controlled by vaccination.
2. The people on the dock was splashed when the boat sped by.
3. The computer and printer are not properly configured for that program.
4. Neither the books nor the folder are wet.
5. The provinces are responsible for education, but is dependent upon transfer payments.
6. The Canadian Armed Forces needs new helicopters.
7. Everybody is going to the Stones concert.
8. The route to the stadium and the airport are clogged with traffic.
9. Ten kilometres are a long distance if you are biking uphill through the mountains.
10. The person who writes well and communicates effectively get the job.

PRONOUN-ANTECEDENT AGREEMENT

Pronouns take the place of nouns, which are their *antecedents*. A pronoun's antecedent must always be clear; otherwise, the reader gets confused. Pronouns must also be of the same gender and number (singular or plural) as the nouns they represent.

Here is a simple example:

When the lawyer arrived at the hearing, she realized that she had forgotten her briefcase. The judge banged his gavel and cleared his throat. Its sound reverberated through the courtroom.

The pronouns in the first two sentences establish the gender of the lawyer and the judge. The pronoun in the third sentence is ambiguous because it's not clear which sound reverberates: the gavel or the throat-clearing.

It struck hard, and the sound reverberated through the courtroom.

The sentence is now much clearer because the reader knows a gavel is an object that strikes. However, it is better not to create a vague reference in the first place. Sometimes the potential for confusion is reduced if the antecedent is placed closer to the pronoun.

The judge cleared his throat and banged the gavel. It struck hard, and the sound reverberated through the courtroom.

Following are a few more examples of common pronoun-antecedent problems.

1. Treat compound antecedents connected by "and" as a plural.

Although Jennifer and Tim were enumerated in the last election, they don't appear on the list.

The University of British Columbia and Simon Fraser University have not solved their parking problems.

An exception occurs when the compound describes the same person or thing and communicates a single idea.

My wife and best friend celebrated her birthday on Monday.

2. If compound antecedents connected by "and" are preceded by "each" or "every," use the singular pronoun. "Each" and "every" always suggest "each one" and therefore communicate a singular meaning.

Each university faculty and department has its budget completed by the spring.

Every club and society must submit its by-laws to the registrar.

3. The indefinite pronouns "each," "every," "anyone," "everyone," "everybody," and "nobody" are always singular.

Each country has jurisdiction over its immigration policies.

Anyone who wants to get a good seat at the parade must set his or her alarm clock.

Everyone wants to find his or her soulmate.

Technically wrong: Everyone wants to find their soulmate.

4. Avoid sexist pronoun usage (see chapter 7). In ordinary conversation, you still hear the masculine "his" or the plural "their" used to signify a collective singular noun. Although the use of "their" in this instance is starting to creep into common usage, it is still not grammatically correct. The sexist pronoun "his" to represent both men and women is never acceptable in formal writing. The following examples should help to illustrate why this is the case.

Every lawyer must have his briefcase searched when entering the courthouse.

Each pilot must bring his health certificate to the hearing.

Every child learns at his own pace.

These examples use language to exclude women—they suggest that all lawyers, pilots, and children are male. Some will argue that it doesn't matter: we all understand that in these cases the masculine pronoun represents a kind of universal person. The point is, there is no reason why the masculine pronoun, any more than the feminine pronoun, should represent both genders. Many men would bristle at the idea of using "she" and "her" as pronouns to represent both genders. At the same time, no one likes the awkward sound of "his or her." The answer is to avoid this kind of structure altogether by making the noun and its antecedent plural whenever possible.

Lawyers must have their briefcases searched before entering the courthouse.

Pilots must bring their health certificates to the hearing.

Children learn at their own pace.

5. When using "or," "nor," "either...or," "neither...nor," or "not only...but also," make sure the pronoun agrees with the antecedent that is closest to it.

Neither the prime minister nor the members of his cabinet inspire confidence by their performance last year.

Either Canada or its trading partners will win their dispute.

The rule works most of the time. In the following example, however, the singular pronoun creates unnecessary ambiguity.

Neither the waiters nor the manager had her clothes stolen.

In this case, it is much clearer to put the plural antecedent closer to the plural pronoun so that it includes both parties:

Neither the manager nor the waiters had their clothes stolen.

Instead of using the rules mechanically, always pay attention to the style and meaning of the sentence so that it flows smoothly and communicates clearly.

6. If a collective noun emphasizes the individual members of the group, use a plural pronoun. Likewise, if a collective noun suggests the group acting as a whole, use a singular pronoun.

The teacher asked the class to put down their pens.

This year, the party will hold its convention in Saint John.

■ *Practice 14-9:* Correct the following sentences. If a sentence has no errors, mark it with a C.

1. Everyone has their own theory about the cause of the crash.
2. The team did not attract enough spectators and lost their contract with the stadium.
3. Each doctor must fill in the report before claiming his expenses.
4. Anyone who has any information about the crime should contact their local RCMP detachment.
5. Neither the woman in the suit nor the two men leaning on the telephone booth know how to coordinate their colours.
6. Every boy and girl must brush their teeth twice a day.
7. The mountain air and the long hike exerted their influence during the drive home.
8. The editor or the writers will give his final report on Thursday.
9. A sports superstar such as Doug Flutie, Doug Gilmore, or Joe Carter earns much more than their ordinary counterparts.
10. Each student must do his own work.

■ *Practice 14-10:* Correct the agreement of tense, subject and verb, and pronoun and antecedent in the following.

CATCH THE VIRUS!

Consider a career in computer technology. They're not as hard to learn as everyone in society think they are. Anyone with an education in computers have hundreds of jobs waiting for them at graduation. Computers won't "byte," even though it has a mouse. And the terminology that seems so hard at first will get easier as you moved along. A class of students learn the basic commands in one week and moved on to word processing one's papers during the first month. Get on-line today!

SPELLING

What can a teacher say about spelling except "Use the dictionary"? Ambrose Bierce called a dictionary "a malevolent device for cramping the growth of language," but he wasn't as bad a speller as most people are. We *need* a dictionary so we don't look stupid. How often do professional writers have to say "i before e except after c"? Probably each time they spell "believe" or "receive." Accept the fact that you will often have to look up "realize" and "surprise."

See if you'd like the following sentences to appear in your work by accident. They're all from actual student papers.

Thoughts rushed at me like a title wave.

Ralph Nader applied pubic pressure on General Motors.

My uncle seldom wears suites anymore.

The jocks can always be found conjugated near the gym.

Just as people judge others based on looks or clothes, so readers judge ideas and writing skills partly by the surface appearance of a paper. Fair or not, it's done. So the final task before typing or printing any paper is to circle all the words you're not *100%* sure of and check their spelling. It'll be worth the two minutes it takes. By the way, don't rely on your word processor's spell-checker to catch more than 75% of your misspellings. "My hat was a white pail" looks just fine to most spell-checkers, even though you meant "My cat has a white tail."

Another complicating factor has to do with the conventions of Canadian spelling. Some people insist that Canadian spelling is exactly like British spelling—that we must always spell "colour," "theatre," "honour," and "centre" correctly as a kind of political statement about Canadian identity. The truth is that Canadian spelling is in flux and tends to mix British and American forms. Check with your instructor to find out whether this is a major issue. Above all, keep your spellings consistent—don't switch from one version to the other.

DICTIONARY OF USAGE

THE 25 MOST COMMONLY MISUSED WORDS IN ENGLISH

advice, advise

> *Advice* is a noun meaning "guidance."
>
>> His father's advice was to study liberal arts.
>
> *Advise* is a verb meaning "counsel" or "give advice to."
>
>> His father advised him to study liberal arts.

affect, effect

> *Affect* is a verb that means "influence."
>
>> The government's budget cuts affected education.
>
> *Effect* may be either a noun or a verb, although it is used as a noun about 99% of the time. As a verb, it means "accomplish."
>
>> The government's cuts effected two million dollars in savings.
>
> As a noun, *effect* means "impact" or "result."
>
>> The cuts have had three effects locally: difficult access, higher tuition, and larger classes.

all right, alright

> *All right* is standard English; *alright* isn't.

a lot, allot

> *A lot* is the only way it should appear; don't use *alot*.
>
>> Don't make a lot of spelling mistakes.
>
> *Allot* is a verb meaning to "distribute shares."
>
>> I must allot the duties of each member.

among, between

> *Among* is used with three or more items or persons.
>
>> After graduating, he had to choose among a career in business, working for his father, and continuing for a master's degree.
>
> *Between* is used with two items or persons.
>
>> After graduating, he had to choose between a career in business and working for his father.

amount, number

> *Amount* is used with uncountable things. It applies to bulk volume or weight. (If you *count* the grains of sand in your navel someday, it will be a number, not an amount.)

An amazing amount of work goes into completing a course.

Number is used with countable things. It applies to people, years, dollars, and so on.

What number of hours do you study on average for a course?

beside, besides

Beside means "next to."

My husband stands beside me.

Besides means either "in addition to" or "also."

He does the laundry and babysits. Besides, he listens to my complaints.

conscience, conscious

Conscience refers to moral sense.

Her conscience bothered her.

Conscious refers to awareness.

She was conscious of a problem.

etc.

Try to avoid using *etc.* It sounds lazy. If you do use it, don't write "and etc." It already means "and others."

farther, further

Farther means "a greater distance." It should only be used to refer to space or time.

If I have to travel any farther between classes, I'm going to wear roller skates to school.

Further means "more" or "besides." It's used with ideas or abstractions.

Our professor is always saying, "Let's go into that further." And after we exhaust the topic, he always seems to say, "Further, we should consider...."

few, little

Few is used with countable items.

Few students know that this college was once a prison farm.

Little is used with uncountable items.

Some would say how little the place has changed.

good, well

Good is an adjective and should always modify a noun, never a verb.

Correct: Her essay makes several good proposals.

Wrong: She runs good. She feels good. She talks good.

Well is an adverb and should modify a verb.

He runs well, feels well, and talks well.

its, it's

Its is the possessive of "it"; *it's* is the contraction of "it is."

It's a shame a deer can't shoot back at its hunters.

lie, lay

Lie means "to recline" and should be used if the reclining object or person can be thought of as doing it under its or his own power.

He lies down. The dog lies in the shade.

Lay means "to put in place" and should be used if another person or force puts the object in that position.

Mom lays the baby in the crib. I lay the book on the table.

Lie and lay are complicated because they're irregular verbs, and the past tense of lie is the same as the present tense of lay.

Lie	*Lay*
I lie down. (today)	I lay it down. (today)
I lay down. (yesterday)	I laid it down. (yesterday)
I have lain down.	I have laid it down.
I am lying down.	I am laying it down.
I was lying down.	I was laying it down.

might of…

Might of, could of, would of, should of, and *must of* do not exist as English verbs. "Of" should be the helping verb "have."

Inez should have used "have" when she wrote the note to her teacher that said: "I must of got 100% on the test—I studied all afternoon."

We may get confused because the contraction "might've" *sounds* like the incorrect form.

raise, rise

The difference between *raise* and *rise* is similar to that between lay and lie. You raise an object or a person, but you rise yourself.

Bill raised his fist when he won the 100-metre dash.

Peter had to rise from where he'd fallen on the track to see his opponent celebrate.

set, sit

Another pair similar to lay and lie. You *set* an object down, but you *sit* yourself down.

I love to sit beside the pond on spring nights; sometimes I set a little stick on the water and watch it float away.

than, then

Than is comparative.

Prince Edward Island has fewer people than Ontario.

Then refers to time.

Then we drove home.

that, which, who

That and *which* are used to refer to things or ideas; who should be used to refer to people.

Correct: Amy, who led the team to the provincial finals last year, broke her ankle in the final minutes of the regular-season game, an accident that cost the team its playoff game.

Wrong: The man that lives next door is bald.

there, they're, their

There refers to a place, they're is the contraction of "they are," and *their* is the possessive of "they."

They're going to take their tennis game over there to court three.

to, too

If you mean "very" or "also," use *too*. (Hint: the extra "o" suggests excess.)

It's too hot to go anywhere; it's humid too.

try to

People often say "try and" when they mean *try to*.

We'll try to start the engine.

unique

Unique means one of a kind, not just unusual.

Moe is unique if he has antennae and speaks Martian.

very, so

Avoid using either of these words to intensify description. Usually, you can find a better word altogether, or just leaving out the *very* or *so* will make the description stronger.

Weak: The very strong wind blew Paul across the courtyard.

Better: The strong wind blew Paul across the courtyard.

Best: The howling gust blew Paul across the courtyard.

your, you're

> Misusing these words is a professional embarrassment. *Your* is the possessive of "you"; *you're* is the contraction of "you are."

> You're going to get in trouble if you misuse your words, but you're going to be a star if your writing is correct as well as lively.

SUPPLEMENTAL EXERCISES

■ *Practice 14-11:* Correct any errors of usage and spelling in the following.

ATTENTION!! JOB OPENING!!
COMMUNICATIONS MANAGER FOR SMALL COMPANY

Young company desperately requires writing advise. We do alright with manufacturing, but our lack of a communications manager has begun to effect sales alot.

If your graduating and are a very, very good writer, forward you're resume to us by June 15. Depending on the total amount received, we will notify applicants of interviews by July 1. Applicants that are successful should of written reports, letters, etc.

We'll look farther into the qualifications of the best three applicants at the interview. Their going to lie down ten rules for good writing and than demonstrate what affect each rule will have on business communications. The person we hire should speak good and be ambitious. The best between the three finalists can start immediately. We need all the help we can get.

CONTACT: Human Resources Department
Wordsmith Sign Company

■ *Supplemental Exercise:* Write a sentence for each of the following instructions.

1. Start with "because," "since," or "if."
2. Use "however" in the middle.
3. Join two independent clauses with "and."
4. Use a colon.
5. Include a quotation.
6. Include a complete date and address.
7. Use a singular possessive.
8. Use a plural possessive.
9. Insert a non-essential phrase.
10. Use a dash or two.
11. Use an intentional sentence fragment.
12. Include two words from the usage section that you've had trouble with.
13. Use a semicolon.
14. Include two words you frequently misspell.

■ *Practice 14-12:* Correct any errors in punctuation, sentence structure, spelling, or usage in the following.

Wade Biggs
Personnel Director
Fudge Motors, Inc.
Blacksky, Ontario
T5E 6K6

September 30, 1995

Dear Mr. Biggs,

Attached to this letter you will find my resume. Which lists my employment and academic background. I hope your still considering me for the job in the swedish division of the company.

I used to make alot of errors in English but I received some good advise from one of my prof's at college, and now I write good. My prof told me the kind of affect bad grammar has on a potential employer who has hundreds of people to choose between. I know I'll go farther if I know how to use a semicolon; as in this sentence. Its important, to, knowing the difference among words such as "amount" and "number." When you study wrighting since Third Grade as I have you soon learn to punctuate and use correct sentence structure. Although its hard sometimes if you hav'nt lain the rules down in front of yourself

Commas for instance should mark two sentences connected with a conjunction. They also set off interrupters, these words block the flow of a sentence. Sitting like a frog flattened on the road, my prof told us to watch out for the sentence fragment. "Beware the galloping run-on he lectured us and shun the frivolous, comma." After I memorized these rules I knew I'd be an employee any company would of been proud to hire.

Sincerely,

Gustov Osterly.

■ *Practice 14-13:* Correct any errors in comma use in the following.

THE PERFECT EXCUSE

Farley Quiddick had a problem. His history paper was late. To tell the whole truth he hadn't even begun to write it, and didn't know when he would. As his roommate always said "Writing makes a person sweat." He needed an excuse not just any excuse but a real knock-down eye-popping excuse. He considered a cold a car accident and a death in the family. He could kill off Grandma. He hadn't used that one since last semester in Mrs. Finch's English class and his current teacher Mr. Roberts probably wouldn't discuss his late paper with her. But he felt ashamed to turn in such an unimaginative common excuse.

I can do better than that thought Farley as he bit his lip. He began to write a fake letter for October 21 1995 the day his paper was due. For all the work I'm doing faking it he realized I might as well write the history paper.

■ *Practice 14-14:* Correct any errors in comma, colon, and semicolon use in the following.

DATES

Sally Slosh
Social Scene Editor, <u>The Campus News</u>

There are five types of blind dates you women may run into on campus; the Hunk the Nerd the Octopus the Cheapskate and the Mama's Boy. I've been out with all of them; and know them well.

The Hunk makes you glow but you're not the only one he excites himself too and always studies his favourite person in his favourite reference work a mirror.

You can spot the Nerd coming a block away; he trips over cracks in the sidewalk and talks like this "I believe quarks will be the growth industry of the future."

The Octopus usually has a flashy car, however, he also has tentacles that wrap around you as soon as you get in. You should be in good shape therefore before dating him.

The Cheapskate believes a date is: walking around a mall watching bag ladies rummage for pop cans, and having the woman pay her way so she doesn't feel like a sex-object, however, there's no need to worry because I've never felt like a sex-object within a kilometre of a Cheapskate.

The Mama's Boy doesn't get his driver's licence until he's 21; for fear of accidents. So you have to pick him up; and usually Mama waves goodbye and wipes her eye as you abduct him. When you say goodnight; you can kiss his forehead and offer to tuck him in.

■ *Practice 14-15:* Correct any errors in the following.

Dear Mom:

Well, Iv'e just about finished my first semester and I cant tell you how exciting its been. Urban View college is not just a High School with ashtrays it's got a video screen and ping pong tables.

The courses are Fantastic. In english we're reading classic twentieth-century novels—"Jaws" and "Revenge of the Nerds." My teacher said

I'm doing so well that next semester I can enrol in Advanced Semicolons. We took a biology field trip wednesday to the Greenwell museum and a Succotash farm South of Webster. I'm also taking an interdisciplinary course that combines Business and Chemistry, the professors first lecture was Alchemy for Fun and Profit.

In my Soc. class—thats short for sociology we have deep discussions. The other day the Professor asked "Well, how do you feel about collective sublimation?" "Uh?" one student thoughtfully pondered. "Mnn. Hmm" the teacher said.

That class was cool. And my math teacher!!! Something else!!

Love,

P.S. Would you please send back Jane's laundry and some fresh money?

■ *Practice 14-16:* Correct any errors in word use in the following.

WOMEN CLOBBER MEN

Flash Giddiup
Sports Editor, The Campus News

I might not of believed it if I hadn't witnessed it myself, folks! On Monday when the Cream Valley College athletic team buses didn't show up, our men's and women's soccer teams decided not to shower and go home. Instead, they played a very, very competitive game against each other.

The women battled through the first half even though their an average of 18 kilos lighter. They pressured the men's defence, particularly the woman who goes steady with Number 29. But the men led 3-1 at the half.

In the second half, the men ran alot of power plays besides they're own bench. The benchwarmers grabbed a few women, which were then taken out of play. The male refs said, "Its alright; your not going to enforce all the rules."

Meanwhile, further downfield, two women stole the soccer ball, which lay out of bounds, and replaced it with a tennis ball. Then they played really good! Between three women, seven goals were scored in two minutes. The men kicked themselves a large amount of times going after the little ball. They ignored their coaches' advise to stop playing dirty to.

As the score piled up to the 12-4 final, the women's coach set smiling on the bench. When the game was over, the women raised there coach to their shoulders.

APPENDIX

Abbreviated Comments on Your Papers

Teachers commonly abbreviate their comments on papers. To help you improve your writing, you should review all comments carefully and revise for each error or suggestion. The point is to learn. If you don't understand, look the problem up in the text, talk to your professor, or go to your college's writing centre. It *will* help.

Agree or **Ag**—Agreement. Nouns, verbs, or pronouns don't match each other. See pp. 270–76.

Awk—Awkward. Something is clumsy, and your professor doesn't have a category for it.

C—Comma error. See pp. 259–64.

CAP—Capitalization. See pp. 268–70.

G—Good work here.

MM—(1) Mixed metaphor. See pp. 104–05.
      (2) Misplaced modifier. See pp. 257–58.

Org—Organization. Two points mixed together or one point split apart. See Ch. 4 and p. 83.

¶—Paragraph needed. See Ch. 3.

?—Confusing section. Look for missing words, awkward sentences, illogical idea, or misused words.

Red—Redundant. Needs cutting. See pp. 107–108.

RO or **CS**—Run-on or comma-spliced sentence. Needs a period or semi-colon. See pp. 255–57.

Ref—Reference. Usually unclear pronoun reference. See pp. 246 and 272–75.

SF—Sentence fragment. See pp. 254–55.

SS—Sentence structure. May be awkwardness or non-parallel construction. See pp. 105–06 and 248–54.

Tense—Verb tenses don't match. See p. 270.

TS—Topic sentence needed or unclear. See pp. 43–47.

Thesis—Thesis needed or unclear. See pp. 52–55.

Trans—Transition needs improvement. See pp. 47–48.

Vague—Needs clarification or more detail. See pp. 82–84 and 101–105.

VG—Very good writing here.

Wordy—Be more concise. See pp. 107–108.

WW—Wrong word used. See Dictionary of Usage, pp. 272–81.

Yes! or **!!!** or ***—Well done!

Index

READER REPLY CARD

We are interested in your reaction to *Ideas and Details: A Guide to Writing for Canadians*, first Canadian edition, by M. Garrett Bauman and Clifford Werier. You can help us to improve this book in future editions by completing this questionnaire.

1. What was your reason for using this book?

    ☐ university course   ☐ college course   ☐ continuing education course
    ☐ professional   ☐ personal   ☐ other (please specify)
        development   interest   _____

2. If you are a student, please identify your school and the course in which you used this book.

3. Which chapters or parts of this book did you use? Which did you omit?

4. What did you like best about this book? What did you like least?

5. Please identify any topics you think should be added to future editions.

6. Please add any comments or suggestions.

7. May we contact you for further information?

Name: _____

_____

Address: _____

_____

_____

Phone: _____

_____

(fold here and tape shut)

MAIL ➣ POSTE

Canada Post Corporation / Société canadienne des postes

Postage paid
If mailed in Canada

Port payé
si posté au Canada

**Business
Reply**

**Réponse
d'affaires**

0116870399   01

0116870399-M8Z4X6-BR01

Heather McWhinney
Publisher, College Division
HARCOURT BRACE & COMPANY, CANADA
55 HORNER AVENUE
TORONTO, ONTARIO
M8Z 9Z9

A TROUBLE-SHOOTING GUIDE TO WRITING

NOTE: Many of these "problems" are normal procedure for most writers.

Problem	*Possible Cause*	*Possible Cures*	*Book Reference*
I don't know what to write about.	Unclear about assignment or purpose in writing.	Reread text. Reread assignment. Ask professor.	Chs. 9–13
	Unclear about audience.	Visualize an audience and write to it.	Chs. 1, 11, 12, 13
I can't get started.	No ideas or vague ideas. Insufficient detail or visualization.	Try brainteasers. Think in ideas and details.	Chs. 1–2
	Introduction jitters.	Start with main idea.	Ch. 5
	Insecure about thinking. Fear of risk.	Overcome blocks.	Ch. 2
I start but then stall.	Ideas fuzzy or incomplete.	Try more brainteasers.	Ch. 2
	Poor writing environment. Fear of messiness/risk.	Overcome these blocks.	Ch. 5
I can't put my ideas or notes together.	No main point or heading for notes.	Work on thesis/ outline.	Ch. 4
I keep writing around the same idea—going nowhere.	Insufficient ideas/details.	Try more brainteasers.	Chs. 1–2
	Redundancy.	Cut to essential idea.	Chs. 6–7
I know what I want to say but not how to say it.	Word paralysis.	Freewrite, loop, or try oral composition.	Chs. 4–5
I start ok but can't stop; it keeps getting longer.	Topic is too broad.	Restrict thesis more.	Chs. 4–6